Post-TRC Prosecutions in South Africa

Post-TRC Prosecutions in South Africa

Accountability for Political Crimes after the Truth and Reconciliation Commission's Amnesty Process

By

Ole Bubenzer

MARTINUS
NIJHOFF
PUBLISHERS

LEIDEN • BOSTON
2009

This book is printed on acid-free paper.

Library of Congress Cataloging-in-Publication Data

Bubenzer, Ole.
Post-TRC prosecutions in South Africa : accountability for political crimes after the Truth and Reconciliation Commission's amnesty process / by Ole Bubenzer.
p. cm.
Includes bibliographical references and index.
ISBN 978-90-04-17703-1 (hardback : alk. paper)
1. Political crimes and offenses—South Africa. 2. Truth commissions—South Africa. 3. Amnesty—South Africa. I. Title.

KTL4415.B83 2009
342.6808'50264—dc22

2009027442

ISBN 978 90 04 17703 1

PRINTED IN THE NETHERLANDS

Contents

Abbreviations

ANC	African National Congress
APLA	Azanian Peoples Liberation Army
AZAPO	Azanian Peoples Organisation
BGHSt	Decisions in criminal matters of the *Bundesgerichtshof* (German Federal Supreme Court)
CDF	Ciskei Defence Force
CSVR	Centre for the Study of Violence and Reconciliation
DSO	Directorate of Special Operations ("Scorpions")
GDR	German Democratic Republic
ICJ	International Court of Justice
ILR	International Law Reports
IFP	Inkatha Freedom Party
MK	*uMkhonto weSizwe*
NDPP	National Director of Public Prosecutions
NEC	National Executive Committee
NGO	non-governmental organisation
NP	National Party
NPA	National Prosecuting Authority
NPA Act	National Prosecuting Authority Act no. 32 of 1998
PAC	Pan Africanist Congress
PAJA	Promotion of Administrative Justice Act no. 3 of 2000
PCLU	Priority Crimes Litigation Unit
PEBCO	Port Elizabeth Black Civic Organisation
SADF	South African Defence Force (the apartheid state's military)
SANDF	South African National Defence Force (the military of the democratic South Africa)
SAPA	South African Press Association
SAP	South African Police (the apartheid state's police)
SAPS	South African Police Service (police service of the democratic South Africa)

SSC	State Security Council
SWAPO	South-West African People's Organisation
TRC	Truth and Reconciliation Commission
TRC Act	Promotion of National Unity and Reconciliation Act no. 34 of 1995
UDF	United Democratic Front
UN	United Nations

Preface

This book arose from my interest in South Africa, its transition to democracy and the remarkable Truth and Reconciliation Commission process over many years. It began as a doctoral study, completed at the Humboldt University of Berlin (Humboldt-Universität zu Berlin) in early 2009. During the work on this book, I received support from many people whom I would like to thank.

First of all, I am indebted to my PhD supervisor, Professor Gerhard Werle, who inspired my work, supported and advised me throughout the research process and gave me excellent input on how to improve it. I also want to thank my external supervisor, Professor Lovell Fernandez at the University of the Western Cape, who was ever helpful and supportive. I am grateful for the generous funding for a research stay in South Africa in 2006 by the German Academic Exchange Service (Deutscher Akademischer Austauschdienst) and thank Professor Francois du Bois for providing me with access to the University of Cape Town's law library during that period. I appreciate the assistance I received from the staff of Martinus Nijhoff publishers, particularly from Lindy Melman.

I would particularly like to acknowledge the extensive help I received from many people in South Africa, which was vital to familiarise me with different aspects of the political background, to get in touch with important figures involved and to compile the firsthand information contained in this book. I would like to thank all of those who generously took time to talk with me and give interviews. I am also indebted to those who continued to provide me with information on new litigation and political events and patiently answered my further queries once I returned to Germany. Their generous assistance was absolutely essential to the success of this book.

I would like to mention a special thank you to my friends Cecilia and Henry Franke from Cape Town, who invited me to stay at their home many times and showed me great hospitality, openness and generosity.

Many thanks also to Anastasia Duscha for her unfaltering moral support and for accompanying me along the way. I want to thank Tino Glass, Sarah and Girma for the proofreading of the text. I also want to gratefully acknowledge Gwen Petersen's vital assistance in South Africa and help with the Afrikaans translations.

Last but not least I want to express gratitude to my parents, whom I cannot thank enough for their unfaltering and generous support over many years, which has made this book possible.

Introduction

The South Africa of the present has a history of violent conflict. The past century was dominated by the struggle against apartheid, institutionalised segregation, discrimination, oppression and exploitation of the majority of the population on racial grounds. As the quest for the liberation of the country from the abhorred system intensified, state security forces attempted to tackle the wave of opposition by means that became increasingly violent. The basic human rights of thousands were grossly violated during this struggle.

After the country embarked on a course of transition towards democracy and a system of equal rights in the late 1980s and early 1990s, pressing questions remained on how to deal with the crimes of the past. As was the case in many other societies, which moved from a system of dictatorship and oppression towards democracy and human rights, the options for dealing with the past generally ranged from criminal prosecutions in the style of the Nuremberg trials, which normally seems to be appropriate in a country adhering to the rule of law, to blanket amnesties.

South Africa struck a balance between these competing extremes. The human rights violations of the past were dealt with by the Truth and Reconciliation Commission (hereinafter TRC) aimed at establishing a public record of the human rights atrocities. A unique combination of criminal accountability and amnesty proceedings embedded in the TRC was employed. Amnesty for political crimes of the past was only granted subject to conditions and in exchange for full disclosure on the particulars of the deeds in question. Amnesty was not the exclusive way of dealing with past crimes, however. Criminal trials accompanied the TRC process. The South African amnesty scheme provided that the normal course of criminal justice must come into play after the conclusion of the TRC's work whether amnesty had been denied or not even applied. This unique way of dealing with past wrongs has largely characterised the South African transition to justice. It has earned the country international praise and admiration for having upheld accountability and for having withstood the pressure to ignore the past and to grant widespread impunity.

The remarkable TRC process has been subject to extensive national and international scholarly examination.[1] However, little or no attention has as yet been paid to the question of whether the concluding chapter of dealing with past political crimes has been accomplished. This is the question of whether those who were denied amnesty for their politically motivated crimes have been held criminally liable after the conclusion of the TRC (hereinafter post-TRC prosecutions). The issue of post-TRC prosecutions is of paramount importance for an evaluation of the legitimacy and justice of the whole amnesty scheme, which was inextricably linked to a threat of prosecution.[2] This book will examine this issue of post-TRC prosecutions. It is guided by the legal scheme on amnesty, which logically requires prosecutions in the wake of the TRC as part of the overall process of dealing with the past. The book will examine the question of whether post-TRC prosecutions were implemented sufficiently in terms of the South African system of

[1] See e.g. A. Boraine *A country unmasked* (2000); A. du Bois-Pedain *Transitional amnesty in South Africa* (2007); S. Garkawe 'The South African Truth and Reconciliation Commission: a suitable model to enhance the role and rights of victims of gross human rights violations?' (2003) 27 *Melbourne University Law Review* 334–80; L.S. Graybill *Truth and reconciliation in South Africa: miracle or model?* (2002); E. Hahn-Godeffroy *Die Südafrikanische Truth and Reconciliation Commission* (1998); F. Kutz *Amnestie für politische Straftäter in Südafrika* (2001) 144; J. Sarkin *Carrots and sticks: the TRC and the South African amnesty process* (2004); W. Verwoerd and C. Villa-Vicencio (eds) *Looking back reaching forward—Reflections on the Truth and Reconciliation Commission of South Africa* (2000); G. Werle 'Without truth no reconciliation' (1996) 29 *Verfassung und Recht in Übersee—Law and politics in Africa, Asia and Latin America* 58–72.

[2] The approach is often referred to as 'carrot and stick' (see further V. Nerlich 'Lessons for the International Criminal Court: the impact of criminal prosecutions on the South African amnesty process' in G. Werle (ed.) *Justice in transition* (2006) 55 at 56; Truth and Reconciliation Commission (ed.) *Truth and Reconciliation Commission of South Africa report* (hereinafter *TRC Report*) vol. 6 (2003) s. 3, chap. 1, paras. 15–19.

dealing with past wrongs. Attention will thereby be paid to the conflicting factors of what is factually possible versus what is legally as well as morally desirable.

Chapter One will provide a brief historical background to the issues under discussion. The issue of post-TRC prosecutions will also be described in greater detail from the perspective of the overall legal and conceptual context of the TRC and its amnesty proceedings in order to clarify the basic guiding principle of this book. Finally, the criminal trials which ran parallel to the amnesty proceedings will be described briefly.

The main objective of this book is to document the present situation in South Africa regarding post-TRC prosecutions. The emphasis, thus, lies in Chapters Two and Three. Chapter Two will describe all efforts at prosecutions and trials, which have taken place thus far, after the work of the Amnesty Committee. All criminal proceedings in cases for which amnesty was denied or not applied and which fell in the legal ambit of the Amnesty Committee will be considered.

In Chapter Three the focus will be on the politics of prosecutions. As such, an overview of the political and public debates will be provided. Further, political negotiations between the government and the former state security forces will be described. As will become apparent, the topic is, to a great extent, influenced by considerations of *realpolitik*. It is therefore of paramount importance in evaluating the issue of post-TRC prosecutions to analyse the politics of prosecutions. The chapter will subsequently provide an analysis of a specific policy approach and the considerations and possible viewpoints of the government.

Chapter Four will deal with the prospects for further TRC-related prosecutions. While considering future prospects, certain legal issues, such as a constitutional and/or international law obligation to prosecute or statutes of limitation, will become relevant and will be dealt with accordingly in this chapter. General prospects will be assessed on the basis of the information contained in the preceding chapters. A brief collection of possibly prosecutable cases shall demonstrate the practical scope of future trials especially with regards to the interests of victims and victim families.

In the last chapter a summary of the findings along with conclusions will be put forward. The conduct and scope of prosecutions as well as the government's political approach will be evaluated with regard to the South African approach to dealing with past wrongs. The role of victims in this scheme will thereby be recognised as well as their interests and demands concerning prosecutions.

The information contained in this book was, to a large extent, gathered during a four month research trip to South Africa in 2006. During the research stay the relevant court documents, which were in some instances not yet transcribed, were obtained. Since written materials were available to a lesser extent and the events on the subject were rather current, it was vital to include interviews as they proved to be a very important source of information. Over 20 interviews were conducted with persons who were and are in some way concerned with the subject and in many instances were able to provide information, which, thus far, had not yet reached the public domain.

Chapter One

Dealing With the Legacy of the Past—Transitional Justice in South Africa

1. *The Apartheid Conflict*

Practically since the first Europeans settled in South Africa in the late 17th century, the native African population was disadvantaged and discriminated against.[1] Control over political instruments, the economy, natural resources and the majority of the land was reserved to whites. After the National Party (hereinafter NP), a predominantly *Afrikaner*[2] nationalist party, won the elections in 1948, the situation was aggravated further as the state of racial segregation and economic exploitation was institutionalised into law.[3] Black and coloured South Africans had

---

[1] If not stated otherwise, the general historical information contained in this subchapter derives from R. Davenport and C. Saunders *South Africa* (2000) and *TRC Report*, vol. 1, chap. 2; vol. 3, pages 12–33. See on the discrimination and human rights violations on racial grounds which occurred before 1948: *TRC Report*, vol. 1, pages 25–28.

[2] The *Afrikaner* population descends from an amalgamation of the earliest European settlers, mainly coming from the Netherlands, Germany and France.

[3] Racial segregation and discrimination was based on a range of acts, mainly the Population Registration Act of 1950, which provided for the classification of each South African according to four racial categories and the duty to carry a pass of racial identification; the Group Areas Act, which partitioned the whole country into zones for exclusive inhabitation by one of the racial groups and which provided for the eviction of millions of black and coloured South Africans from their land and property and the forced removal into townships and poor *bantustan* homelands; the Prohibition of Mixed Marriages Act of 1949; and the 1950 Immorality Amendment Act, which prohibited not only inter-racial marriages but all forms of sexual contacts between the

practically no political or economic rights, yet were simultaneously exploited as cheap labourers, a practice which was vital for the thriving economy. Officially independent states were created on minimal and poor parts of the country which were intended to serve as homelands for the respective African ethnic groups. This racist system of so-called *apartheid*[4] became a guiding principle of South African government politics for the following decades.

Inevitably, resistance grew to white supremacy and apartheid. An opposition organisation, which in 1923 became the African National Congress (hereinafter ANC), formed in 1912. In 1959 the other major opposition movement, the Pan Africanist Congress (hereinafter PAC), was established. The opposition was faced with an intransigent commitment to apartheid and white supremacy. Peaceful political protest was greatly obstructed by the authorities. The opposition movement therefore resorted to militant means of protest. In 1961 the ANC formed its armed wing, *uMkhonto weSizwe*[5] (hereinafter MK) which attacked the security forces and directed acts of sabotage at important state facilities.

The legitimate quest for equal rights was perceived by the government merely as a terrorist onslaught[6] on the integrity of the state and

---

ethnic groups. See for a comprehensive account of the legislation: *TRC Report*, vol. 1, chap. 2, paras. 25–40. See on the socio-economic effects of apartheid on the new democracy: K. Naudaschder-Schlag and H.R. Schillinger 'Von der Rassentrennung zur Regenbogennation' in R. Zugehör (ed.) *Kap der besseren Hoffnung?* (1994) 9–62. See for a survey of the gross human rights violations committed during apartheid: M. Coleman (ed.) *A crime against humanity* (1998) and *TRC Report* vols 1–7.

4 Apartheid in Afrikaans means separate- or apart-ness. The term refers to the official government policy and system of racial segregation, discrimination and white political hegemony, introduced by the NP in 1948 (R.B. Beck *The history of South Africa* (2000) 125). See generally on apartheid R.B. Beck *The history of South Africa* (2000) 125–53; P. Bonner et al. (eds) *Apartheid's genesis—1935–1962* (1993); W Beinart and S. Dubow *Segregation and apartheid in twentieth-century South Africa* (1995).

5 *UMkhonto weSizwe* means "spear of the nation".

6 Interview with Jan Wagener in Pretoria (May 8, 2006). The perceptions within security police are illustrated in H.D. Stadler *The other side of the story* (1997).

was increasingly met by force.[7] The resulting violent conflict reached its climax in the mid-1980s. During 1984 and 1989, 5600 people died as a result of political unrest.[8] Tens of thousands of people were detained during this period for political reasons without trial or court order.[9] Although security legislation had already been hugely extended, the state forces increasingly resorted to means that were criminal under South African law.[10] The South African Police (hereinafter SAP) abducted, tortured and murdered political opponents within and outside of South African borders. Secret death squads were established for this purpose.[11] Thus, the legitimate struggle of the black majority for equality and political as well as economic rights resulted in a violent conflict during which many gross human rights violations were committed on all sides.[12] The apartheid conflict extended to the South African

---

7 The opposition to apartheid was seen as part of a communist 'total onslaught' on South Africa which was to be countered by a 'total strategy' of force (*TRC Report*, vol. 2, chap. 1, paras. 108–11; M. Coleman (ed.) *A crime against humanity* (1998) 7–9).

8 M. Coleman (ed.) *A crime against humanity* (1998) 42. Security force activities and vigilantism accounted for the majority of deaths. Vigilante groups operated in black communities. They were unofficial, yet directed and supported by the government to violently act against anti-apartheid activists.

9 *TRC Report*, vol. 3, page 25. Cases of death in detention occurred frequently (M. Coleman (ed.) *A crime against humanity* (1998) 12 and 53–67; *TRC Report*, vol. 2, chap. 3, paras. 166–95).

10 See for an elaboration on the scope of state crimes in South Africa: V. Nerlich *Apartheidkriminalität vor Gericht* (2002) 9–14.

11 M. Coleman (ed.) *A crime against humanity* (1998) 118. The most notorious of these units was "Vlakplaas", named after a farm close to Pretoria where it was based. It operated from 1979 to the early 1990s (*TRC Report*, vol. 6, s. 3, chap. 1, paras. 157–79; F. Kutz *Amnestie für politische Straftäter in Südafrika* (2001) 23; V. Nerlich *Apartheidkriminalität vor Gericht* (2002) 116–17). Revelations on such hit-squad activities were first made by Almond Nofomela, a former member of Vlakplaas, in 1989. This was followed by revelations of his former commander Dirk Coetzee and others (M. Coleman (ed.) *A crime against humanity* (1998) 119).

12 G. Werle 'Alternativen zur Aufarbeitung von Systemunrecht' in H. Hof and M. Schulte (eds) *Wirkungsforschung zum Recht* vol. III (2001) 291 at 293.

protectorate of South-West Africa, now known as Namibia.[13] Other neighbouring countries also suffered from what the TRC described as a 'reign of terror and destruction'[14] in that South Africa either waged war on unwanted governments, supported rebel movements to overthrow such governments or periodically attacked the ANC abroad.

2. *The Negotiated Transition and the Work of the TRC*

Heightening internal unrest and international pressure brought the last apartheid President F.W. de Klerk, who had come into power in September 1989, to start a process of democratic reform. After Nelson Mandela was released from prison in March 1990,[15] a period of negotiations began between representatives of the ANC and the government.[16] The consultations were aimed at facilitating the transition to a democratic state and establishing a new constitution. After an agreement was reached on the first democratic and human rights oriented constitution,[17] Nelson Mandela was elected President and the ANC won a majority of parliamentary seats in the first democratic elections in April 1994.

---

[13] *TRC Report*, vol. 1, chap. 2, para. 53.

[14] Ibid., para. 21.

[15] Mandela had been sentenced to life imprisonment for high treason in 1963.

[16] The negotiations were accompanied by massive outbursts of violence, mainly resulting from clashes between supporters of the Zulu Inkatha Freedom Party and ANC members or sympathisers in Natal. Such conflicts were often instigated and fuelled by the state security forces. About 14,000 people died as a result of prolonged political conflicts all over South Africa during the negotiation period (*TRC Report*, vol. 2, chap. 7, para. 7), which is in total more than during the preceding decades of conflict (*TRC Report*, vol. 5, chap. 6, para. 126).

[17] The Interim Constitution (Act 200 of 1993) entered into force in April 1994 and was in 1997 replaced by the Constitution (Act 108 of 1996).

This heralded a period of transitional justice,[18] demanding that the legacy of apartheid—human rights violations and crimes—would not be ignored.[19] It was decided that such matters would be dealt with by a truth commission.[20] The Promotion of National Unity and Reconciliation Act[21] (hereinafter TRC Act) established the Truth and Reconciliation Commission.[22] The brief of the TRC was '[t]o provide for the investigation and the establishment of as complete a picture as possible of the nature, causes and extent of gross violations of human rights committed' between 1 March 1960 and 6 December 1993.[23] Under the terms of the act, a gross human rights violation constitutes any act of killing, abduction, torture or severe ill-treatment of any person or any attempt, conspiracy, incitement, instigation, command or procurement to commit such an act.[24]

---

[18] Transitional justice basically circumscribes the way a democratic government takes over power from an oppressive regime and the choices taken in the course thereof with respect to, *inter alia*, the transition of state organs and the dealing with human rights violations committed under the former regime (D.A. Crocker 'Truth commissions, transitional justice, and civil society' in R.I. Rotberg and D. Thompson (eds) *Truth v. justice* (2000) 99 at 99; M. Fenwick 'Dilemmas of transitional justice' (2003) 35 3 *The Seinan Law Review* 1 at 1). See generally on transitional justice N.J. Kritz (ed.) *Transitional justice* vol. I (1995); A.J. McAdams (ed.) *Transitional justice and the rule of law in new democracies* (1997); G. Werle (ed.) *Justice in transition* (2006).

[19] A. Boraine 'Truth and reconciliation in South Africa' in R.I. Rotberg and D. Thompson (eds) *Truth v. justice* (2000) 141 at 142.

[20] The initiative to establish a truth commission was taken by the ANC, various human rights non-governmental organisations and leading personalities of the human rights sector (A. Boraine *A country unmasked* (2000) 11–46; E. Hahn-Godeffroy *Die südafrikanische Truth and Reconciliation Commission* (1998) 56–57).

[21] Act 34 of 1995. The act is available at http://www.doj.gov.za/trc.

[22] The process of establishing the legal framework of the TRC was accompanied by extensive debates in Parliament and the general public, which gave the TRC a high degree of democratic legitimacy (G. Werle 'Neue Wege' in P. Bock and R. Wolfrum (eds) *Umkämpfte Vergangenheit* (1999) 269 at 287).

[23] Preamble of the TRC Act.

[24] Section 1 of the TRC Act.

The Commission's work started when its commissioners were appointed in December 1995.[25] It consisted of three committees: a committee on human rights violations, a committee on reparations and a committee on amnesty—the work of the latter is the most relevant for the goals of this book. The commission's operation terminated in 1998. In October 1998 it issued a five volume final report[26] in which it published the findings it reached from its hearings and investigations on the nature, extent and causes of human rights violations committed during its mandate period. Since the work of the Amnesty Committee was only concluded later, two further volumes were published in March 2003.

The TRC found that the state and its security agencies accounted for the majority of gross human rights violations.[27] It found that during the political struggle between the late 1970s and early 1990s, state bodies increasingly made use of criminal measures in terms of the laws at the time. For example, occurrences such as extra-judicial killings of opposition members took place.[28] The Commission further found that the use of torture was systematic and widespread within the ranks of the SAP.[29] Many cases were recorded by the TRC where opposition members had been abducted, tortured and often killed by the security forces.[30] Such practices were condoned and authorised by leading police and security branch officials.[31] The Inkatha Freedom Party (hereinafter IFP) supported the state in its criminal activities.[32] The TRC found

---

[25] See *TRC Report*, vol. 1, chap. 3, paras. 1–6 and chap. 6, para. 4.

[26] See sections 3(1)(d), 4(e), 43(1)(b) and 44 of the TRC Act.

[27] *TRC Report*, vol. 6, s. 5, chap. 2, para. 7.

[28] *TRC Report*, vol. 5, chap. 6, para. 77; *TRC Report*, vol. 6, s. 5, chap. 2, paras. 72–90; *TRC Report*, vol. 2, chap. 3, paras. 221–320, 509. See for testimonies received in amnesty applications and hearings on death squad activities of the various regional security branches *TRC Report*, vol. 6, s. 3, chap. 1, paras. 155–307.

[29] *TRC Report*, vol. 2, chap. 3, para. 220; *TRC Report*, vol. 6, s. 5, chap. 2, para. 16.

[30] *TRC Report*, vol. 6, s. 5, chap. 2, paras. 50–71; *TRC Report*, vol. 2, chap. 3, paras. 278–424. The security branch sometimes also killed its own members when it believed they were unloyal (*TRC Report*, vol. 2, chap. 3, paras. 425–56).

[31] *TRC Report*, vol. 6, s. 5, chap. 2, para. 17.

[32] *TRC Report*, vol. 5, chap. 6, para. 77.

that the IFP was responsible for numerous killings in attacks on often unarmed ANC members and supporters and other gross human rights violations under the auspices of government policies.[33] With respect to the ANC and MK, the Commission took into account that it was the declared policy of the ANC to avoid the loss of civilian lives, but found nonetheless that civilians were killed and that MK members independently targeted persons outside of the ANC official policy in a manner which resulted in gross human rights violations.[34]

3. *Accountability for Past Human Rights Violations in the South African Context: Conditional Amnesties and Prosecutions*

The concept of amnesty within the TRC process is of paramount importance for the present research. Its parameters will be outlined in the following.

The question of criminal accountability was highly controversial at the negotiations.[35] The former government, the NP and the security forces of the apartheid state lobbied strongly for a general amnesty.[36] Although sympathies for a general amnesty could also be found among leading ANC members, such an approach was mostly seen as untenable.[37] A

---

[33] Ibid., para. 121.

[34] Ibid., para. 136; *TRC Report*, vol. 6, s. 5, chap. 3, paras. 28–47. See generally on the liberation movement *TRC Report*, vol. 5, chap. 6, paras. 130–50.; *TRC Report*, vol. 6, s. 5, chaps. 3 and 5.

[35] See for the debates on amnesty: A. Boraine *A country unmasked* (2000) 275–86; J. Sarkin *Carrots and sticks: the TRC and the South African amnesty process* (2004) 53; L. McGregor 'Individual accountability in South Africa: cultural optimum or political facade?' (2001) 95 *American Journal of International Law* 32 at 32–35; P. Parker 'The politics of indemnities, truth telling and reconciliation in South Africa' (1996) 17 1–2 *Human Rights Law Journal* 1 at 1–7.

[36] Interview with Jan Wagener in Pretoria (May 8, 2006); L. McGregor 'Individual accountability in South Africa: cultural optimum or political facade?' (2001) 95 *American Journal of International Law* 32 at 34.

[37] A. Boraine 'Truth and reconciliation in South Africa' in R.I. Rotberg and D. Thompson (eds) *Truth v. justice* (2000) 141 at 143.

general amnesty was felt to be counterproductive to the establishment of a human rights culture and unconducive to the consolidation of the new democratic order, which demanded recognition of and reconciliation with the legacy of the past.[38] Many ANC members demanded strict prosecution of those responsible for apartheid crimes and Nuremberg-style trials of the leaders.

However, a concession had to be made in this regard in order to secure the support of the security forces during the negotiation period and to facilitate a peaceful transition to democracy with the support of the former elites.[39] It was agreed that amnesty should be granted in some form for gross human rights violations committed during the conflicts of the past.[40] The post amble of the Interim Constitution, headed National Unity and Reconciliation, eventually incorporated the following statement concerning amnesty:

> In order to advance such reconciliation and reconstruction, amnesty shall be granted in respect of acts, omissions and offences associated with political objectives and committed in the course of the conflicts of the past. To this end, Parliament under this Constitution shall adopt a law determining a firm cut-off date, which shall be a date after 8 October 1990 and before 6 December 1993, and providing for the mechanisms, criteria and procedures, including tribunals, if any, through which such amnesty shall be dealt with at any time after the law has been passed.[41]

As no specific agreement could be reached, the determination of the precise form of the amnesty had to be left open for later implemen-

---

[38] Ibid., 142; J. Sarkin *Carrots and sticks: the TRC and the South African amnesty process* (2004) 52.

[39] G. Werle 'Neue Wege' in P. Bock and R. Wolfrum (eds) *Umkämpfte Vergangenheit* (1999) 269 at 275. It is commonly accepted that a compromise on amnesty was the price which invariably had to be paid in order to avoid civil war and in order to make a negotiated settlement possible at all. (Mbeki as cited in A. Boraine 'Truth and reconciliation in South Africa' in R.I. Rotberg and D. Thompson (eds) *Truth v. justice* (2000) 141 at 143; A.M. Omar 'Foreword by A.M. Omar' in M.R. Rwelamira and G. Werle (eds) *Confronting past injustices* (1996) vii at x).

[40] G. Werle 'Without truth no reconciliation' (1996) 29 *Verfassung und Recht in Übersee—Law and politics in Africa, Asia and Latin America* 58 at 64–65.

[41] Post amble of the Interim Constitution of South Africa, Act 200 of 1993.

tation. The amnesty model eventually incorporated in the TRC Act empowered the Amnesty Committee to grant amnesty only on certain conditions and restrictions.[42] First of all, violators had to apply for amnesty.[43] According to section 20(1)(b) of the TRC Act, amnesty could only be granted for an act, omission or offence which was associated with a political objective and was committed in the course of the conflicts of the past during the period of 1 March 1960 to 10 May 1994.[44] Applications for amnesty could only be submitted until 30 September 1997.[45] An additional decisive precondition in section 20(1)(c) of the TRC Act for attaining amnesty stated that the applicant had to make a full disclosure of all relevant facts concerning the crime to which the application related.[46] Thus, if any of the preconditions, most notably the full disclosure or political objective requirements, were not satisfied, amnesty would be denied. This legal mandate applied to all crimes, regardless of whether they were committed by the liberation movements or the state security forces.[47]

Despite the extensive public and parliamentary debates which preceded the enactment of the amnesty legislation, the amnesty scheme was not based on popular and political consensus. Many victims strongly contested the basic notion of amnesty and demanded retributive justice, prosecutions and trials.[48] The former apartheid government and security force representatives, however, perceived the TRC to be a one-sided

---

[42] Sections 16–22 of the TRC Act.

[43] Section 18 of the TRC Act.

[44] The time frame for amnesty had later been extended. The political objective criteria is more concretely outlined in sections 20(2) and 20(3) of the TRC Act. See further on these so-called 'Noorgaard Criteria' and the political offence criteria J. Sarkin *Carrots and sticks: the TRC and the South African amnesty process* (2004) 37–8, 63 and 278–335; F. Kutz *Amnestie für politische Straftäter in Südafrika* (2001) 221–61.

[45] F. Kutz *Amnestie für politische Straftäter in Südafrika* (2001) 144.

[46] See on this criteria: J. Sarkin *Carrots and sticks: the TRC and the South African amnesty process* (2004) 249–78; F. Kutz *Amnestie für politische Straftäter in Südafrika* (2001) 261–70.

[47] A. Boraine *A country unmasked* (2000) 69.

[48] A. Boraine 'Truth and reconciliation in South Africa' in R.I. Rotberg and D. Thompson (eds) *Truth v. justice* (2000) 141 at 149.

exercise of victor's justice and a raw deal for their side.[49] They had expected what they had advocated for all along, a general amnesty.[50] As will become apparent below, such positions still strongly influence the political discussions on post-TRC prosecutions.

However, the TRC was and continues to be held in high regard internationally. This is because with conditional amnesty and especially the onus to make a full disclosure it introduced a unique and unprecedented way of dealing with past atrocities in a transitional society.[51] The model was heralded as an innovative moral and legal achievement.[52] While many other countries adopted a course of blanket amnesty and forgetting of the past,[53] South Africa put in place a scheme by which it could uphold accountability, avoid total impunity[54] and unearth the truth regarding past human rights violations.

Amnesty was not designed to replace prosecutions entirely. It was only to be granted in exchange for a process of public truth telling. Criminal and amnesty proceedings, thus, ran parallel to each other. In the wake of the TRC, it clearly follows as a logical consequence from this concept as well as from the legal setup of the amnesty provisions that those perpetrators who were not granted amnesty for their politically motivated crimes must be prosecuted.[55] After the work of the Amnesty

---

[49] Interview with Johan van der Merwe in Pretoria (May 5, 2006); Interview with Jan Geldenhuys in Pretoria (May 10, 2006); F.W. de Klerk as cited in A. Boraine *A country unmasked* (2000) 275 at footnote 10.

[50] Ibid.

[51] A. Boraine *A country unmasked* (2000) 269; J. Sarkin *Carrots and sticks: the TRC and the South African amnesty process* (2004) 3; G. Werle 'Neue Wege' in P. Bock and R. Wolfrum (eds) *Umkämpfte Vergangenheit* (1999) 269 at 287. See for other truth commissions: P.B. Hayner 'Fifteen truth commissions' in N.J. Kritz (ed.) *Transitional justice* vol. I (1995) 262–89.

[52] E. Kiss 'Moral ambition within and beyond political constraints' in R.I. Rotberg and D. Thompson (eds) *Truth v. justice* (2000) 68 at 76.

[53] A. Boraine *A country unmasked* (2000) 269. See also K. Ambos *Straflosigkeit von Menschenrechtsverletzungen* (1997) 23–159.

[54] A. Boraine *A country unmasked* (2000) 283.

[55] M.E. Bennun 'Some procedural issues relating to post-TRC prosecutions of human rights offenders' (2003) 16 *South African Journal of Criminal Justice* 17 at 17.

Committee was concluded in May 2001,[56] the TRC accordingly recommended in its final report that:

> Where amnesty has not been sought or has been denied, prosecution should be considered where evidence exists that an individual has committed a gross human rights violation. In this regard, the Commission will make available to the appropriate authorities information in its possession concerning serious allegations against individuals (excluding privileged information such as that contained in amnesty applications). Consideration must be given to imposing a time limit on such prosecutions. Attorneys-general must pay rigorous attention to the prosecution of members of the South African Police Service (SAPS) who are found to have assaulted, tortured and/or killed persons in their care. In order to avoid a culture of impunity and to entrench the rule of law, the granting of general amnesty in whatever guise should be resisted.[57]

Equally President Mandela on the occasion of the tabling of the TRC Report in Parliament in February 1999 stated that '[a]ccountability does need to be established and where evidence exists of a serious crime, prosecution should be instituted within a fixed time frame.'[58]

Against the background of this concept the importance of post-TRC prosecutions for the whole process of dealing with past human rights abuses in South Africa becomes obvious. Since the concept of amnesty in South Africa was premised on the fact that those who were not granted impunity would be prosecuted, the issue of post-TRC prosecutions strongly affects the credibility and legitimacy of the entire process.[59] The amnesty process would be rendered paradoxical and might 'unravel into a farce', as Fernandez puts it strongly, if no prosecutions

---

[56] Due to the workload and ongoing amnesty hearings the Amnesty Committee's operation had to continue (*TRC Report*, vol. 6, s. 1, para. 3).

[57] *TRC Report*, vol. 5, chap. 8, para. 14.

[58] Opening address by President Nelson Mandela in the special debate on the report of the Truth and Reconciliation Commission (National Houses of Parliament) (Feb. 25, 1999).

[59] G. Werle 'Alternativen zur Aufarbeitung von Systemunrecht' in H. Hof and M. Schulte (eds) *Wirkungsforschung zum Recht* vol. III (2001) 291 at 297; G. Werle 'Neue Wege' in P. Bock and R. Wolfrum (eds) *Umkämpfte Vergangenheit* (1999) 269 at 282.

take place in the aftermath of the TRC.[60] An evaluation of the success or failure and the overall justice of the TRC process must therefore inevitably take into account whether and how post-TRC prosecutions take place.[61] It is the purpose of this book to provide the basis for such an evaluation by examining the scope of post-TRC prosecutions in the following chapters.

7115 applications were registered by the TRC.[62] Of this total, 5143 applications were refused administratively, without a public hearing, mostly since no political objective was found to exist in the events referenced.[63] 1973 applications were dealt with in public hearings in terms of section 19(3)(a) and (b) of the TRC Act, meaning that the applications conveyed a prima facie politically related offence and a gross human rights violation in terms of the TRC mandate.[64] This number of applications relates to 1701 individual applicants. 1100 amnesty decisions were published in respect thereof.[65] 857 applicants of those were aligned to the ANC, 85 to the IFP, 116 to the PAC or the

[60] L. Fernadez 'Post-TRC prosecutions in South Africa' in G. Werle (ed.) *Justice in transition* (2006) 65 at 79; M.E. Bennun 'Some procedural issues relating to post-TRC prosecutions of human rights offenders' (2003) 16 *South African Journal of Criminal Justice* 17 at 36.

[61] R.C. Slye 'Comment on the papers by Lovell Fernandez, Jeremy Sarkin and Volker Nerlich' in G. Werle (ed.) *Justice in transition* (2006) 83 at 84; G. Werle 'Alternativen zur Aufarbeitung von Systemunrecht' in H. Hof and M. Schulte *Wirkungsforschung zum Recht* vol. III (2001) 291 at 301.

[62] *TRC Report*, vol. 6, s. 1, chap. 3, para. 4. See for an empirical study of the amnesty decisions: A. Pedain 'Was amnesty a lottery?' (2004) 121 *South African Law Journal* 785–828.

[63] J. Sarkin 'The amnesty hearings in South Africa revisited' in G. Werle (ed.) *Justice in transition* (2006) 43 at 47. About 65 per cent of the applications were received from persons who were already convicted and served jail terms (*TRC Report*, vol. 6, s. 1, chap. 2, para. 74).

[64] J. Sarkin 'The amnesty hearings in South Africa revisited' in G. Werle (ed.) *Justice in transition* (2006) 43 at 48.

[65] A. Pedain 'Was amnesty a lottery?' (2004) 121 *South African Law Journal* 785 at 795. Pedain points out that all applications concerning *prima facie* political conduct were published on the Commission's website (http://www.doj.gov.za/trc).

Azanian Peoples Liberation Army (hereinafter APLA) and 289 to the security forces.[66] Very few applications were received from the South African Defence Force (hereinafter SADF).[67] 1499 of those applicants submitted applications which concerned offences falling in the ambit of the committee's jurisdiction in terms of section 20(1) of the TRC Act.[68] Of the remainder, 105 applicants were high-ranking ANC members, whose applications generally related to political activities, but were refused since they did not specify a specific violation or circumstance to be considered.[69] Of the applications that were dealt with in public hearings, 1164 were granted, 806 were denied.[70]

The figures give an indicator of how many cases, potentially worthy of prosecution, might arise from the TRC amnesty proceedings. Considering the scale of human rights violations in the period of South Africa's history, which is relevant for the TRC's inquiries, the number of amnesty applications must be considered rather low.[71] Thus there are potentially hundreds of cases for which amnesty was not applied that could be relevant to future criminal prosecutions. The amnesty proceedings suffered especially from a lack of applications by figures from the upper ranks of politics and commanders of the security forces of the apartheid state.[72] The vast majority of amnesty applicants, especially from the state security forces, were ordinary rank and file officers.

---

[66] A. Pedain 'Was amnesty a lottery?' (2004) 121 *South African Law Journal* 785 at 804. Pedain points out that the numbers are by no means representative for the number of human rights violations committed by each respective group.

[67] *TRC Report*, vol. 6, s. 3, chap. 1, para. 4.

[68] A. Pedain 'Was amnesty a lottery?' (2004) 121 *South African Law Journal* 785 at 804–5.

[69] Ibid., 805.

[70] J. Sarkin 'The amnesty hearings in South Africa revisited' in G. Werle (ed.) *Justice in transition* (2006) 43 at 48.

[71] Ibid., 46.

[72] A. Pedain 'Was amnesty a lottery?' (2004) 121 *South African Law Journal* 785 at 806–7.

There was basically no participation by the military.[73] Significantly, the amnesty process also lacked the participation of IFP members, despite the fact that IFP members were the second most active group of perpetrators with respect to gross human rights violations.[74] In 1998, however, the TRC handed over to the prosecution authorities a list containing approximately 300 references to names and cases, resulting from the various TRC hearings, which the Commission considered worthy for further criminal investigation.[75]

4. *Criminal Trials During the 1990s*

As has been pointed out above, criminal proceedings took place before and during the operation of the Amnesty Committee.[76] However, very few trials took place regarding the former security forces and only two convictions of former security police members were recorded during the 1990s.[77] After the confessions surrounding the death squad unit Vlakplaas,[78] initial investigations were launched into the apartheid state's secret hit squad activities.[79] Subsequently, a special prosecution team headed by Transvaal Attorney-General Dr. Jan D'Oliveira was established to conduct the investigation and prosecution of hit-squad

[73] M. Fullard and N. Rousseau 'Truth, evidence and history' in C. Villa-Vicencio and E. Doxtader (eds) *The provocations of amnesty* (2003) 195 at 199.

[74] Ibid., 200.

[75] E. Kiss 'Moral ambition within and beyond political constraints' in R.I. Rotberg and D. Thompson (eds) *Truth v. justice* (2000) 68 at 78.

[76] See on the tense relationship of the Amnesty Committee, its investigation unit and the prosecutors: V. Nerlich *Apartheidkriminalität vor Gericht* (2002) 240–41; *TRC Report*, vol. 1, chap. 11, para. 93.

[77] See for the only comprehensive study on the prosecution of apartheid crimes during the 1990s: V. Nerlich *Apartheidkriminalität vor Gericht* (2002).

[78] See *supra* Chapter 1 note 11.

[79] The Harms- and later the Goldstone-Commissions were charged with conducting such investigations (V. Nerlich *Apartheidkriminalität vor Gericht* (2002) 116–22; F. Kutz *Amnestie für politische Straftäter in Südafrika* (2001) 77–84.

activities.[80] The team consisted of prosecutors and investigators, and could therefore, contrary to the normal process, conduct its own investigations. This was vital in order to maintain a high degree of independence and efficiency.[81]

The first trial involved Eugene de Kock, former commander of Vlakplaas from 1985 to 1993.[82] De Kock was charged in February 1995 on 121 counts, 12 of which related to murder.[83] De Kock had been a central figure in a wide range of secret security force operations. He was, however, charged mainly for crimes which did not have a primarily political background.[84] De Kock was found guilty on 89 charges in August 1996 and was sentenced to two terms of life and 212 years of imprisonment.[85] After his conviction de Kock cooperated intensively with the prosecution authorities and testified on secret hit squad activities and concomitant command structures.[86]

In another case, the investigations of the D'Oliveira Unit led to charges against the former Eastern Cape security policemen Gideon Nieuwoudt, Gerhard Lotz, Wybrand du Toit, Jacobus Kok and Marthinus Ras in August 1996. They were charged with the murder of three black members of the police service and an *askari*[87] in December 1989.[88]

---

[80] V. Nerlich *Apartheidkriminalität vor Gericht* (2002) 122–24.

[81] Interview with Jan D'Oliveira and others in Pretoria (May 2, 2006).

[82] *TRC Report*, vol. 2, chap. 3, appendix, para. 19 at page 317.

[83] See on the de Kock trial: V. Nerlich *Apartheidkriminalität vor Gericht* (2002) 124–34.

[84] This in part was due to the fact that such crimes were less difficult to prove but also since it was still unclear at the time how politically motivated crimes would be dealt with on a political level (ibid., 223–43).

[85] *TRC Report*, vol. 6, s. 3, chap. 1, para. 16. See for an analysis of the verdict: V. Nerlich *Apartheidkriminalität vor Gericht* (2002) 129–34.

[86] De Kock's testimonies also contributed chiefly to the amnesty process in that they urged perpetrators to apply for amnesty. According to the TRC de Kock accounted for about 48 per cent of all applications from security branch personnel (*TRC Report*, vol. 6, s. 3, chap. 1, para. 16).

[87] *Askari* is a term used for black members of the security police, who were liberation movement activists 'turned' to security policemen.

[88] V. Nerlich *Apartheidkriminalität vor Gericht* (2002) 134–37.

The case became known as "Motherwell-Four".[89] Nieuwoudt, du Toit and Ras were sentenced in June 1996 to 20, 15 and 10 years imprisonment respectively. The three later applied for amnesty and never had to serve their respective prison sentences.

In a trial closely connected to the de Kock prosecution, the security policemen Peter McIntyre, Andries Venter, Jaques Else and their superior Philip de Beer were charged in November 1996 with the murder of Sweet Sambo, who died in police custody in 1991.[90] As McIntyre, Venter and Else had already been charged and acquitted on assault charges in connection with Sambo's death in 1994, they successfully pleaded *autrefoi acqui*[91] and were accordingly acquitted.[92]

In April 1997, former Vlakplaas commander Dirk Coetzee and four other policemen were charged with the murder of lawyer and political activist Griffiths Mxenge in Durban in 1981.[93] Coetzee and two others were found guilty in May 1997 but shortly thereafter all received amnesty by the TRC.[94]

The investigations of the D'Oliveira team also concerned other security branches and the military. In October 1996 General Jack Cronjé and Jaques Hechter of the Northern Transvaal security branch were charged on 33 counts, including 27 counts of murder and four of attempted murder between 1986 and 1987.[95] Cronjé and Hechter immediately tendered amnesty applications, including the crimes in

---

89 *TRC Report*, vol. 6, s. 1, chap. 4, paras. 111–19; *TRC Report*, vol. 3, chap. 2, para. 301.

90 V. Nerlich *Apartheidkriminalität vor Gericht* (2002) 144.

91 See for the double jeopardy pleas: *infra* Chapter 2(2.4).

92 De Beer's indictment hinged on the other charges and could thus not be pursued (V. Nerlich *Apartheidkriminalität vor Gericht* (2002) 145).

93 V. Nerlich *Apartheidkriminalität vor Gericht* (2002) 146–53. The revelations of Nofomela and Coetzee in 1989 (see *supra* Chapter 1 note 11) related to the Mxenge murder. The prosecution was not conducted by the D'Oliveira team but by KwaZulu-Natal Attorney-General Tim McNally.

94 V. Nerlich *Apartheidkriminalität vor Gericht* (2002) 149. Decision no AC/97/0041. Transcripts of decisions of the Amnesty Committee are available at http://www.doj.gov.za/trc/amntrans/index.htm.

95 V. Nerlich *Apartheidkriminalität vor Gericht* (2002) 153–54.

question, which were eventually successful.[96] The trial was therefore not concluded.[97]

Ferdinand Barnard, a member of the special unit Civil Cooperation Bureau,[98] which was attached to the SADF, was charged in September 1997 with the murder of human rights activist David Webster in May 1989, the attempted murder of the later ANC Minister of Justice, Dullah Omar, and a number of other political and non-political deeds.[99] Barnard was convicted in 1998 on 25 counts, including the murder and attempted murder counts. He was sentenced effectively to life imprisonment.[100]

The trial with the highest political impact started in Durban in December 1995. It resulted from investigations of the independent Investigative Task Board and Investigative Task Unit into the political violence between IFP and ANC supporters in KwaZulu-Natal before and during the negotiation period.[101] The last apartheid Minister of Defence, Magnus Malan, and 29 others, among them former high-ranking SADF generals such as former SADF chief Jan Geldenhuys and Jacobus "Kat" Liebenberg, were charged with their alleged involvement in the murder of 13 ANC supporters in Natal in 1987, the KwaMakutha massacre, and for conspiracy to murder various ANC and United Democratic Front (hereinafter UDF)[102] activists during the late 1980s. During the so-called "Operation Marion", which took place in the Namibian Caprivi Strip in 1986, the SADF instructed and trained about 200 Inkatha supporters in paramilitary combat techniques to fight the ANC.[103] The charges alleged that the murders were committed by the Caprivi recruits with

96 Decisions no. AC/99/0031 and AC/99/0030.

97 V. Nerlich *Apartheidkriminalität vor Gericht* (2002) 154.

98 CCB. The CCB's initial task was to attack opposition members abroad but it later also operated in South Africa.

99 V. Nerlich *Apartheidkriminalität vor Gericht* (2002) 158–67.

100 Ibid., 167.

101 Ibid., 184–211.

102 The UDF was an association of various anti-apartheid organisations, founded in 1983 (R. Davenport and C. Saunders *South Africa* (2000) 495).

103 *TRC Report*, vol. 2, chap. 5, paras. 236–56.

the support of the SADF generals.[104] The trial ended in an acquittal of the accused due to various circumstances.[105]

On the whole, therefore, the trials contributed very little to the examination of the criminal apartheid past in terms of revealing new information on past conflict related atrocities and crimes.[106] This can be attributed to the fact that, on the one hand, political issues were not sufficiently investigated in most trials or simply ignored, and on the other, only a few trials took place with only two convictions.[107] Nevertheless, the prosecutions, which took place parallel to the amnesty process, contributed significantly to the work of the TRC as they had a major effect on the number of amnesty applications. The threat of prosecution was the decisive incentive for the vast majority of perpetrators from the security police to apply for amnesty. Many only applied for amnesty when they became aware of an imminent threat of being charged or when they were implicated in a criminal trial concerning former colleagues.[108] Without concomitant criminal trials, the number of amnesty applications for apartheid-state sponsored crimes would, thus, have been significantly lower.

---

[104] V. Nerlich *Apartheidkriminalität vor Gericht* (2002) 191–95.

[105] Ibid., 205. See for an analysis of the judgment: H. Varney and J. Sarkin 'Failing to pierce the hit-squad veil: an analysis of the Malan-trial' (1997) 10 *South African Journal of Criminal Justice* 141–61.

[106] V. Nerlich *Apartheidkriminalität vor Gericht* (2002) 328.

[107] Ibid.

[108] For a statistical analysis of this point see V. Nerlich *Apartheidkriminalität vor Gericht* (2002) 30 and 294–319.

Chapter Two

Prosecution of Political Crimes After the TRC

This chapter documents the prosecutions arising out of and/or connected with the TRC that have been initiated since the conclusion of its work. The chapter will also describe the various special units within the prosecutorial service, which were established for this purpose. The analysis will embrace all proceedings concerning crimes that were committed during the time period relevant for the Amnesty Committee's mandate from 1960 to 1994 and which potentially also fall within its legal mandate. Such crimes were, thus, at least politically motivated and connected with the apartheid conflict. The discussion therefore focuses on two types of crimes: those for which amnesty has been applied but was refused or those for which amnesty was not applied at all. Although the issue of post-TRC prosecutions in fact became more salient after the Amnesty Committee finished its work in 2001, the focus will be on all trials that were instituted after the deadline for amnesty applications had lapsed in 1997.

The first four documented cases concern proceedings that were conducted and initiated by the regional prosecution authorities independent of any central or special units in Pretoria. The following four cases, starting with the Terre'Blanche case, contain descriptions of prosecutions that were instituted and conducted by the special Priority Crimes Litigation Unit. Both sets of cases will be presented in chronological order.

1. *Special Units for Post-TRC Prosecutions*

In 1998 the work of the team headed by Jan D'Oliveira came to an end. In the course of that year the prosecution authorities were completely restructured. A new centralised National Prosecution

Authority (hereinafter NPA), headed by a National Director of Public Prosecutions (hereinafter NDPP), was established in Pretoria.[1] The first NDPP was Bulelani Ngcuka who was succeeded in early 2005 by Vusi Pikoli.[2] D'Oliveira became one of the deputy NDPP and was no longer involved with prosecutions related to the apartheid conflict.[3] In September 1999 most of the members of his unit were integrated into the newly established Directorate of Special Operations (hereinafter DSO),[4] the so-called "Scorpions", which was in urgent need of skilled investigators and prosecutors.[5] However, the question remained, what should happen with the TRC-related cases with which the D'Oliveira Unit had been dealing.

1.1 *The Human Rights Investigative Unit*

In early 1999 a working group called the Human Rights Investigative Unit was established within the NPA on the initiative of then Minister of Justice Dullah Omar. The unit's mandate was to review, investigate and possibly prosecute all cases falling within the ambit of the TRC Act for which amnesty had been refused or was not applied,[6] thus, to continue the work of Jan D'Oliveira.

---

[1] See for a comprehensive study of the NPA: M. Schönteich *Lawyers for the people* (2001).

[2] Ngcuka resigned as a result of political conflicts over the prosecution of former Deputy President Jacob Zuma. Pikoli was suspended in September 2007 for political reasons and replaced by Mokotedi Mpshe.

[3] Interview with Jan D'Oliveira and others in Pretoria (May 2, 2006).

[4] The DSO was an Investigating Directorate according to section 7 of the National Prosecuting Authority Act 32 of 1998 (hereinafter NPA Act) (for the capacities of the DSO see Chapter 5 of the NPA Act). It was the only prosecutorial entity capable of conducting its own investigations. According to section 7(1A) of the NPA Act the President may appoint two further Investigating Directorates, which as yet has not happened. Meanwhile the DSO has been disbanded on the initiative of the ANC. Most likely this happened for political reasons, since the DSO successfully targeted a number of high profile ANC leaders for corruption. See *End of the road for Scorpions* SAPA, Oct 10, 2008.

[5] V. Nerlich *Apartheidkriminalität vor Gericht* (2002) 214.

[6] Interview with Vincent Saldanha in Cape Town (April 26, 2006).

The unit was headed by Vincent Saldanha; and his deputy was former Witwatersrand prosecutor Brink Ferreira.[7] According to Saldanha, four lawyers worked basically on a full or part time basis for the unit.[8] He sensed intense political support for his work, especially from the Department of Justice, led by Dullah Omar. Distinctions were not to be made between perpetrators of the political groups.[9] The composition of the unit further reflected, according to Saldanha, an approach that was extremely human rights- and victims-orientated. He himself comes from the human rights sector and was involved in a number of TRC hearings as an attorney for victims.[10] Some of the other members of the unit had prior work experience with the TRC or with human rights non-governmental organisations (hereinafter NGO).[11] The drafting of personnel from outside the ordinary prosecution structures also guaranteed for a high degree of independence.[12]

In November 1999 all dockets concerning criminal cases were moved from the D'Oliveira Unit to the Human Rights Investigative Unit.[13] Furthermore, some prosecution dockets from the regional NPA offices concerning TRC-related cases as well as all relevant dockets from the TRC were gathered at the latter unit. Although the dockets often concerned ongoing investigations, which in some cases had reached a very advanced stage, there was strangely no consultation or cooperation between D'Oliveira and the Saldanha team.[14]

It was intended that Saldanha would head the unit for a short period. After the conclusion of his secondment from his primary place of work, the Legal Resources Centre in Cape Town, he left the unit, having

---

[7] V. Nerlich *Apartheidkriminalität vor Gericht* (2002) 213.

[8] According to Nerlich it was initially intended to assign three deputy directors and five senior state advocates to the unit (ibid.).

[9] Interview with Vincent Saldanha in Cape Town (April 26, 2006).

[10] V. Nerlich *Apartheidkriminalität vor Gericht* (2002) 213.

[11] Ibid.

[12] Interview with Vincent Saldanha in Cape Town (April 26, 2006). However, the unit had to appoint police to conduct investigations and had to appoint NPA prosecutors once a case was ready for indictment.

[13] V. Nerlich *Apartheidkriminalität vor Gericht* (2002) 213.

[14] Interview with Jan D'Oliveira and others in Pretoria (May 2, 2006).

served for only one year. Until then all investigations were still ongoing and no charges had been laid.[15] Among the cases under scrutiny some were very high profile, such as the case of the torture and killing of Steve Biko.[16] Moreover, a number of persons from the upper echelons of the former security apparatus were among those under the scrutiny of the unit.[17] The rationale behind the fact that nobody was charged lay, according to Saldanha, with the complexities of such high profile cases, which required meticulous preparation and the fact that a great number of cases were still handled by the Amnesty Committee. Once Saldanha's tenure lapsed, the unit's work only continued for a brief time. The setup of the unit was probably not ideal. Saldanha worked only on a part-time basis for the unit and lacked experience as a prosecutor.

However, thereafter the responsibility for TRC cases was again allocated to a working group within the DSO, the so-called Special National Projects Unit headed by Advocate Chris Macadam.[18] It is doubtful whether any significant and/or ongoing work was done on the issues during that time as it was probably only Macadam who worked on post-TRC prosecutions on a part time basis.[19] Again, no court proceedings were instituted. TRC cases apparently did not enjoy high priority at that time. Macadam asserts that, again, it was the ongoing amnesty proceedings that acted as the main barrier to progressing with prosecutions.[20]

Whereas the D'Oliveira Unit had been well-staffed and well-equipped, the resources allocated to post-TRC prosecutions after 1998 were absolutely minimal, which naturally contributed to their slow progress.[21]

---

[15] Interview with Vincent Saldanha in Cape Town (April 26, 2006).

[16] See text accompanying *infra* Chapter 4 note 166.

[17] Interview with Vincent Saldanha in Cape Town (April 26, 2006).

[18] Interview with Torie Pretorius and others in Pretoria (May 2, 2006). Macadam had previously also worked for the TRC as head of the Commission's witness protection programme.

[19] Interview by Gerhard Werle with Jan D'Oliveira in Pretoria (March 2004).

[20] Interview by Gerhard Werle with Chris Macadam and others in Pretoria (Feb 27, 2004).

[21] Interview by Gerhard Werle with Jan D'Oliveira in Pretoria (March 2004).

The NPA did not want to commit resources to cases which might eventually collapse due to amnesty applications being granted to those under investigation.[22] Yet it seems probable that there were also a significant number of potential cases for which amnesty had not been applied or that the D'Oliveira team had already prepared, such as the investigations against General Krappies Engelbrecht, the former commander of Eugene de Kock.[23] By 1999 the D'Oliveira Unit had allegedly already prepared about 20 charge sheets.[24]

According to Macadam, the NPA wanted to await the presentation of the last volumes of the TRC Report. This could not, however, have constituted an obstacle in a legal sense, especially considering the clear recommendations the TRC had already made with regards to criminal accountability in 1998. However, the NPA tried to avoid interfering with the President's response to the TRC Report with respect to policy approaches to tackle TRC-related crimes, including the possible pardoning of certain perpetrators.[25] This and the lack of resources could explain why, although the Amnesty Committee's work ended in May 2001, still by 2003, when the last TRC Report volumes were published, criminal proceedings had yet to be instituted. Moreover, the structures put in place for post-TRC prosecutions were not ideal, as was especially the case when matters were placed with the DSO,[26] which was primarily an elite unit for the investigation and prosecution of serious economic crimes, corruption, organised crime and terrorism.[27]

In conclusion it must be stated that the work on post-TRC prosecutions within the central NPA office between 1998 and 2003 was insignificant.

---

22 Interview by Gerhard Werle with Chris Macadam and others in Pretoria (Feb 27, 2004).

23 See V. Nerlich *Apartheidkriminalität vor Gericht* (2002) 154–55.

24 Ibid., 154.

25 Interview by Gerhard Werle with Chris Macadam and others in Pretoria (Feb 27, 2004).

26 Interview with Madeleine Fullard in Pretoria (May 4, 2006).

27 M. Schönteich *Lawyers for the people* (2001) 64.

1.2 *The Priority Crimes Litigation Unit*

The pace of developments did indeed pick up, however, after the last two volumes of the TRC Report[28] had been tabled in Parliament on 15 April 2003. President Mbeki stated in a speech before Parliament on this occasion that it was in the hands of the NDPP to pursue any cases arising from the TRC that he considered prosecutable as is normal practice in criminal justice.[29] This apparently provided the clarification the NPA had awaited to proceed on TRC cases.

One month prior to this statement the responsibility for TRC prosecutions had been transferred again. On 24 March 2003, three days after the final Report volumes had been presented to the President, Advocate Anton Ackermann was appointed Special Director of Public Prosecution[30] and head of the newly founded Priority Crimes Litigation Unit (hereinafter PCLU).[31] According to the respective presidential proclamation, the PCLU is responsible for managing and directing the investigation and prosecution of crimes dealt with in the Implementation of the Rome Statute of the International Criminal Court Act no 27 of 2002, serious national and international crimes, including acts of terrorism and sabotage, high treason, sedition, mercenary activities and other priority crimes to be determined by the NDPP.[32] No mention is made of post-TRC prosecutions. However, at the inception of the PCLU the NDPP declared all crimes relating to the TRC for which

---

[28] *TRC Report*, vols 6 and 7. See also section 44 of the TRC Act.

[29] Statement by President Mbeki to the National Houses of Parliament and the Nation, at the Tabling of the Report of the Truth and Reconciliation Commission (April 15, 2003).

[30] According to section 13(1)(c) of the NPA Act the President may appoint Directors of Public Prosecutions to exercise certain powers, carry out certain duties and perform certain special functions.

[31] Proclamation by the President of the Republic of South Africa of 24 March 2003 (No. 46 of 2003).

[32] Ibid. The PCLU is also responsible for prosecutions relating to the non-proliferation of weapons of mass destruction (nuclear, chemical and biological) and regulations of conventional military arms (National Prosecuting Authority, *Annual report 2005/2006*).

amnesty had not been granted as priority crimes in the context of the proclamation, which made the PCLU the agency responsible for dealing with such crimes.[33] In fact, TRC matters initially made up the main proportion of the unit's work.

In mid-2006 the PCLU effectively consisted of six prosecutors: its head Anton Ackermann, his deputy Torie Pretorius, Chris Macadam, who was previously responsible for TRC matters in the DSO, Shawn Abrahams, Susan Bukau and the then newly appointed Mtunzi Mhaga, who had previously been involved in two TRC-related trials in the Eastern Cape.[34] The composition of the unit shows a high degree of continuity. Ackermann and Pretorius had worked under D'Oliveira. Prior to that Pretorius had worked for the Goldstone commission.[35] As already stated, Macadam had been involved with TRC cases before 2003 and had gathered experience by working for the TRC.

When Ackermann took over matters, he instituted an audit of all available cases. The result was that some 459 cases[36] could be registered from the material, contained in dockets concerning the cases handed over from the TRC or the D'Oliveira Unit. About 160 cases were immediately deemed not to warrant further proceedings. Only about 16 cases were identified as worthy of pursuing prosecution.[37] At least three were prepared almost immediately for indictment.[38] It would, however, be totally unrealistic to expect all of the hundreds of cases, especially those submitted by the TRC, to warrant criminal proceedings.[39] The list handed over by the TRC does not significantly contribute to the work of the PCLU in general, as most cases had already been known to the D'Oliveira Unit.[40] By the end of 2006 the PCLU was

[33] E-mail from Anton Ackermann (Oct 18, 2005).

[34] Interview with Torie Pretorius and others in Pretoria (May 2, 2006).

[35] V. Nerlich *Apartheidkriminalität vor Gericht* (2002) 123.

[36] National Prosecution Authority, *Annual report 2002/2003.*

[37] Interview with Anton Ackermann in Pretoria (May 11, 2006).

[38] Ibid.

[39] Interview with Jan D'Oliveira and others in Pretoria (May 2, 2006).

[40] Interview with Torie Pretorius and others in Pretoria (May 2, 2006).

working on 16 cases in total, five of which were considered to be of high priority and had been prepared to an advanced stage.[41]

As far as the general approach to post-TRC cases is concerned, the PCLU focuses first on cases in which amnesty has been denied, since it is generally easier to identify a case worthy for prosecution. The PCLU's secondary focus is cases where amnesty was not applied at all.[42] Cases that involve the use of egregious violence and which resulted in the death of more than one person are naturally of higher priority than those which, for instance, were only directed at non-human entities, such as sabotage attacks of the liberation movement.[43] However, according to its senior members, the PCLU attempts to ignore as much as possible political implications and to resist distinguishing between the political groups of liberation movement and apartheid state forces. The approach taken is strictly dependent on the availability of evidence and the egregiousness of the crime, regardless of political affiliation of the perpetrator.[44]

Besides this, there is also a working group within the NPA which works on the exhumation of missing persons who were killed during the struggle against apartheid and secretly buried. The primary aim of the exhumation work is to return the remains to the victims' relatives. It is not driven by criminal investigations but occasionally new information can come to light that is relevant for prosecutions.[45]

---

41 E-mail from Anton Ackermann (June 19, 2006). It is unclear what happened to the above mentioned 20 indictments allegedly prepared already in 1999 or in how far those overlap with the 16 cases.

42 Interview by Gerhard Werle with Chris Macadam and others in Pretoria (Feb 27, 2004).

43 Interview with Anton Ackermann in Pretoria (May 11, 2006).

44 Interview with Torie Pretorius and others in Pretoria (May 2, 2006); Interview with Anton Ackermann in Pretoria (May 11, 2006).

45 Interview with Madeleine Fullard in Pretoria (May 4, 2006). Valuable information was uncovered in the case concerning the death of Ntombi Khubeka, who was a member of MK. In 1987 she was arrested by the security police in Natal and beaten during her interrogation. The policemen at their amnesty hearing claimed that she had suddenly died of a heart attack. However, when her remains were discovered

The biggest obstacle facing the PCLU is the severe lack of resources.[46] Apart from TRC matters, the unit is responsible for a range of other issues. As such, cases pertaining to the illegal trafficking of nuclear material and knowledge by South Africans took up a particularly large proportion of the unit's resources in recent times. Until the end of 2006, TRC matters took up on average only about 30 to 50 per cent of the unit's work.[47] Considering the already small number of prosecutors in the PCLU, this proportion is rather modest. Furthermore, the minimal resources devoted to the unit's investigative work is a major problem. Some cases had already been fully investigated, others needed more investigation. The D'Oliveira team included about 20 carefully selected, highly skilled and experienced police investigators, who were not suspected of sympathising with their former colleagues accused of political crimes.[48] Whereas this unit could thus conduct investigations independent of the police, the PCLU has to rely on the assignment of investigators and the conduct of investigations by the South African Police Service (hereinafter SAPS) or the meanwhile disbanded DSO.[49] The gathering of evidence concerning TRC cases is especially

---

and exhumed, a bullet hole in her temple was detected which, of course, exposed the police testimony presented as false (See *TRC Report*, vol. 6, s. 4, chap. 2).

46 Interview with Anton Ackermann in Pretoria (May 11, 2006); Interview with Torie Pretorius and others in Pretoria (May 2, 2006). See also N Rousseau 'Prosecutions' in E. Doxtader (ed.) *Provoking questions* (2005) 37 at 47.

47 Interview with Torie Pretorius and others in Pretoria (May 2, 2006).

48 V. Nerlich *Apartheidkriminalität vor Gericht* (2002) 123; Interview by Gerhard Werle with Jan D'Oliveira in Pretoria (March 2004).

49 Interview with Torie Pretorius and others in Pretoria (May 2, 2006). Traditionally investigations, which are basically the independent responsibility of the police, and prosecutions are quite strictly separated (M. Schönteich *Lawyers for the people* (2001) 41). Only with the establishment of the NPA was this traditional separation eased since with the DSO investigative powers were permanently introduced to the NPA. Furthermore, with the NPA Act prosecutors were granted greater influence on investigations. According to section 24(4)(c) of the NPA Act, a Director of Public Prosecutions, such as Ackermann, may in some bounds direct the responsible investigator who is according to section 24(7) of the NPA Act obliged to follow requests. It is also interesting to note that the first steps towards a combination of investigation and prosecution capacities occurred at the investigation of apartheid

demanding of investigators. The crimes often happened secretly without independent witnesses and were covered up meticulously. Thus, as was the case with the D'Oliveira team, the PCLU relies to a great extent on state witnesses in order to bring cases before the courts.[50] Again, incriminating evidence has to be compiled in order to urge the conspirators to cooperate.

Such circumstances and the political implications of TRC cases place special demands on the skills, commitment and experience of investigators. In contrast to the abilities of the investigators working for the D'Oliveira team, the PCLU has major problems recruiting such investigators.[51] Although it was intended for the DSO to provide the PCLU with investigators, the DSO declined to cooperate.[52] Thus, the unit has to rely on the police, who are obliged to cooperate. However, a request to the police of early 2004 to assign investigators on an ongoing basis was not followed.[53] The investigators, who were assigned to

crimes through the D'Oliveira team and the Investigative Task Unit in Natal which was necessitated by the during the 1990s still largely untransformed police service (V. Nerlich *Apartheidkriminalität vor Gericht* (2002) 123).

[50] Interview with Anton Ackermann in Pretoria (May 11, 2006). According to section 204 of the Criminal Procedure Act no 51 of 1977 arrangements can be made for participants in a crime to testify on behalf of the state against their accomplices to secure a conviction. If the state witness testifies frankly and honestly in the opinion of the court, he may be discharged from criminal liability for the offence in question. According to Ackermann, Pretorius and D'Oliveira evidence gathered by the TRC in comparison is not helpful and plays no significant part in the work of the PCLU. See also V. Nerlich *Apartheidkriminalität vor Gericht* (2002) 327 and 244.

[51] Interview with Torie Pretorius and others in Pretoria (May 2, 2006).

[52] Ibid.

[53] Ibid. It has to be borne in mind that the SAPS also suffers from a major lack of resources and availability of skilled investigators. The focus of the SAPS is clearly on tackling the high present-day crime rate. It is thus not willing to assign resources for cases which mostly took place more than 20 years ago. (Interview with Jan D'Oliveira and others in Pretoria (May 2, 2006)). Added to this power struggles between police commissioner Jackie Selebi and the NDPP, which came to a head at the prosecution of former deputy President Jacob Zuma, tainted the relationship between the SAPS and the NPA (Interview with Torie Pretorius and others in Pretoria (May 2, 2006)).

investigate certain matters, often lacked the necessary skill, determination and experience.[54] Compared to this problem, a possible lack of development and change in the police service or the reluctance of certain officers to investigate their former colleagues no longer plays an influential role.[55]

From early 2006 all post-TRC prosecutions were concentrated at the PCLU and the regional prosecutors are obliged to refer such cases to the NPA in Pretoria. A centralised prosecution certainly has the advantage of enabling the achievement of consistent progress. Moreover, it certainly makes sense to concentrate the experience in prosecuting TRC-related cases in one central unit. The advantages of centralised prosecutions were highlighted by the D'Oliveira team and also by the prosecution of systematic crimes committed by the socialist regime in the former German Democratic Republic (hereinafter GDR).[56]

2. *The Wouter Basson Case*

On 4 October 1999 the trial of Dr. Wouter Basson was opened at the High Court of Pretoria.[57] Basson was the leader of South Africa's secret programme on chemical and biological warfare also referred to as "Project Coast".[58] Project Coast was established by the SADF in the early 1980s initially with the intention of providing the country with the defensive capacity to react to chemical and biological warfare attacks.[59] Especially due to the activities of Basson, the project became increasingly involved in criminal activities in relation to the countering of opposition efforts against apartheid in Namibia, South Africa and various other countries.

---

[54] Interview with Torie Pretorius and others in Pretoria (May 2, 2006).

[55] Ibid.

[56] K. Marxen and G. Werle *Die strafrechtliche Aufarbeitung von DDR-Unrecht* (1999) 233–34.

[57] V. Nerlich *Apartheidkriminalität vor Gericht* (2002) 167.

[58] *TRC Report*, vol. 2, chap. 6 C, paras. 1–2.

[59] Ibid., para. 40.

The trial against Wouter Basson is not a genuine post-TRC case. It is rather connected to the prosecutions of the 1990s since it was conducted by Ackermann and Pretorius, both members of the D'Oliveira Unit at that time. The amnesty hearings were still in full swing when it was started. However, Basson failed to apply for amnesty and the deadline for applications had lapsed by the time charges were laid. Moreover, the Basson case was significant due to its links to other post-TRC cases, such as the attempted murder of Frank Chikane which will be described below, and the scope and seriousness of the charges, which were of great significance. The litigation only came to an end in late 2005. It went through the Supreme Court of Appeal and the Constitutional Court. The ruling of the Constitutional Court potentially has great effects for post-TRC prosecutions in general. The trial court litigation has already partly been analysed by legal scholars and was generally well documented in the public.[60] The following subchapter will thus only outline the charges and give an overview of how the case progressed. The Constitutional Court's judgment will then be analysed in greater detail.

2.1 *The trial and quashed charges*

Basson was initially charged with 64 counts, 24 of which pertained to non-political fraud offences allegedly committed by Basson while managing Project Coast.[61] Further counts pertained to drug offences.[62] Of special importance are 29 counts which concerned murder.[63] According to the prosecutors, the murders in which Basson participated were aimed at killing enemies of the apartheid state. Most of these incidents were distinctly connected to a political objective and were allegedly

---

[60] See especially V. Nerlich *Apartheidkriminalität vor Gericht* (2002) 167. For a comprehensive overview of the development of the trial see http://ccrweb.ccr.uct.ac.za/archive/cbw/cbw_index.html.

[61] *S. v Wouter Basson* (T) Case no. 32/1999 11 April 2002, unreported, at para. 16. See for a comprehensive summary of the indictment: V. Nerlich *Apartheidkriminalität vor Gericht* (2002) 169–74.

[62] *S. v Wouter Basson*, akte van beskuldigung, vol. II, aanklagte 25–30.

[63] Ibid., aanklagte 31–36, 38–43, 45–50, 52–58, 60–63.

committed in the fight against the opposition movement's anti-apartheid struggle.[64]

Targets for such murders were detainees in Namibia, the then South-West Africa, who belonged to the rebel movement South-West African People's Organisation (hereinafter SWAPO), members of the South African state's own forces who were believed to be a security risk, ANC members such as Ronnie Kasrils and Pallo Jordan[65] and various other persons believed to be enemies of the apartheid state.[66] One of the gravest incidents concerned the poisoning of about 200 SWAPO detainees in Namibia.[67] Basson allegedly provided the poison. Apparently many corpses were later dumped from a plane into the sea off the Namibian coast.[68] In another incident Basson allegedly provided cholera bacteria, which were introduced to a drinking water well in a SWAPO refugee camp.[69] The aim was to disturb the first free elections in Namibia.[70] Basson was allegedly involved mostly in organising the murders and especially providing the poison.[71]

After an extensive and very costly trial he was eventually acquitted on all charges by the trial judge, Mr Justice Hartzenberg, on 11 April 2002.[72]

---

64 See for a summary of the wide ranging charges against Basson: *S. v Basson* (CC) Case no. CCT 30/03 9 September 2005 at para. 192.

65 Pallo Jordan served the ANC as a senior member in exile in London and Lusaka and later inhibited various posts as a minister in the cabinet (P. van Niekerk and B. Ludman (eds) *A-Z of South African politics 1999* (1999) 133–35).

66 *S. v Wouter Basson*, akte van beskuldigung, vol. II, aanklagte 31–36, 38–43, 45–50, 52–58, 60–63.

67 V. Nerlich *Apartheidkriminalität vor Gericht* (2002) 170.

68 *S. v Wouter Basson*, akte van beskuldigung, vol. II, opsomming van wesentlike feite, aanklag 31, para. 16.

69 Ibid., aanklag 61.

70 The bacteria were unexpectedly killed due to a high proportion of chlorine in the water.

71 V. Nerlich *Apartheidkriminalität vor Gericht* (2002) 171–73.

72 *S. v Wouter Basson* (T) Case no. 32/1999 11 April 2002, unreported. The judgment stretches over more than 1400 pages. The trial was one of the most extensive ones in South African history. 140 witnesses were heard. The costs for the state totalled several million Rand. The state also had to cover the costs of Basson's defence team, since he was still a state employee.

The failure to secure a conviction can be attributed mainly to the fact that Hartzenberg rejected most of the evidence and witnesses testifying on behalf of the State as unconvincing and untrustworthy.[73] The judge was criticised for being biased and generally hostile towards the prosecutors but also for erring on several legal issues.[74]

However, three issues emerged during the trial which were of central relevance in the Appeal Court and Constitutional Court litigations. The first of the three issues emerged about three months after the start of the trial. The prosecutors applied for the recusal of Judge Hartzenberg. They claimed that Hartzenberg was biased and could not rule on the case objectively.[75] The judge, however, refused to recuse himself.[76] The second issue pertains to the prosecutors' intention to introduce records of a bail hearing regarding the fraud charges to the trial. Hartzenberg ruled that the bail records were inadmissible in the trial.[77]

The third and most important issue for the purposes of the present discussion, concerns the objection made by Basson's defence team to certain charges before the trial had commenced.[78] The attorneys applied for nine of the charges to be quashed on the grounds that they would not concern criminal offences.[79] The judge granted the application with respect to seven charges.[80] Six of these quashed charges, counts 31, 46, 54, 55, 58 and 61, concern acts of conspiracy to commit murder in terms of section 18(2) of the Riotous Assemblies Act no 17 of 1956.[81] The

[73] Interview with Torie Pretorius and others in Pretoria (May 2, 2006).

[74] Ibid.; M. Fullard and N. Rousseau 'An imperfect past: the Truth and Reconciliation Commission in transition' in J. Daniel et al. (eds) *State of the nation* (2003) 78 at 92; V. Nerlich *Apartheidkriminalität vor Gericht* (2002) 179–82.

[75] *S. v Basson* (CC) Case no. CCT 30/03 9 September 2005 at para. 3.

[76] *S. v Basson* [2000] 3 All SA 59 (T).

[77] *S. v Basson* (CC) Case no. CCT 30/03 10 March 2004 at para. 4.

[78] See for a summary of this issue: *S. v Basson* (CC) Case no. CCT 30/03 9 September 2005 at paras. 13–18. See for a legal evaluation: V. Nerlich *Apartheidkriminalität vor Gericht* (2002) 174–83.

[79] The application was based on section 85(1)(c) of the Criminal Procedure Act.

[80] *S. v Basson* [2000] 1 All SA 430 (T).

[81] *S. v Basson* (CC) Case no. CCT 30/03 10 March 2004 at para. 5. The provision reads as follows:

charges contained the most serious of the accusations against Basson. Count 31 concerned the poisoning of the SWAPO detainees. Count 46 concerned the conspiracy to murder a high-ranking administrative official in northern Namibia. Count 54 related to the unsuccessful conspiracy to murder the later ANC ministers Pallo Jordan and Ronnie Kasrils in London. Counts 55 and 58 concerned a conspiracy to murder ANC members in Mozambique and Swaziland. Count 61 concerned the conspiracy to murder the SWAPO refugees with cholera bacteria.

As is evident, these charges concern cases of murder or attempted murder that took place beyond South Africa's borders. Since South African courts have no jurisdiction to try crimes which were committed abroad,[82] prosecutors were relegated to pursuing convictions for Basson's participation in the conspiracy that took place in South Africa.[83] However, Basson's defence argued that the conspiracy to commit crimes abroad would according to the definition of the crime itself not constitute a criminal offence, even if this conspiracy took place in South Africa.[84] Hartzenberg accepted the defence's arguments and held that conspiracies to commit crimes abroad were not covered by section 18(2) of the Riotous Assemblies Act.[85] Should this legal opinion prevail it would have serious consequences for all cases in which a similar indictment is intended. The litigation proceedings concerning this point will now be examined.

---

(2) Any person who

(a) conspires with any other person to aid or procure the commission of or to commit; or

(b) incites, instigates, commands, or procures any other person to commit, any offence, whether at common law or against a statute or statutory regulation, shall be guilty of an offence and liable on conviction to the punishment to which a person convicted of actually committing that offence would be liable.

82 *S. v Basson* (CC) Case no. CCT 30/03 9 September 2005 at para. 223.

83 V. Nerlich *Apartheidkriminalität vor Gericht* (2002) 175. Nerlich points out that the prosecutors in the trial of Eugene de Kock successfully exercised this approach in respect of certain charges.

84 Ibid., 175.

85 *S. v Basson* [2000] 1 All SA 430 (T) at 444g.

2.2 *The appeal litigation*

Immediately after the judgment had been handed down, the State applied for judgment to be reserved on certain questions of law[86] for resolution by the Supreme Court of Appeal.[87] The application concerned the three issues outlined above. Subject to certain conditions, Hartzenberg reserved the recusal and bail record issues for consideration by the Supreme Court of Appeal. However, he refused to reserve the question of whether he erred in law concerning his ruling to quash the aforementioned charges.[88] The NPA in June 2002 appealed against the judgment concerning the questions of law reserved by the trial judge and simultaneously applied to the Supreme Court of Appeal to reserve the issue of the quashing of the charges for consideration.[89] However, this specific application was seriously defective in various procedural aspects.[90] The prosecutors then applied for condonation regarding the non-compliance with the procedural requirements.[91] Due to the appeal application's clear and serious violations with respect to the Supreme Court of Appeal rules, the Court refused condonation, and, thus, did not even consider the merits of the legal question of whether the charges were correctly quashed, nor did it answer the other questions in favour of the State.[92]

---

[86] See section 319(1) of the Criminal Procedure Act.

[87] *S. v Basson* (CC) Case no. CCT 30/03 10 March 2004 at para. 8. For a comprehensive summary of the litigation up to the Constitutional Court see *S. v Basson* (CC) Case no. CCT 30/03 10 March 2004 paras. 1–14 and *S. v Basson* (CC) Case no. CCT 30/03 9 September 2005 paras. 1–18.

[88] *S. v Basson* [2002] JOL 9680 (T) at 19–20.

[89] *S. v Basson* (CC) Case no. CCT 30/03 10 March 2004 at para. 10.

[90] *S. v Basson* 2003 (2) SACR 373 (SCA) at 379. See on defects of the application also: *S. v Basson* (CC) Case no. CCT 30/03 9 September 2005 paras. 157–160.

[91] *S. v Basson* 2003 (2) SACR 373 (SCA) at para. 379; *S. v Basson* (CC) Case no. CCT 30/03 10 March 2004 at para. 11.

[92] *S. v Basson* 2003 (2) SACR 373 (SCA) at para. 118. The Supreme Court of Appeal held that the bail record and recusal issues concerned questions of fact and not of law as required for an appeal litigation.

2.3 *The Constitutional Court litigation*

After the appeal had failed, the prosecutors applied for special leave to appeal against the judgment of the Supreme Court of Appeal in mid-2003 and for leave to appeal the judgment of the High Court directly at the Constitutional Court.[93] The application again concerned the three central issues: bias of the trial judge; admissibility of the bail records; and the quashing of six charges, which had already been before the Supreme Court of Appeal.[94] The focus here will be on the quashing of the charges.

In a preliminary judgment the Constitutional Court ruled that even though the conduct in question had taken place before the Constitution had come into force, the issues concerned constitutional matters within the jurisdiction of the Court.[95] Apart from various complex procedural issues,[96] the crucial issue to be considered by the Constitutional Court was whether the Supreme Court of Appeal exercised its discretion wrongly in not considering the respective question and whether it was in the interest of justice to grant leave to appeal on this question.[97] The Court therefore found it crucial to consider the seriousness of the charges in light of South Africa's international obligations regarding the maintenance of fundamental principles of international humanitarian law.[98] Since the crimes in question were very grave and had been committed abroad, the question arose whether South Africa had an obligation to prosecute under international law. In its preliminary judgment, the Court had stated, without dealing exhaustively with the issue, that international law obliged South Africa to prosecute crimes against humanity and war crimes.[99] In its final judgment, however, it

---

[93] *S. v Basson* (CC) Case no. CCT 30/03 10 March 2004 at para. 1. The application was unique in that it was the first time that a state organ, the NPA, appealed to the Constitutional Court against a judicial decision.

[94] *S. v Basson* (CC) Case no. CCT 30/03 9 September 2005 at para. 1.

[95] *S. v Basson* (CC) Case no. CCT 30/03 10 March 2004 at para. 79.

[96] *S. v Basson* (CC) Case no. CCT 30/03 9 September 2005 at paras. 128–187.

[97] Ibid., at paras. 185–186.

[98] Ibid., at para. 171.

[99] *S. v Basson* (CC) Case no. CCT 30/03 10 March 2004 at para. 37.

confined itself to evaluating the importance of the charges in general terms with regard to South Africa's obligations under international humanitarian and human rights law.

The Court was of the opinion that no country ought to allow the planning of cross-border criminal activities.[100] The Court then elaborated in general terms on the great significance of international humanitarian law, thereby quoting the decision of the International Court of Justice on the legality of the threat or use of nuclear weapons,[101] which highlighted humanitarian law as a fundamental and intransgressible aspect of international law.[102] The Court further made it clear, with reference to the decision of the International Criminal Tribunal for the former Yugoslavia in the *Dusko Tadic* case, that the distinction in international law between internal and international conflict had become increasingly blurred.[103] Thus, since the minimum standards for internal and international conflicts were identical, the Court neglected to determine how the conflict between SWAPO and the SADF in Namibia should be classified.[104] Due to the growing overlap of international human rights and humanitarian law the precise characterisation of the participants' legal status was also left open.[105] However the Court pointed out that South Africa, as a party to the Geneva Conventions, was bound to respect the principles outlined therein and was bound to respect fundamental principles of customary humanitarian law.[106] Such rules had also to be obeyed in the Namibian conflict. The subjection of captives to asphyxiation through poison under the guise of medical care and the insertion of cholera bacteria in the water supply of hundreds

---

100 *S. v Basson* (CC) Case no. CCT 30/03 9 September 2005 at para. 170. The Court pointed out that this factor has neither been considered by the Supreme Court of Appeal in any regard, nor had it been brought to the attention of the Supreme Court of Appeal.

101 *Legality of the Threat or Use of Nuclear Weapons* (Advisory Opinion) [1996] ICJ Rep 226.

102 *S. v Basson* (CC) Case no. CCT 30/03 9 September 2005 at para. 174.

103 Ibid., at para. 175.

104 Ibid., at para. 178.

105 Ibid., at para. 179.

106 Ibid., at para. 177.

suspected opponents of the regime grossly transgressed even the most minimal standards of international humanitarian law.[107] According to the Constitutional Court, the Supreme Court of Appeal had failed to consider these grave breaches and the, what it termed 'international consensus on the normative desirability to prosecute war criminals'.[108] The application of the State thus succeeded.

The Court went even further and examined whether the quashing of the six charges was based on a proper interpretation of section 18(2) of the Riotous Assemblies Act. The Court initially referred to the main arguments of counsel for the State[109] that the Military Discipline Code[110] criminalised certain conduct of SADF members even if the acts were committed beyond the borders of South Africa, that section 19A of the Riotous Assemblies Act provided that the Riotous Assemblies Act was also applicable in South-West Africa and most importantly, that South African Courts generally had jurisdiction to try crimes committed abroad when there was a sufficient connection between the crime and South Africa.[111]

According to the Court, section 47 of the Military Discipline Code[112] determines that any SADF member who commits a civil offence, meaning an offence not criminalised by military law but by common South African law, is criminally liable in terms of the code even if the crime was

---

[107] Ibid., at paras. 179–182.

[108] Ibid., at paras. 184–185.

[109] Counsel for the state were Wim Trengrove, A. Cockrell and N. Fourie.

[110] The code is part of the Defence Act (Act no. 44 of 1957).

[111] *S. v Basson* (CC) Case no. CCT 30/03 9 September 2005 at para. 210.

[112] The section provides that:

> 'Any person who beyond the borders of the Union commits or omits to do any act in circumstances under which he would, if he had committed or omitted to do that act in the Union, have been guilty of a civil offence, shall be guilty of an offence under this Code and liable on conviction to such penalty applicable in respect of that civil offence as could be imposed under section ninety-one of this Code.' The Code was in force during the time in that the offences were allegedly committed and during the time of the trial. According to section 104(5) of the Defence Act, the Code applies to all members of the Permanent Force of the Defence Force.

committed abroad.[113] Any member of the army who commits murder beyond South Africa's borders is liable to prosecution in a military as well as an ordinary court in South Africa.[114] Thus, provided the murders were to be carried out by members of the SADF, South Africa has jurisdiction to try the conspiracy.[115] This was especially relevant for counts 55, 54 and 58 that pertained to murders in Mozambique, London and Swaziland.[116] In terms of the Defence Act and the Military Discipline Code, Namibia was in any case considered part of South Africa, which had certain specific implications for the matter.[117]

In any event, the Court did not take this further and turned to a general rule concerning the jurisdiction over crimes committed abroad. It basically stated that the rule that South African courts have no jurisdiction over crimes that are committed abroad, based on the principle of international comity, is not absolute.[118] The Constitutional Court then approved and followed the ruling of the Canadian Supreme Court on the same legal issue.[119] The Canadian Supreme Court had ruled that Canadian courts have jurisdiction to try conspiracies concerning crimes to be committed abroad when a significant portion of the activities constituting the offence took place in Canada or when there is a real and substantial link between the conspiracy to commit the crime and the country itself.[120] The Constitutional Court confirmed the existence of such a real and substantial link in the Basson case[121] and based this opinion on the following grounds, which can be partitioned in two groups.

---

[113] *S. v Basson* (CC) Case no. CCT 30/03 9 September 2005 at para. 214.

[114] Ibid., at para. 216.

[115] Ibid., at para. 219.

[116] Ibid.

[117] Ibid., at paras. 220–222. See section 1(xxii) of the Defence Act.

[118] *S. v Basson* (CC) Case no. CCT 30/03 9 September 2005 at paras. 223 and 225. International comity in this sense means the respect for another country's sovereignty in terms of exclusively exercising jurisdiction over crimes committed on its territory.

[119] *Libman v The Queen* [1985] 2 SCR 178.

[120] *S. v Basson* (CC) Case no. CCT 30/03 9 September 2005 at para. 226.

[121] Ibid., at para. 228.

The first group encompasses factors pertaining to the special situation of Namibia at the time. A number of findings show that there was a real and substantial link between the conspiracy to commit the crime and South Africa, including the following: Namibia was administered by South Africa; the Riotous Assemblies Act was applicable in Namibia; at all material times, the SADF was deployed in Namibia in terms of the Defence Act, which deems Namibia part of South Africa; certain charges pertain to the murder of detainees who were held captive by the SADF; and that the Defence Act generally criminalises acts of SADF members even if committed abroad.[122]

The other set of factors indicating the real and substantial link to South Africa are broader in nature and are not confined to the Namibian situation. They include: the mere fact that the conspiracy was entered into in South Africa; that it was organised and directed by members of the South African military; that the means for the implementation of the killings were provided and prepared in South Africa; and that the respective instructions were issued from there.[123]

The Court rejected the arguments of Basson's legal counsel.[124] Accordingly the Constitutional Court unanimously held on 9 September 2005 that South African courts have jurisdiction to try the crimes in question

---

[122] Ibid., at 227.

[123] Ibid.

[124] The main argument was based on the hypothetical situation that if section 18(2) of the Riotous Assemblies Act was construed in the way desired by the State, the conspiracy to smoke cannabis in the Netherlands, which is not criminal there, would be criminal in South Africa as well as the situation where the conspiracy to consume alcohol in a Muslim country, in some countries a criminal offence, would be criminal in South Africa. This argument was rejected on the basis that there anyways is not a sufficient connection between South Africa and the acts to warrant jurisdiction and that they are by no means comparable to the murder of detainees by SADF personnel held captive in a country administered by South Africa. The second argument, namely that the acts were covered by an amnesty proclaimed in Namibia in 1989, was rejected on the basis that the proclamation has no application for South African courts. See *S. v Basson* (CC) Case no. CCT 30/03 9 September 2005 at paras. 237 and 244.

and ordered that the quashing of the charges be set aside.[125] The judgement thereby clarified to a certain degree the question concerning section 18(2) of the Riotous Assemblies Act.

The Court obviously viewed international law, more precisely the international law obligation to prosecute this case, as a decisive factor in coming to the conclusion that the Supreme Court of Appeal should have granted the State leave to appeal against the trial court's judgment. Nevertheless, in this regard the Court's elaborations remained of a rather broad and general nature. It did not analyse in any detailed way whether there is a strict obligation to prosecute such crimes under international law. Although this issue is relevant for the decision on whether South African courts have jurisdiction to try crimes of the gravity and international relevance such as in the Basson case, or the concomitant conspiracy, it did not analyse whether the crimes and conspiracies could also have been prosecuted on the basis of the international law principle of universality.[126] According to the principle of universality, any state's courts have jurisdiction to try a person accused of an international crime, regardless of the place where the crime was committed or the nationality of the victim or alleged perpetrator.[127] This principle is accepted under international customary law for war crimes, crimes against humanity, genocide and also with regard to crimes committed in civil wars.[128] The Constitutional Court had pointed out that the crimes of which Basson was accused would violate even the most minimal standards of international humanitarian law and would

---

[125] *S. v Basson* (CC) Case no. CCT 30/03 9 September 2005 at para. 265. The applications regarding the recusal and the admissibility of the bail record were dismissed.

[126] See on the issue of universal jurisdiction and generally international law in the Basson case: M. Swart 'The Wouter Basson prosecution: the closest South Africa came to Nuremberg?' (2008) 68/1 *Heidelberg Journal of International Law* 209–26. The Court expressly states that it does not consider it necessary to examine these issues in detail (*S. v Basson* (CC) Case no. CCT 30/03 9 September 2005 at para. 172). It apparently sufficed for the Court to approach the topic on the basis of South African law.

[127] A. Cassese *International criminal law* (2003) 284.

[128] G. Werle *Principles of international criminal law* (2005) para. 174.

thus constitute horrendous war crimes.[129] Against this background, it is incomprehensible why the Court did not elaborate on the principle of universality, which would clearly have provided for the jurisdiction of South African courts and would have rendered as incorrect the quashing of the charges.

2.4 *A new trial?*

With respect to the six quashed charges, the NPA won its case. The Constitutional Court had stated that the previously quashed indictment stands and that it was up to the State to charge Basson anew.[130] The way seemed clear for a new trial on the basis of the six charges. Yet rather surprisingly, especially considering the time and effort required to reach this result, the NPA announced in October 2005 that it would not recharge Wouter Basson on the six counts.[131] The reason provided for this decision was that a new trial on the basis of the six charges would violate the double jeopardy rule, which in this case would be an inescapable procedural obstacle for a new indictment.[132]

The principle of double jeopardy is laid out in section 35(3)(m) of the Constitution. Its roots lie in the basic principle common to most legal systems that no one shall be punished for the same offence more than once.[133] In criminal procedure, the rule is embodied in the pleas of *autrefoi acqui*, if the accused has previously been acquitted, or *autrefoi convict*, if the accused has previously been convicted for the offence in question in terms of section 106(c) and (d) of the Criminal Procedure Act. However, the rules on these pleas provide that the accused must

---

129 *S. v Basson* (CC) Case no. CCT 30/03 9 September 2005 at paras. 179–180.

130 Ibid., at para. 260.

131 W. Menges *'Dr Death' is off the hook in South Africa* The Namibian, Oct 24, 2005.

132 NPA, press statement *NPA decides not to re-charge Wouter Basson* (Oct 19, 2005).

133 P.M. Bekker et al *Criminal procedure handbook* 7ed (2005) 220; *S. v Basson* (CC) Case no. CCT 30/03 10 March 2004 at para. 61. See generally on the double jeopardy rule M.L. Friedland *Double jeopardy* (1969); Law Reform Commission of Canada *Double jeopardy, pleas and verdicts* (1991).

have been in danger of conviction in the first trial[134] which was never the case with Basson, since the specific charges were not admitted.[135] The NPA's decision must therefore have been based on a different aspect of the double jeopardy rule, which is the plea of *res judicata.*[136] The doctrine of *res judicata*, known in England and Canada as issue estopple, in the United States as collateral estoppel,[137] is part of the double jeopardy rule in criminal procedures of common law countries.[138] It holds that if issues of ultimate fact, including those concerning evidence such as the credibility of witnesses and the like, have already been determined by a valid and final judgment of a trial court, these issues cannot be made the subject of another criminal litigation between the parties.[139]

In the present case, the six charges, which had been set aside, were all materially also covered by an umbrella charge (count 63), which encompassed virtually all conspiracy charges, those relating to crimes to be committed abroad and those relating to crimes to be committed in South Africa.[140] According to Pretorius, who mainly led the evidence in question at the trial, the evidence supporting the quashed charges

[134] *S. v Basson* (CC) Case no. CCT 30/03 9 September 2005 at para. 254. See on the preconditions of the pleas *autrefoi acqui* and *autrefoi convict*: P.M. Bekker et al. *Criminal procedure handbook* 7ed (2005) 220–25; E. Du Toit et al. *Commentary on the Criminal Procedure Act* service 36 (2006) 15–28 to 15–34.

[135] *S. v Basson* (CC) Case no. CCT 30/03 9 September 2005 at para. 256.

[136] The Constitutional Court only briefly touched upon this issue when it stated that the question could arise whether the quashed charges, were they subject of a new indictment, could be rendered susceptible to a plea of *res judicata* (ibid. at para. 257).

[137] Law Reform Commission of Canada *Double jeopardy, pleas and verdicts* (1991) 13.

[138] See generally M.L. Friedland *Double jeopardy* (1969) 117–60; Law Reform Commission of Canada *Double jeopardy, pleas and verdicts* (1991) 13–14; C.F. Stuckenberg *Double jeopardy* (2001) 26–28.

[139] Law Reform Commission of Canada *Double jeopardy, pleas and verdicts* (1991) 13; C.F. Stuckenberg *Double jeopardy* (2001) 26. The principle is accepted in most English speaking countries (M.L. Friedland *Double jeopardy* (1969) 117), obviously including South Africa.

[140] NPA, press statement *NPA decides not to re-charge Wouter Basson* (Oct 19, 2005). Count 63 basically concerned all charges where Basson had to provide the poison (Interview with Torie Pretorius and others in Pretoria (May 2, 2006)).

equally supported the relevant parts of the umbrella charge.[141] Thus, for the purpose of count 63, the State led all the evidence, including especially witness statements, on which also the six quashed charges were almost entirely based.[142] Judge Hartzenberg refers to this situation in the final judgment when he states that:

> Although I initially ruled that conspiracies to commit crimes abroad are not justiciable in this court and a number of charges had therefore been quashed, it made no difference to the evidence the State has led, because the State has led evidence to support the charges, as it was required of the State, to prove the wider conspiracy (charge 63) the accused allegedly had committed.[143]

The trial judge considered the evidence and rejected it as being not credible enough to support the guilt of the accused with respect to count 63.[144] The Court, therefore, had ruled on issues of ultimate fact. Thus, there was the peculiar situation that, although the six charges had not been admitted to the trial, the Court apparently nevertheless heard virtually all evidence in respect thereof. Before the trial, Basson's defence had also applied for the quashing of count 63, which was refused by Hartzenberg since it also concerned conspiracies regarding crimes to be committed in South Africa.[145] Nevertheless, Hartzenberg ruled that the defence had the right to object to all evidence, which was led in connection with count 63, that is only aimed at proving conspiracies to commit crimes abroad, which according to the judge

---

141 Interview with Torie Pretorius and others in Pretoria (May 2, 2006). See also *S. v Basson* (CC) Case no. CCT 30/03 9 September 2005 para. 257.

142 Pretorius estimates that only about 5 per cent of the evidence concerning the six charges has not been led in the trial.

143 *S. v Wouter Basson* (T) Case no. 32/1999 11 April 2002, unreported, at para. 1610 (abstract translated from Afrikaans).

144 Interview with Torie Pretorius and others in Pretoria (May 2, 2006). The dismissal of the evidence was made on factual not legal grounds and could thus only be taken on review not on appeal. However, a review of the judges rulings on the evidence would have provided a gross irregularity which was not given (Interview with Susan Bukau and others in Pretoria (May 2, 2006)).

145 *S. v Basson* [2000] 1 All SA 430 (T) at 436h.

do not disclose criminal offences.[146] Apparently either the defence did not object to the leading of evidence in this regard or the evidence that was actually led in the trial always concerned both justiciable and non-justiciable conspiracies. Thus, since the judge at the trial had ruled over all relevant evidence and no fresh evidence was available to sufficiently sustain the charges,[147] further charges would be vulnerable of a plea of *res judicata.*

It is difficult to comprehend, why the NPA applied for leave to appeal in respect of the six charges at the Constitutional Court at all, when a new indictment would be exposed to a double jeopardy plea anyway. The specific issue had already been raised during the Supreme Court litigation. The NPA must have been aware of such implications. Furthermore, the Constitutional Court did not state that these circumstances completely precluded a new prosecution. Instead, the Court appeared much more encouraging stating that it would be up to the judge in a newly convened trial to determine in the light of the new charges and the record of the previous criminal proceedings whether the mass of evidence led previously indeed particularly covers the new charges.[148] However, the Court also left it up to the NPA to decide on a fresh charge.[149] Although the prosecutors are naturally well able to consider this question, a ruling by a new trial court, after careful consideration of the criminal records, would have had greater authority, which would probably have made it easier for many victims concerned to find closure on the issue.

The reason for the decision not to proceed with the trial after the NPA had succeeded on the issue of the six quashed charges probably lies in the fact that this issue was only one of three that were taken to the Constitutional Court. The NPA had also applied at the Constitu-

[146] Ibid. at 443e and 444h.

[147] Interview with Torie Pretorius and others in Pretoria (May 2, 2006).

[148] *S. v Basson* (CC) Case no. CCT 30/03 9 September 2005 at paras. 169, 258 and 260. The court expressly refrained from tackling this complex task in the proceedings before it since it had no effect on its decision to grant leave to appeal (*S. v Basson* (CC) Case no. CCT 30/03 9 September 2005 at para. 258).

[149] *S. v Basson* (CC) Case no. CCT 30/03 9 September 2005 at para. 260.

tional Court for a ruling on the refused recusal of Judge Hartzenberg and his alleged bias, which did not succeed. A successful ruling in this regard might have led to the setting aside of the judgment and would have enabled the NPA to proceed with a new trial regardless of the double jeopardy rule. However, it is not possible to conclude with certainty what the considerations of the NPA were in this regard. The independent decision of the NPA has not been accepted by many victims.[150] Basson continued to work as a member of the South African National Defence Force (hereinafter SANDF) and as a cardiologist in various hospitals.[151]

2.5 *Conclusion*

In the view of many apartheid victims, the trial against Wouter Basson was very promising. That it did not succeed was equally disappointing for many. The case had the potential to become one of the most significant prosecutions of apartheid era crimes. It offered the possibility of focussing more closely on the secret activities of the military, which had thus far not received the same attention as the security police.[152] The acquittal prevented the achievement of definite clarity on such criminal activities. It also had a negative impact on further post-TRC prosecutions. Since the costs of millions of Rand were not "balanced" by a conviction, the government might become increasingly reluctant to push for other trials. Also, a number of state witnesses who had testified extensively against Basson were nevertheless not granted immunity by Hartzenberg in terms of section 204 of the Criminal Procedure Act, which might generally impact negatively on the willingness of co-perpetrators to cooperate with the prosecutors.[153]

---

150 Interview with Marjorie Jobson in Pretoria (May 9, 2006).

151 *Defence confirms Basson's suspension payments* SAPA, Sep 13, 2006; *Wouter Basson to defend himself against complaints* SAPA, Feb 26, 2007.

152 V. Nerlich *Apartheidkriminalität vor Gericht* (2002) 174.

153 M. Fullard and N Rousseau 'An imperfect past: the Truth and Reconciliation Commission in transition' in J. Daniel et al. (eds) *State of the nation* (2003) 78 at 93.

However, one positive aspect is that the Constitutional Court dealt with the matter and made a number of statements with regards to the relevance of international human rights law for the prosecution of apartheid era crimes. It is also of great importance for other post-TRC trials regarding the conspiracy issue. It concerns all similar situations in which crimes were organised in South Africa but were carried out abroad. These include the numerous cross border raids of the security police during which opposition members and other civilians were killed in neighbouring countries. The judgment is also generally relevant for all crimes committed by SADF members abroad.

The Court outlined that South African courts have jurisdiction over conspiracies in terms of section 18(2) of the Riotous Assemblies Act to commit crimes abroad when there is a real and substantial link between the conspiracy and South Africa. However, it did not formulate general criteria to determine the existence of a real and substantial link. One can nevertheless conclude from the factors applied by the Court with respect to the Basson case, the general criteria that are relevant should such factors mutually occur. Accordingly, apart from the factors that pertained to the special situation in Namibia, a real and substantial link exists when the conspiracy was entered into in South Africa, when it was organised and directed by members of the South African state forces, when the relevant orders emanated from South Africa and when the means for the implementation of the crime were provided from within South Africa. Such circumstances probably existed in most criminal cross-border activities of the security police. The conspiracy to commit such acts would thus be prosecutable.

Additionally it is implicit from the judgment that South African courts have jurisdiction to try all crimes committed by former SADF members covered by the Military Discipline Code. Conspiracies to commit crimes in Namibia generally fall under the jurisdiction of South African courts due to the Court's strong emphasis on the close connection between Namibia and South Africa at the time.

3. *The Bisho-Massacre*

In October 2001 a criminal trial commenced at the High Court of Bisho in the Eastern Cape that dealt with the Bisho-massacre, one of the most serious and tragic political killings in the South African transition period.

3.1 *The massacre*

The events commonly referred to as the Bisho-massacre occurred on 7 September 1992 in the immediate vicinity of Bisho, capital of the then homeland Ciskei.[154] The ANC had organised a protest march from the Eastern Cape city of King Williams Town towards the adjacent town of Bisho. The rally, in which about 70,000 to 80,000 people participated, was intended to proceed into Bisho in order to press for the resignation of then Ciskei leader, Oupa Gqozo.[155] However, the marchers only received permission to enter a stadium right behind the Ciskei border.[156] The organisers of the march, among them prominent ANC members such as Chris Hani, Ronnie Kasrils[157] and Cyril Ramaphosa, nevertheless were adamant that they would proceed into Bisho.[158] The assigned route to the stadium was marked off by razor wire fencing and approximately 200 Ciskei Defence Force (hereinafter CDF) soldiers were lined up in the surroundings.[159] The situation was, due to recent intense violent clashes between ANC supporters and Ciskei authorities, very tense.[160]

---

154 *TRC Report*, vol. 3, chap. 2, paras. 368–69.

155 Ibid., para. 369.

156 Ibid., para. 374.

157 Kasrils became deputy Minister of Defence in the new government in 1994 (P. van Niekerk and B. Ludman (eds) *A–Z of South African politics 1999* (1999) 139). In 1999 he was appointed Minister of Water Affairs and Forestry.

158 *S. v Mkosana and another* 2003 (2) SACR 63 (BCH) at 74.

159 *TRC Report*, vol. 3, chap. 2, paras. 369 and 374.

160 Numerous warnings that the march is in danger of ending in a bloodshed were made by prominent politicians from all sides and reported in the media (*S. v Mkosana and Gonya*, indictment, summary of substantial facts, pages 20–22).

However the marchers were clearly unarmed and the rally proceeded peacefully.[161]

Events took a turn when a group of marchers, headed by Ronnie Kasrils, noticed a gap in the fence and decided to break through.[162] Some hundred marchers then ran towards a CDF battalion that was lined up at a distance. Commander Vakelele Archibald Mkosana gave the order to fire.[163] What ensued was uncontrolled and indiscriminate shooting.[164] Without warning of the order to fire the shooting was joined by most of the other soldiers employed around the march.[165] 29 protestors and one CDF soldier died, dozens others were injured.[166] Many were shot either when running away or while already lying on the ground.[167]

The massacre was subject to various investigations and TRC hearings.[168] The TRC found that Gqozo and the CDF were accountable for the massacre but also criticised the ANC leadership for having lacked prudence in the volatile situation.[169] Indictments were drafted shortly after the massacre concerning CDF soldiers and even Ronnie Kasrils.[170] However due to political circumstances, charges were not instituted and it was only in 1996 that a new police investigation docket was submitted to the Attorney-General.[171] The proceedings were pending the outcome of amnesty applications, received from Vakele Archiebald

161 Decision no. AC/2000/122; *S. v Mkosana and another* 2003 (2) SACR 63 (BCH) at 74.

162 *TRC Report*, vol. 2, chap. 7, para. 180.

163 Ibid., para. 182.

164 Over 400 shots and four rifle grenades were fired.

165 *TRC Report*, vol. 3, chap. 2, para. 375.

166 Ibid. para. 369. The prosecutors of the case list 67 injured (*S. v Mkosana and Gonya*, indictment, annexure D, page 17). Other sources refer to about 300 injured (J. Sarkin *Carrots and sticks: the TRC and the South African amnesty process* (2004) 377).

167 *TRC Report*, vol. 2, chap. 7, para. 184.

168 The TRC had held two extensive public hearings on the Bisho-massacre in September and November 1996, during which about 60 witnesses testified (See especially *TRC Report*, vol. 3, chap. 2, paras. 368–99).

169 *TRC Report*, vol. 3, chap. 2, para. 399.

170 Ibid., para. 397.

171 Ibid., para. 398.

Mkosana and Mzamile Thomas Gonya, who were both concerned by the investigations.[172] Both applications were refused in 2000.[173] In 2001 the newly appointed Director of Public Prosecutions of the area, Johan Bezuidenhout, took the matter up again.[174]

3.2 *The indictment*

In October 2001, Mkosana and Gonya were both charged with one count of murder and two counts of attempted murder. Mkosana was also charged with culpable homicide.[175]

Mkosana was the field commander of the CDF soldiers employed in the operation on the particular day in question and was stationed directly behind the CDF line facing the approaching protestors who had broken through the gap.[176] He allegedly radioed his superiors for instructions and reported, as he later admitted, that shots were fired by the approaching protestors. He then received permission to fire single shots in return to turn back the crowd.[177] Following this, Mkosana allegedly ordered the line in front of him to open fire on the approaching group.[178] The State based the charges against him on the claim that he lied when he reported the shots.[179] He had supposedly known that the situation did not pose such a compelling threat as to justify the shooting and he had failed to ensure that only single shots were fired, knowing that his conduct would result in many deaths.[180] Due to the chaotic nature of the events it was not possible to determine exactly who was shot by which group of soldiers.[181] At least one victim from

[172] Applications no. AM/4458/96 and AM/7882/97.

[173] Decision no. AC/2000/122.

[174] *S. v Mkosana and another* 2003 (2) SACR 63 (BCH).

[175] *S. v Mkosana and Gonya*, indictment.

[176] Ibid., preamble, at page 5.

[177] Ibid. at page 6.

[178] Ibid.

[179] Ibid. at page 7.

[180] Ibid. at pages 8–9.

[181] Ibid. at page 7.

the group of protestors, which had run through the fence, was allegedly killed by the CDF line in front of Mkosana.[182] Accordingly, he would be guilty of murder of this one protestor and also of attempted murder of an undeterminable number of other demonstrators.[183] Furthermore, Mkosana would be guilty of having negligently caused the death of all other victims shot dead at other places around the stadium (culpable homicide count), since he had failed to ensure that the other soldiers would not join in the shooting without specific orders.[184]

Gonya was a soldier armed with a rifle grenade launcher, employed in the CDF line facing the approaching protestors.[185] He allegedly fired two grenades, without orders to do so, into the approaching group or in the direction thereof with the intention to kill members of the group.[186] He was accordingly charged with murder of one victim who died through grenade shrapnel and with the attempted murder of an undeterminable number of persons.[187]

The prosecutor was initially not convinced that the case against the accused would be strong. The indictment was rather the result of the great significance of the massacre and the expectations among victims and the public since amnesty had been denied to the accused. An inquest was not conducted since it was feared that public expectations would rise even more should the inquest result in a recommendation to charge the suspects.[188]

---

182 Ibid. at page 10.

183 Ibid. at page 11.

184 Ibid. at page 9. Allegedly Mkosana's order was transmitted by radio and was also audible to at least some of the other lines engaged in the shootings, who then mistook it as being directed at them (Telephone interview with Johan Bezuidenhout in June 2006).

185 *S. v Mkosana and Gonya*, indictment, page 10.

186 Ibid.

187 Ibid. at page 11. It appears contradictory that on the one hand Mkosana was charged with murder by having ordered the line to shoot and on the other hand Gonya, who allegedly killed the only one protestor in the group charged with murder for acting without any order to shoot.

188 Telephone interview with Johan Bezuidenhout in June 2006.

3.3 *The judgment*

Exploring the Bisho-massacre confronted the Court with a major task. After 43 court days during which the events were dealt with thoroughly, Judge White delivered his ruling on 13 March 2002.[189] Both accused were found not guilty and were acquitted on all charges.[190]

The crucial issues were whether the accused were entitled to act in self-defence and whether the limits of self-defence had been observed.[191] The Court confirmed both issues. The ruling took into account that all soldiers were very anxious of possible attacks due to the row of violent clashes[192] and had beforehand been advised that the marchers could be armed.[193] With respect to the examination of whether a situation of self-defence existed, the Court found no evidence of shots being fired from the protestors.[194] Mkosana had suggested that he might have mistaken the rotor sound of a helicopter, flying above the march, for shots.[195] After examining closely the evidence and testimony on this question, the Court found it reasonably possible, especially considering the tense and agitated conditions, that the sounds were indeed mistaken for shots.[196] On this basis the Court was of the opinion that a situation justifying actions taken in self-defence existed.[197] With regard to the question of whether the limits of self-defence had been exceeded, the Court found that to order shots immediately was indeed appropriate.

---

189 *S. v Mkosana and another* 2003 (2) SACR 63 (BCH) at 66. The state had submitted an extensive list of 134 state witnesses (*S. v Mkosana and Gonya*, indictment, list of state witnesses).

190 *S. v Mkosana and another* 2003 (2) SACR 63 (BCH) at 95.

191 Ibid. at page 87.

192 Ibid. at page 67.

193 Ibid. at page 1.

194 Ibid. at page 63.

195 This possibility had already been raised at the TRC (*TRC Report*, vol. 3, chap. 2, para. 383).

196 A special *in loco* inspection was undertaken by the Court after which it found that there was considerable similarity between the sounds (*S. v Mkosana and another* 2003 (2) SACR 63 (BCH) at 88). A number of protestors also mistook the rotor sounds for shots during the march.

197 *S. v Mkosana and another* 2003 (2) SACR 63 (BCH) at 90.

Less stringent measures, such as warning shots etc., could not have been considered since the crowd was running towards the soldiers and was already relatively close.[198] The Court thereby also took into account that senior commanders had expressly prohibited the use of warning shots.[199] The charge of culpable homicide was rejected since the Court could not find proof that Mkosana had submitted his order to shoot to the line in front of him via radio, which could, thus, not have been mistaken by other CDF groups as being directed at them.[200] With regard to Gonya the Court could not find proof that it was exactly the grenade fired by Gonya that killed the one specific victim.[201] It appeared possible that the death was caused by grenades that might have been fired by other soldiers.[202]

3.4 *Conclusion*

The Bisho massacre is an example of the clashes that occurred at the mass rallies during the early 1990s. It is not representative of the secret state activities against political activists. It had already been examined extensively due to its scope, the great public attention and the investigations of the TRC. It was doubtful whether the trial could contribute further to the findings already made by the TRC. However, the call for retributive justice from victims and from many in the public was still strong.[203]

There is a strong impression from the judgment that the judge was of the opinion that the events were merely a tragic coincidence of various unfortunate factors rather than a crime for which a specific person could be held accountable. This becomes clear when the Court refers to the events as an inevitable 'clash between an irresistible force and an immovable object'.[204] Moreover, the judge apparently found it

---

198 Ibid. at page 91.

199 Ibid. at page 92.

200 Ibid. at page 93.

201 Ibid.

202 Ibid. at page 94.

203 Telephone interview with Johan Bezuidenhout in June 2006.

204 *S. v Mkosana and another* 2003 (2) SACR 63 (BCH) at 68.

inappropriate to blame only the two accused, although he presumably found others equally or even more responsible. The Court for instance heavily criticised the leadership of the ANC for taking the irresponsible decision to break through the gap in the fence and run towards Bisho.[205] It also made it clear that the prosecution should have rather focussed on CDF soldiers in other positions surrounding the march, who had shot in a totally defenceless and harmless crowd, which had caused the vast majority of deaths and injuries on that day.[206] Such action was described as 'a wanton and brutal slaying of innocent people'.[207] According to the prosecutor,[208] the willingness of the Court to punish the accused diminished further when Ronnie Kasrils made statements during the trial in which he once again called strongly for closing the books on the massacre and indicated his lack of vindictiveness.[209]

Against this background, it appears that the Court accepted too easily that Mkosana acted in self-defence when he ordered the line in front of him to open fire. The Court simply accepted that warning shots had not been appropriate since they had been forbidden for whatever reason by the CDF leadership. Warning shots would generally have been insufficient to stop the crowd. The judge went further to state that even if Mkosana had not thought the protestors were firing he would have been exonerated by the defence of self-defence by the plain fact that some hundred marchers running towards them in a distance of about 150 meters constituted a real danger.[210] Furthermore, he stated that it would be 'churlish for a Court to blame an accused who has, through no fault of his own, been placed on the horns of a dilemma as to the exact steps he must take to protect himself and those in his care'.[211]

It is hard to accept this. Mkosana was a senior officer of the CDF who was in command on the ground on that day. One requires a high degree

---

[205] Ibid. at page 77. Indeed Kasrils had already expressed a deep sense of moral responsibility for the events before the TRC (*TRC Report*, vol. 2, chap. 7, para. 181).

[206] *S. v Mkosana and another* 2003 (2) SACR 63 (BCH) at 81.

[207] Ibid. at page 80.

[208] Telephone interview with Johan Bezuidenhout in June 2006.

[209] *S. v Mkosana and another* 2003 (2) SACR 63 (BCH) at 74.

[210] Ibid. at page 91.

[211] Ibid. at page 93.

of prudence and responsibility of an officer in such a high position of the army. Furthermore, a distance of 150 meters seems far enough to fire warning shots or single shots. Kasrils had stated that they would have stopped right away if there had been warning shots.[212] The Court's findings on self-defence are in stark contrast to the findings of the TRC and especially to the findings of the Amnesty Committee. The Amnesty Committee refused amnesty to Mkosana and Gonya on the grounds that their actions were totally disproportionate to the dangers they faced.[213] The committee had described the firing under the circumstances as totally irrational and unjustified.[214] However, in the end, the acquittal is consequent as it is clear from the judgment that the judge had to acquit the accused due to the principle of *in dubio pro reo.*

4. *The Trial of Michael Luff*

In November 2001 the policeman Michael Phillip Luff was charged with murder in the Regional Court of Worcester in the Western Cape. He was accused of having shot the 17-year-old William Dyasi in Zwelethemba township in 1985. At the time, Luff was a young member of the so-called Unrest Unit of the Worcester police, a riot squad that was dealing primarily with containing unrest in the townships of the region.[215]

According to the prosecutor, events unfolded as follows.[216] In early November 1985, Luff and a colleague were called while on duty in the

[212] *TRC Report*, vol. 2, chap. 7, paras. 180–81.

[213] Decision no. AC/2000/122. According to section 19(3)(f) of the TRC Act the proportionality of the act *inter alia* determines the political character of the offence. The offences were on this basis not considered to be political.

[214] Decision no. AC/2000/122.

[215] MMM Mackay *Outrage as amnesty reject gets off in court* Cape Argus, May 7, 2002.

[216] The following information derives from an interview with prosecutor Themba Velem on 21 June 2006 in Paarl, if otherwise is not stated. The judgment and the charge sheet concerning the trial have been destroyed after the lapse of two years since Luff had been acquitted. Velem's account, often differs from information

township to deal with a rioting group of protestors who were stoning a local beer hall.[217] When confronting the protestors, the policemen fired shots and Dyasi, who was among the crowd, was seriously injured by a lead gun-shot in his chest. Dyasi managed to escape. Two women gave him shelter in a nearby house. Later that evening, Luff and his colleague were informed that he was hiding in the house. Dyasi was found by the two policemen, who wanted to arrest him. Luff took the heavily bleeding youth outside while his colleague was still inside the house with the two women. Luff then shot Dyasi outside of the house. The prosecutor claimed that Luff intentionally shot Dyasi without justification.

Already in early 1986, an inquest was conducted by the Worcester Magistrate's Court in order to establish whether an indictment of Luff was worthwhile. It was found that Luff was criminally liable for Dyasi's death and that the Attorney-General should institute a prosecution.[218] However, the Attorney-General declined to charge Luff, most likely for political reasons. Only in December 1996 was the decision reversed and a trial set to begin. This was due to intervention by the TRC. Dyasi's death and the subsequent events had been the subject of a TRC Human Rights Violations Committee hearing, in which his parents told their story.[219] Luff, however, immediately applied for amnesty.[220] The criminal proceeding was pending at that time. At the amnesty hearings, Luff testified that Dyasi had tried to escape when they had gone outside. He admitted to having shot him in the back only in order to effect an arrest.[221] Amnesty was refused in 2000 mainly because the offence lacked a political objective.[222] However, the Amnesty Committee also raised serious doubts regarding Luff's version of events. It found it especially

deriving from TRC proceedings. An exact account of the events is thus under the circumstances impossible.

217 Beer halls in townships were perceived by political activists as an apartheid instrument to keep Africans quiet.

218 Decision no. AC/2000/005.

219 *TRC Report*, vol. 3, chap. 5, para. 144.

220 Application no. AM/3814/96.

221 Decision no. AC/2000/005.

222 Ibid.

improbable that Dyasi was able to run away at all considering his severe injuries caused by the first shots at the beer hall. These doubts were not further explored since the criminal proceedings were still pending.

After the refusal of amnesty, the case was resumed and went to trial in November 2001. The prosecution was conducted without any involvement by the unit for TRC prosecutions in Pretoria. The prosecutor, Themba Velem, intended to base the charges mainly on the evidence provided by the two women of the shack in which Dyasi was hiding, one of whom could be traced, and most importantly on the testimony of a doctor who had conducted the post-mortem examination of the corpse in 1986. He had also testified at the inquest in 1986. This testimony contradicted Luff's version of events. For example, the doctor there had stated that Dyasi's injuries would probably not have allowed him to walk or run away at all. In a meeting with the doctor right before the trial, Velem convinced himself that the evidence given at the inquest in 1986 would be repeated. When testifying at the trial, however, the witness made a complete about turn, according to Velem, and his new recount of events was no longer consistent with his previous testimony.

Luff was eventually acquitted by Magistrate van Rensburg in May 2002. According to Velem, the Court could not find sufficient proof that Dyasi was shot by Luff at all. Velem stated that Luff had testified at the inquest that he had accidentally shot Dyasi in the back while stumbling outside the shack. Strangely, however, Luff never had to testify at the trial. The main reason for a lack of proof was that the doctor testified differently. A number of other important witnesses also could not be traced. Furthermore, Velem sensed a strong reluctance on the part of the police to investigate the case thoroughly. Initially only a junior officer, who had even attended shooting lessons led by Luff, was assigned to investigate the case. A senior, more independent officer later replaced him. Certain witnesses were only traced after Velem intervened personally. He also had the impression that the Magistrate van Rensburg was very reluctant to conduct the trial. For example, on many occasions the judge strangely did not grant applications for adjournments by Velem in order to trace other witnesses. The judge also apparently made certain derogative statements about the fact that Luff was prosecuted at all.

The case was certainly loaded with political implications and emotions. After the acquittal, the judge was accused of racism by Dyasi's relatives and representatives of the black population in the area.[223] The victim's relatives found it especially difficult to accept that there was insufficient proof that Luff killed Dyasi since they had attended the amnesty hearings in which Luff admitted to having killed Dyasi.[224] The trial raised much racial tension and emotion in the area. The exact circumstances of Dyasi's death were not established. There were indications that there was a politically motivated reluctance on the side of the police and the Court to convict Luff, who continues to work as an inspector at the Ceres police. However, even the prosecutor admitted that under the circumstances the evidence was probably not sufficient to secure a conviction.

5. *The Case of Tyani and Gumengu*

In 2004 two former members of the Transkei homeland security police, Aron Mtobeli Tyani and Pumelele Gumengu, were each charged in the Butterworth Circuit Court[225] with one count of attempted murder and one count of murder. The two were charged with having murdered Sithembele Zokwe on 8 August 1987.[226] Zokwe was a political activist and member of MK. He had undergone military training abroad. The indictment alleged that the accused and other members of the local security police arrested Zokwe in Umtata in August 1987 and took him to a remote quarry where they shot him in the neck and head.

---

223 M.M.M. Mackay *Outrage as amnesty reject gets off in court* Cape Argus, May 7, 2002.

224 Such self-incriminating evidence is according to section 31(3) of the TRC Act inadmissible in a criminal trial.

225 Umtata High Court.

226 *S. v Tyani and Gumengu*, indictment. The charges were conducted by M. Mhaga, who later shifted to the PCLU in Pretoria.

Zokwe, who was severely injured, miraculously survived the attack. He later managed to call for help and was brought to a hospital.[227] After his release from hospital, he was again arrested by the security police in January 1988. Gumengu and Tyani took Zokwe to a house where he was allegedly asked to point out where he was hiding hand grenades. On this occasion, he was shot by Tyani inside the house. The accused then allegedly placed the dead body on a hand grenade, which was activated in the house to create the impression that Zokwe had tried to throw the grenade at them so that they had to shoot him in self-defence.[228]

After they had already previously been charged for the murder both applied for amnesty in relation to it in 1996.[229] Gumengu simultaneously applied for amnesty regarding the previous murder attempt. The prosecution was then pending the amnesty decision and only continued after amnesty had been denied in March 2000.[230] The Amnesty Committee found that the applicants had presented highly improbable and contradictory versions of the events and accordingly denied amnesty for a lack of full disclosure.[231] At trial, the accused nevertheless presented the same account of events. They claimed that when they had brought Zokwe to the quarry he attempted to escape which they tried to prevent by shooting in the air and in his direction without intending to kill him.[232] With regard to the actual murder they claimed that Tyani shot at Zokwe since he had tried to attack them with a hand grenade. Both pleaded not guilty.[233] The versions were again rejected as obviously false and highly improbable considering the various pieces of evidence and the post-mortem examination.[234] The judge was certain that Zokwe was

227 *S. v Tyani and Gumengu*, indictment, summary of substantial facts.

228 Ibid.

229 Applications no. AM/3786/96 and AM/3610/96.

230 Decision no. AC/2000/042.

231 Ibid.

232 *S. v Tyani and Gumengu* (Transkei division) Case no. 76/2004, unreported, at para. 55.

233 Ibid. at para. 4.

234 Ibid. at para. 76.

not killed in self-defence[235] and that both acted with a common purpose when Zokwe was shot.[236] Gumengu and Tyani were found guilty of murder.[237] Only Gumengu was found guilty of attempted murder whereas Tyani was discharged on that count for a lack of evidence.[238] Both were sentenced to 25 years imprisonment.[239]

Although a conviction was secured, it is rather disconcerting that the judgment did not clarify the truth regarding the facts of the case. There is no proper examination of why exactly Zokwe was murdered. While the amnesty decision clearly stated that Gumengu had been ordered by his superiors to eliminate Zokwe, there is no mention of such implications and the intentions behind the deed in the judgment. The political background is only touched upon in the trial judge's judgment when he mentions that Zokwe was indeed a very active member of MK and that it was the common goal of Gumengu and Tyani to subdue him since he was considered a dangerous terrorist.[240] The judgment is also largely confined to rejecting the accused' versions of events. It does not clarify in detail how Zokwe's murder took place. It also fails to clarify whether Zokwe was brought to the quarry with the sole purpose of killing him there. However, it is most likely that the judge did not consider it necessary to elaborate on these questions since he was convinced that the case against the accused was strong and clear.[241] Moreover, it is not the purpose of a criminal trial to deal with the political background of a crime, if this does not contribute to establishing the guilt of the accused. The case nevertheless provides evidence that the security forces also engaged in the practice of murdering opposition members in the officially independent homelands.

---

235 Ibid. at para. 79.

236 Ibid. at para. 81.

237 Ibid. at para. 83.

238 Ibid.

239 Telephone interview with Advocate Quitsi in June 2006.

240 *S. v Tyani and Gumengu* (Transkei division) Case no. 76/2004, unreported, at paras. 42 and 79.

241 Ibid. at para. 83.

6. *Eugene Terre'Blanche*

The first TRC-related trial conducted by the PCLU concerned the right wing organisation *Afrikaner Weerstandsbeweging* leader, Eugene Terre'Blanche. Terre'Blanche was accused of various terrorist attacks aimed at thwarting the negotiations during the early 1990s which potentially fell in the TRC amnesty mandate but for which he had failed to apply for amnesty. He had entered into a plea agreement with the PCLU in terms of section 105A of the Criminal Procedure Act. On 12 November 2003 he pleaded guilty to five counts of terrorism in contravention of section 54(1)(i) of the Internal Security Act[242] in the Regional Court of Potchefstroom and was sentenced to six years imprisonment, which was wholly suspended.[243] The case did not demand extensive investigations. Since it concerned isolated acts of right-wing terrorist violence and not the violence of the liberation movement and the security forces during the apartheid conflict, it is only of minor relevance for the present research. Thus it is not examined in detail.

7. *The PEBCO-Three Case*

Soon after the PCLU was established, Ackermann decided to press charges in early 2004 in the first major TRC case, the murder of the so-called PEBCO-Three. In May 1985 Sipho Hashe, Champion Galela and Qaqawuli Godolozi were abducted, tortured and killed by the security police.[244]

During the mid-1980s the Eastern Cape was heavily disrupted by political unrest. After a visit to the region in 1985, a high-ranking delegation of security force officials expressed concern, which signalled to the local security police branch, based at Port Elizabeth, that they

[242] Act no. 74 of 1982.

[243] E-mails from Shaun Abrahams of 30 May 2007 and 6 June 2007.

[244] Unless otherwise is stated the following information derives from the amnesty decision no. AC/99/0223 and from *TRC Report*, vol. 2, chap. 3, paras. 240–44.

should drastically intensify their efforts. The three victims were leading members of the Port Elizabeth Black Civic Organisation[245] (hereinafter PEBCO), an important regional political organisation with close ties to the UDF and ANC. The security forces considered PEBCO to be a mere extension of the ANC and a major author of the political unrest and anti-apartheid movement in the region. The Port Elizabeth security branch, thus, decided to eliminate Hashe, Godolozi and Galela in a concerted effort with a Vlakplaas unit that was operating in the area at that time in order to break the opposition in the region.[246] On 8 May 1985, the three were lured to Port Elizabeth airport, from which they were abducted to a defunct police station in Post Chalmers, close to the town of Cradock. There they were interrogated. During the interrogation they were continuously and severely tortured. Eventually, on the 9 or 10 May they were shot dead.

In 1996 the Amnesty Committee received amnesty applications of Gideon Nieuwoudt, Harold Snyman, Hermanus Barend Du Plessis, Johannes Martin van Zyl and Gerhardus Johannes Lotz of the Port Elizabeth security branch[247] as well as of Johannes Koole[248] and some other members of the Vlakplaas group[249] for their involvement in the events.[250] In the amnesty hearings contradictory testimony was given. The applicants of the Port Elizabeth security police stated that no torture had taken place during the interrogation, which had been conducted by van Zyl, Lotz and Nieuwoudt. They further claimed that the Vlakplaas members only took part in the abduction, not in the interrogation and murder. This evidence was contradicted by the Vlakplaas *askaris*,

---

245 Godolozi was the President, Galela the General Secretary and Hashe the Secretary of PEBCO (*S. v Nieuwoudt and others*, konsep akte van beskuldiging).

246 The operation was commanded by the Port Elizabeth security branch.

247 Applications no. AM/3920/96; AM/3918/96; AM/4384/96; AM/5637/97; AM/3921/96.

248 Application no. AM/3748/96.

249 The group consisted of Roelf Venter, Gerhardus Beeslaar, Kimani Peter Mogoai, Joseph Mamasela and Johannes Koole.

250 Snyman and Du Plessis had not been physically involved in the deed but were the ones who had ordered the actions.

Mogoai, Koole and Mamasela, who claimed to have been present in the interrogation during which the three victims, allegedly, were severely assaulted. The Amnesty Committee found their versions reasonably true. Since other contradictions also emerged, in 1999 amnesty was refused to Nieuwoudt, van Zyl and Lotz for the abduction and killing of the PEBCO-Three for lack of full disclosure.[251] Amnesty was also refused to du Plessis, for conspiring and ordering the abduction and murder, to Beeslaar, for his role in the abduction and assault, and to Koole for the abduction and assault.[252] Later, amnesty was also refused to Venter.[253] Snyman was granted amnesty and has since died. Mogoai was also granted amnesty for his role in the abduction and assault.[254]

7.1 *The indictment and further development*

In February 2004 Anton Ackermann informed the attorney of Gideon Nieuwoudt[255] that he intended to charge his client in connection with the PEBCO-Three murder.[256] Nieuwoudt, who since passed away in August 2005, then appeared for his bail hearing in the Magistrate Court on 11 February 2004. He was released on 3000 Rand bail. The case was postponed to 3 June 2004. Shortly thereafter an arrest warrant was also issued for van Zyl,[257] who, at the time, was working for a company in Cambodia, clearing landmines. Van Zyl then also became a client of Wagener, who arranged for his return to South Africa. He appeared in court in early March 2004 and was released on bail. At the same time

---

[251] Decision no. AC/99/0223.

[252] Ibid.

[253] Decision no. AC/2001/064.

[254] Decision no. AC/99/0223.

[255] Gideon Nieuwoudt came to prominence through his involvement in a range of other cases for which he applied for amnesty and which were interrogated by the TRC such as the torture and killing of Steve Biko, which also involved Snyman, and the murder of the so-called Motherwell-Four.

[256] Unless otherwise is cited, all information contained in this subchapter derives from an interview with the attorney of Nieuwoudt and van Zyl, Jan Wagener, on 8 May 2006 in Pretoria.

[257] *Nieuwoudt charged with murder* SAPA, Feb 11, 2004.

the PCLU had tried to convince Johannes Koole to serve as a state witness in terms of section 204 of the Criminal Procedure Act.[258] However, Koole refused to cooperate and the PCLU decided to charge him as well.[259] In the PEBCO case the PCLU again relies heavily on state witnesses to sustain their case. Roelf Venter, Gert Beeslaar, Joe Mamasela and Peter Mogoai were approached for this purpose and thus for the time being were not included in the charges.[260]

Nieuwoudt, van Zyl and Koole were each to be charged with three counts of abduction, assault and murder respectively.[261] The charges accuse them of the deeds the Amnesty Committee determined they had committed: that they abducted the three deceased at the airport and then took them to Post Chalmers. The indictment further alleges that throughout the night and the following day the PEBCO-Three were severely assaulted. On 10 May 1985 the accused allegedly killed the PEBCO-Three under circumstances that, as the indictment asserts, are unknown to the State.[262] However, after the bail hearings of early 2004 until mid 2007, the Court proceedings made no progress at all. The trial was pending. The delay was caused mainly by an application of van Zyl and Nieuwoudt to review the refusal of amnesty. The circumstances of this application will be outlined in the following subchapter. Adding to this NDPP Bulelani Ngcuka imposed a moratorium in November 2004 on all TRC-related cases.[263] All TRC-related investigations and prosecutions were put on hold, which also affected proceedings in the PEBCO case.[264] The case is since pending. Only in July 2007 did the NPA again make statements on the matter when it was announced that the PCLU

---

[258] Act 51 of 1977. See *supra* Chapter 2 note 50.

[259] Interview with Anton Ackermann in Pretoria (May 11, 2006).

[260] Ibid.

[261] *S. v Nieuwoudt and others*, konsep akte van beskuldiging. Counts one to three relate to the abduction, counts four to six to the murder and counts seven to nine to the assault of the three deceased.

[262] *S. v Nieuwoudt and others*, konsep akte van beskuldiging, opsomming van wesentlike feite, pages 3–5.

[263] The causes and circumstances of the moratorium will be discussed below (Chapter 3(3.1)).

[264] E-Mail from Anton Ackermann (Oct 10, 2005).

also intended to charge Herman du Plessis, Gerhardus Lotz, Gerhardus Beeslaar and Peter Mogoai if they did not cooperate.[265] Mogoai, who had been granted amnesty for the abduction and assault, could only be charged for a possible participation in the murder.

In mid-July 2007 an NPA investigation team found remains of corpses on the farm in Post Chalmers near Cradock in the Eastern Cape where the PEBCO-Three had been kept.[266] These remains are believed to be those of the PEBCO-Three, which would contradict the testimony of van Zyl and other amnesty applicants from the Port Elizabeth security police that the corpses had been burned and thrown into the Fish River.[267] At the date of completing this book it remained to be seen how the case would proceed.

7.2 *The review application*

The decision to apply for a review of Nieuwoudt's and van Zyl's refusal of amnesty was taken shortly after their bail hearings.[268] As will become apparent, this has major implications for the PEBCO-Three prosecution. The review application, which now only concerns van Zyl since Nieuwoudt has passed away, was tendered at the High Court of Pretoria[269] by the attorney Jan Wagener in September 2004.

Considering that the amnesty decisions were already handed down in 1999, the tendering of the review application appears to have been

[265] T. Mtshali *Pebco Three: old cops face charges* The Sunday Times, July 17, 2007.

[266] L. Oelofse *NPA may have found bodies of Pebco Three* SAPA, July 16, 2007.

[267] Decision no. AC/99/0223.

[268] Decisions of the Amnesty Committee can be taken on review at the High Courts by applicants, victims or other parties with a substantial interest in the matter (*TRC Report*, vol. 6, s. 1, chap. 2, para. 68; J. de Lange 'The historical context, legal origins and philosophical foundation of the South African Truth and Reconciliation Commission' in W. Verwoerd and C. Villa-Vicencio (eds) *Looking back reaching forward* (2000) 14 at 26). See further J. Sarkin *Carrots and sticks: the TRC and the South African amnesty process* (2004) 86–88; F. Kutz *Amnestie für politische Straftäter in Südafrika* (2001) 139–41,.

[269] The legal successor of the TRC is the Minister of Justice and Constitutional Development (see section 46(7)(b)(ii) of the TRC Act), seated in Pretoria.

delayed. According to section 7(1) of the Promotion of Administrative Justice Act[270] (hereinafter PAJA), an application for judicial review of an administrative action must be brought no later than 180 days after the person was informed of the administrative action. The High Courts ruled that the Amnesty Committee is part of the executive power and that amnesty decisions are administrative actions.[271] Thus, according to this provision the deadline for applying for review already lapsed six months after the decision was handed down. Section 9(1)(b) PAJA, however, provides that the period of 180 days may be extended by agreement between the parties. This is what happened in the PEBCO-Three amnesty proceedings. Shortly after the applications in question had been refused, some of the applicants approached Wagener for advice on the possibility of reviewing the decision.[272] Wagener then negotiated an agreement with the Justice Department according to which the time limit for instituting judicial review proceedings in the PEBCO amnesty process was extended to the date on which the authorities charge the applicants. While Johannes Koole has never been a client of Wagener and, accordingly, the agreement does not cover him, the criminal proceedings against Koole are also affected since the charges will be tried jointly. The agreement does cover van Zyl and covered Nieuwoudt. Moreover, it not only affects the PEBCO matter, but another eight applications of clients of Wagener in which amnesty has been refused.[273] In the following, the legal and factual effects on the criminal litigation will, therefore, be outlined.

---

[270] Act 3 of 2000. It merely repeats the common law rule which already existed in 1999.

[271] *Nieuwoudt, du Toit and Ras v Chairman, Sub-Committee on Amnesty for the Truth & Reconciliation Commission* 2002 (1) SACR 299 (C) at 311; *Derby-Lewis and another v The Chairman of the Committee on Amnesty and Truth and the Reconciliation Commission and others* 2001 (3) BCLR 215 (C). Whether the Amnesty Committee is an administrative body was rarely discussed in legal literature (see F. Kutz *Amnestie für politische Straftäter in Südafrika* (2001) 113 and 141).

[272] Most of them had not been Wagener's clients during the amnesty proceedings but became his clients thereafter.

[273] E-mail from Jan Wagener (Feb 12, 2007).

The amnesty proceedings and criminal litigation generally run parallel to each other.[274] However, once an application has been lodged the Amnesty Committee may request the appropriate authority to postpone the proceedings pursuant to section 19(7) of the TRC Act[275] pending the consideration and disposal of the amnesty application. In practice the applicant always tenders a request at the criminal court himself[276] and the courts have always granted such requests.[277] However, in this case, an amnesty hearing is not pending and the Amnesty Committee no longer exists. Nevertheless, the review application stays the criminal proceedings. This conclusion derives from a similar case, the Motherwell-Four case. As has been outlined above, Nieuwoudt and two other policemen were convicted of murder in the Motherwell case in 1996.[278] The conviction was immediately appealed to the Supreme Court of Appeal. The three had applied for amnesty simultaneously in relation to their conviction for the Motherwell-Four incident.[279] The appeal proceeding was then postponed pending a final decision on the question of amnesty.[280] After amnesty was eventually denied to all applicants in December 1999,[281] Wagener applied at the High Court in Cape Town for a review of the decision to refuse amnesty.[282] In the still pending appeal of the criminal conviction, the Supreme Court of

[274] F. Kutz *Amnestie für politische Straftäter in Südafrika* (2001) 201.

[275] The section reads: 'If the person who submitted an application under section 18 is charged with any offence constituted by the act or omission to which the application relates, or is standing trial upon a charge of having committed such an offence, the Committee in consultation with the attorney-general concerned, may request the appropriate authority to postpone the proceedings pending the consideration and disposal of the application.'

[276] F. Kutz *Amnestie für politische Straftäter in Südafrika* (2001) 201.

[277] Ibid., 202.

[278] See *supra* Chapter 1(4.).

[279] Applications no AM/3920/96; AM/3381/96; AM/5183/96.

[280] L. Fernandez 'Post-TRC prosecutions in South Africa' in G. Werle (ed.) *Justice in transition* (2006) 65 at 67.

[281] Decision no. AC/99/0345. Thereafter du Toit and Nieuwoudt became clients of Jan Wagener.

[282] Interview with Jan Wagener in Pretoria (May 8, 2006).

Appeal then ruled that this appeal litigation will remain pending until the review litigation concerning the refused amnesty applications has been concluded, since only when such review proceedings are concluded would an amnesty application be disposed of in terms of section 19(7) of the TRC Act.[283] The same applies to the PEBCO-Three case. The prosecution, which was initiated in early 2004, is now pending the final outcome of the review application concerning the rejected amnesty application of van Zyl.

The practical effects of a review application on the PEBCO prosecution, in terms of delay, are again illustrated by the Motherwell-Four case. There, the review application to have the amnesty decision set aside was granted on 23 November 2001.[284] It was ordered that the amnesty decision be set aside and, quite interestingly, that the Minister of Justice had to reconvene a new amnesty committee to hear and consider the amnesty applications afresh, since the Amnesty Committee had meanwhile been disbanded.[285] It took until March 2004 for a new amnesty committee to be constituted in Port Elizabeth.[286] The ad hoc committee consisted of the attorney F Bosman and High Court judges R Pillay and N Motata. The hearing was concluded in September 2004 but the decision on whether to grant amnesty was reserved.[287] Only on 29 August 2005, did the majority of the committee decide that amnesty should be granted to du Toit and Ras but again refused

---

283 E-mail from Jan Wagener (Feb 12, 2007).

284 *Nieuwoudt, du Toit and Ras v Chairman, Sub-Committee on Amnesty for the Truth & Reconciliation Commission* 2002 (1) SACR 299 (C). The court found that the decision of the Amnesty Committee was unstructured, that the evidence had largely been disregarded or only considered on a selective basis. Moreover the amnesty decision did not make it sufficiently clear how the decision had been reached at all.

285 *Nieuwoudt and others v Chairman, Sub-Committee on Amnesty for the Truth & Reconciliation Commission* 2002 (1) SACR 299 (C) at page 304.

286 J. Sarkin *Carrots and sticks: the TRC and the South African amnesty process* (2004) 88. The Promotion of National Unity and Reconciliation Amendment Act (Act no 23 of 2003) was specially enacted to make provisions for the setting up of a new amnesty committee in case applications need to be dealt with afresh.

287 Interview with Jan Wagener in Pretoria (May 8, 2006).

to Nieuwoudt.[288] Nieuwoudt did not hear of the decision since he died shortly before it was handed down. The proceedings illustrate that a review application can lead to drastic delays in the pursuit of criminal justice. Six years have passed from the time the first amnesty decisions were handed down to the time of the final decision on amnesty in 2005. If Nieuwoudt had still been alive, the second refusal would have again been taken on review, if possible.[289] Although the delay in the Motherwell-Four case is also due to the fact that special legislation had to be enacted, providing for the establishment of ad hoc amnesty committees, which only happened in 2003, the example, nevertheless, illustrates that the PEBCO-Three prosecution will be delayed significantly by the judicial review hearings.

At the time of writing, no decision had been reached in the PEBCO-Three review proceedings since 2004. The start of the review litigation is held up by the Department of Justice, which takes an inexplicably long time to file the necessary papers to the court in order to initiate the proceedings. By the end of 2007, years after the review application had been tendered, the Department had yet to file the documents and the criminal matter remained postponed until August 2008.[290] Should the review application succeed, an amnesty committee would need to be reconvened. Should van Zyl's amnesty application eventually succeed, he would be freed of criminal and civil liability in terms of section 20(8) of the TRC Act.

7.3 *Conclusion*

The charges in the PEBCO-Three case aroused strong reactions in the South African public, both welcoming and critical.[291] The PEBCO-Three

[288] The new amnesty hearing also concerned former police general Jacobus Janse Nicolaas ("Nic") van Rensburg, who was also granted amnesty. He has since died. Information on the decision was only provided to the public in December 2005. The decision has not been published yet. It was provided to the author by the Justice Ministry.

[289] Interview with Jan Wagener in Pretoria (May 8, 2006).

[290] E-mail from Jan Wagener (Sep 13, 2007).

[291] See *infra* Chapter 3 (1.2.3).

case is a well-known, high profile case, exemplifying the use of egregious violence by the security police and the cold-blooded murder of political opponents. It was heralded by many as the starting point of a larger body of prosecutions. Indeed, it marked the first major sign of progress on the subject of post-TRC prosecutions after the establishment of the PCLU in 2003. However, as will be pointed out later in this book, it was not the starting point of a larger process. Though it started promisingly, the case quickly stagnated and the review application will prevent it from proceeding. It is probable that it will take years before the criminal trial can continue, if at all.[292]

The interruption of the criminal proceedings through the amnesty review applications was, as described above, unavoidable in procedural terms. However, the Department of Justice can easily avoid long delays until the start of the review litigation. It is inexplicable why the Department of Justice is not filing its affidavits and papers to the High Court and is not taking the steps necessary for the review litigation to start. It thereby deliberately hinders the criminal trial from resuming.

8. *The Blani Case*

In October 2004, Buyile Ronnie Blani, at that time a 40 year-old member of the SANDF, was tried for his involvement in the killing of two people in the Eastern Cape in 1985.[293] Blani had been a member of the Addo Youth Congress during the 1980s, an organisation loosely affiliated to the ANC and UDF.[294] Blani's involvement with the liberation movement was, however, of a basic and minimal nature. He came from a poor and uneducated background and was one of many militant youths who were mobilised and politicised by the wave of mass movement activities during the 1980s.[295] However, in response to a call of

[292] Interview with Jan Wagener in Pretoria (May 8, 2006).

[293] *ANC member charged with murder of farm couple* Cape Times, July 7, 2004.

[294] N. Rousseau 'Prosecutions' in E. Doxtader (ed) *Provoking questions* (2005) 37 at 42.

[295] Interview with Madeleine Fullard in Pretoria (May 4, 2006).

the UDF in the mid-1980s to render the country ungovernable, Blani and other members of the youth congress raided a local farm and killed the elderly farmer couple.[296] Various items were stolen.

In 1985 the case was prosecuted. Blani managed to escape to exile in Angola. Most members of the group were tried and either sentenced to death or to long jail terms. Two death penalties were executed and two were later commuted to live imprisonment. During the negotiation period in the early 1990s, all remaining convicts in the case received either presidential pardons in 1993 or indemnity under the laws of 1990 and 1992.[297] One of Blani's accomplices who had also fled to exile successfully applied for amnesty for his participation in the killings after his return.[298] Blani, however, neither seemed to have recognised the indemnity laws of 1990 and 1992 nor of the TRC as he failed to apply for amnesty after his return from exile in 1992.[299]

When auditing the TRC dockets, Ackermann came across the docket of the Blani case. The case against Blani had already been investigated fully and the evidence was clear and compelling.[300] It was obvious that the case would not require a great effort for the prosecution. Blani was arrested in June 2004 and granted bail. On 12 October 2004 he was charged at the High Court of Grahamstown with two counts of murder and one count of housebreaking with intent to commit robbery and robbery with aggravating circumstances for his part in the conspiracy and execution of the raid and killings.[301] The case was not affected by the said moratorium on all TRC-related prosecutions of November 2004. Whereas the PEBCO-Three case was still in the pre-trial stage, the Blani trial had to continue because by November it was too advanced

[296] N. Rousseau 'Prosecutions' in E. Doxtader (ed) *Provoking questions* (2005) 37 at 42.

[297] See for the indemnity laws of the early 1990s: J. Sarkin *Carrots and sticks: the TRC and the South African amnesty process* (2004) 37–49.

[298] Application no. AM/2707/96; Decision no. AC/99/0264.

[299] *Feud builds up over Kirkwood murders* The Herald, available at http://www.theherald.co.za/herald/2004/07/08/news/n06_08072004.htm.

[300] Interview with Anton Ackermann in Pretoria (May 11, 2006).

[301] *S. v Buyile Ronnie Blani*, indictment.

to be stopped.[302] The prosecution was conducted by M. Mhaga and directed by the PCLU.

The parties agreed on a relatively lenient sentence. On 25 April 2005 Blani was convicted on all charges and sentenced to five years imprisonment, four of which were suspended for five years.[303] The judge took into account the fact that, in contrast to all of his accomplices, Blani neither benefited from the indemnity laws of the early 1990s nor the TRC amnesty legislation. This was due to a lack of legal advice, for which Blani clearly lacked the resources to obtain. Upon returning from exile he basically assumed that the 1992 Further Indemnity Act[304] automatically indemnified him from criminal liability. Had he understood the provisions correctly, he would not have had to face charges at all. He obviously did not have proper access to legal counsel. Even at his trial in 2004, he only obtained legal representation through the legal aid scheme shortly before the trial was to start.[305] Against the background of these mitigating circumstances, the Court considered it to be inappropriate to sentence Blani to a long jail term.[306] The Court further acknowledged the political implications of the matter and took into account the fact that a number of co-perpetrators only benefited from indemnity and amnesty regulations since the crimes in question were associated with a political objective.[307] The prosecutors concurred with this consideration and pleaded for a mild sentence.[308]

There were many critical reactions to the Blani trial.[309] However, the trial shows that the PCLU is intent on prosecuting across the political spectrum by focusing mainly on the availability of evidence and the

---

[302] Interview with Madeleine Fullard in Pretoria (May 4, 2006).

[303] *S. v Buyile Ronnie Blani* (Eastern Cape division) Case no. CC 81/2004 25 April 2005, unreported.

[304] Act 151 of 1992.

[305] D. Bruinders *Postponement granted in 1985 Kirkwood murder case* The Herald, available at http://www.epherald.co.za/herald/2004/10/13/news/n05_13102004.htm.

[306] *S. v Buyile Ronnie Blani* (Eastern Cape division) Case no. CC 81/2004 25 April 2005, unreported.

[307] Ibid.

[308] Interview with Anton Ackermann in Pretoria (May 11, 2006).

[309] See *infra* Chapter 3(1.2.3).

strength of the case. As stated above, the evidence in the case was very strong and the crimes in question, murder and robbery, were serious. Blani's trial was not, however, without political consequences, as it contributed to a debate on priorities and also to the above mentioned moratorium.

9. *The Attempted Murder of Frank Chikane*

In early November 2004, the PCLU was ready to carry out the arrests of three former officers of the South African security police on charges relating to the attempted murder of Frank Chikane in 1989.[310] Frank Chikane, who is now the Director-General of the President's Office, had been the Director-General of the South African Council of Churches, which was the leading organisation in the Protestant opposition to apartheid.[311] He was also a leading member of the UDF and generally a very vocal and popular opponent of the apartheid government.[312] The security forces perceived him to be a considerable threat to the regime.[313] It is believed that there were several attempts to kill him.[314] At his trial in 1995, former Vlakplaas commander Eugene de Kock alleged that the SADF and police had attempted to kill Chikane in a planned and premeditated operation.[315]

The three former policemen, former Major-General Christoffel Smith, Gert Otto and Johannes "Manie" van Staden, were to appear in Pretoria High Court on charges of attempted murder led by the PCLU.[316] They were also to face an umbrella charge of conspiracy to kill a number of unknown opponents of the apartheid state.[317] The accused persons had

[310] Interview with Torie Pretorius and others in Pretoria (May 2, 2006).
[311] P. van Niekerk and B. Ludman (eds) *A–Z of South African politics 1999* (1999) 33.
[312] Ibid.
[313] *S. v Wouter Basson*, akte van beskuldiging, vol. II, aanklag 57, para. 2.
[314] S. Adams *Drama in Chikane's poison case* The Star, Nov 11, 2004.
[315] P. van Niekerk and B. Ludman (eds) *A–Z of South African politics 1999* (1999) 34.
[316] S. Adams *Drama in Chikane's poison case* The Star, Nov 11, 2004.
[317] Interview with Jan Wagener in Pretoria (May 8, 2006).

not applied for amnesty in relation to the charges. The facts concerning the involvement of the three accused in the attempted murder in 1989 emerged during the investigations against Wouter Basson,[318] who himself had been charged in 1999 for his alleged involvement in the murder attempt.[319] The case against the policemen had been almost completely investigated in the course of the Basson investigations.[320] The three had allegedly managed to get access to Chikane's luggage at the airport of Johannesburg in April 1989, when he was about to go on a trip to Namibia. On this occasion Chikane's clothing was apparently saturated with Paraoxon, a lethal nerve poison. The poison had been produced under the supervision of Basson in military laboratories and had been provided to the three accused under his instruction. After putting on his cloths, Chikane experienced severe health disturbances but survived the attack. His condition only improved once he had received hospital treatment and had taken off his clothing. Directly afterwards he went on a scheduled trip to the USA where he again experienced severe health problems after wearing his clothes. When he was treated in hospital the chemicals were eventually detected in his body and it was clear that an attempt on his life had been made.[321]

However the accused never appeared in court in November 2004 and the planned prosecution took a remarkable turn.

9.1 *The arrest suspension*

After the accused persons were informed by the PCLU of their imminent arrest the arrest warrants were suddenly withdrawn and the bail hearing, which was scheduled for the following day, was suspended.[322] The decision was reportedly taken by senior members of the NPA.[323]

---

[318] Interview with Torie Pretorius and others in Pretoria (May 2, 2006).

[319] *S. v Wouter Basson*, akte van beskuldiging, vol. II, aanklag 57.

[320] T. Pretorius *Panel presentation at the Institute for Justice and Reconciliation conference 'The TRC: ten years on'* (April 20, 2006).

[321] See *S. v Wouter Basson*, akte van beskuldiging, vol. II, aanklag 57, paras. 3–10.

[322] Interview with Torie Pretorius and others in Pretoria (May 2, 2006).

[323] S. Adams *Drama in Chikane's poison case* The Star, Nov 11, 2004.

The most likely scenario is that the NDPP Bulelani Ngcuka directed the PCLU to stop the proceedings.[324]

The NPA's official reason given for the sudden reversal of the PCLU's decision to prosecute was that the NPA realised that there was not a clear strategic plan on how to deal with TRC prosecutions and, thus, specific guidelines for these kinds of cases were needed.[325] The events in the case contributed to and are closely linked to the imposition of the said moratorium on all TRC-related investigations and prosecutions in late November 2004.[326] The exact implications of this will be outlined below.[327] However, there is more to the reasons for why the step was taken than what has been officially presented by the NPA. Although the NPA tried to argue that the reasons for the suspension of the arrests were not political,[328] the suspension of the arrests was mainly the result of a political settlement behind the scenes.[329] After the PCLU informed the accused persons of their arrest, their attorney Jan Wagener took immediate steps to prevent this from happening. Wagener intervened at the Office of the President and pressed for a suspension of the arrests.[330] According to Wagener it was President Mbeki who then decided that the proceedings be put on hold. Ngcuka was apparently directed to take the necessary steps. However, there must obviously have been convincing political arguments to influence the decision.[331]

Chikane, who holds a central position in the President's Office, played an active role in the events. In 2003, Chikane wrote letters to the alleged

---

324 The NDPP has great influence on all prosecutorial decisions. According to section 22(1) of the NPA Act, the NDPP exercises directive control over all duties, functions and powers assigned to the prosecuting authorities. According to section 22(2)(c) of the NPA Act, he can review any decision taken by a Director of Public Prosecutions to lay charges.

325 S. Adams *Drama in Chikane's poison case* The Star, Nov 11, 2004.

326 E-mail from Anton Ackermann (Oct 18, 2005).

327 *Infra* Chapter 3(3.1).

328 *Chikane poison case not closed, say Scorpions* SAPA, Nov 11, 2004.

329 Interview with Jan Wagener in Pretoria (May 8, 2006).

330 Ibid.

331 The political influences and considerations of the government will be analysed in Chapter 3(4.).

perpetrators, urging them to come and disclose to him their deeds in order to be liberated from their guilt.[332] Then in late 2006, he announced that they were ready to meet with him and ask for forgiveness.[333] He was convinced that it was more important that the perpetrators tell their story rather than be prosecuted.[334]

The NPA assured at the time that once the question of strategy had been settled, the prosecution would definitely continue[335] and later confirmed that the case was still being considered.[336]

9.2 *The indictment and plea bargain*

It took until early 2007 for new developments on the case to occur. The said moratorium came to an end by January 2006 since the question of strategy had apparently been settled. From then on, the prosecution was subject to a consultation process between the attorney of the accused and the NPA.[337] The NPA and government had meanwhile drafted new prosecution policy guidelines for the exercise of prosecutorial discretion concerning the decision of whether to prosecute TRC-related cases, which will later be analysed in greater detail.[338] The policy document outlines criteria according to which a procedure can be implemented that requires the alleged perpetrator to make full disclosure on the criminal acts in question, which then can lead to a decision of the NDPP not to institute criminal proceedings. Although the NPA made no public announcements whatsoever, it is clear that the three accused in the Chikane case were subject to the new procedure apparently mainly in September 2006.[339]

---

[332] S. Adams *Drama in Chikane's poison case* The Star, Nov 11, 2004.

[333] *I know who tried to kill me—Chikane* SAPA, Oct 2, 2006.

[334] E. Naidoo *No general amnesty for apartheid crimes* The Sunday Independent, July 3, 2005.

[335] *Chikane poison case not closed, say Scorpions* SAPA, Nov 11, 2004.

[336] *Chikane's would-be assassins on NPA's list* SAPA, Jan 24, 2005.

[337] Interview with Jan Wagener in Pretoria (May 8, 2006).

[338] See *infra* Chapter 3(3.).

[339] See for the implications of the prosecution guidelines for the Chikane case: *infra* Chapter 3(3.4).

It later emerged that the case would also concern two formerly high-ranking officials of the security forces and government. In mid-2007 the NPA announced that Adriaan Vlok, who had been Minister of Law and Order in the apartheid government from 1986 to 1991, and Johan van der Merwe, who had been head of the SAP security branch from 1986 to 1988, deputy National Commissioner of the Police from 1988 to 1990 and National Commissioner of the Police from 1990 to 1995, would be indicted.[340] Vlok and van der Merwe had been linked to a number of criminal activities of the security police due to their previous positions. Vlok had apparently already admitted earlier to having played a central role in the crime and had in 2006 apologised to Chikane.[341]

Although no official announcements were made concerning the aforementioned, it is clear that during 2006 Vlok and van der Merwe had joined the three former security police officers, who were initially to be charged, in terms of the guideline's disclosure procedure in order to make representations on their involvement in the case.[342] The fact that they came forward, however, was allegedly not prompted by imminent charges or the discovery of implicating evidence against them, but was done entirely voluntarily.[343] Their motives for this move will be outlined below. However, in January 2007 the NPA eventually informed the three alleged perpetrators that their prosecution would go ahead and apparently intended to also focus on Vlok and van der Merwe,[344] which obviously means that the guidelines procedure did not result in a decision of the NPA against prosecution. In August 2007, van der Merwe, Vlok, Otto, van Staden and Smith were charged with one count of attempted murder of Frank Chikane, alternatively with the conspiracy to murder Chikane in contravention of section 18(2)(a)

---

340 *Court date for Vlok expected Tuesday: NPA* SAPA, June 25, 2007.

341 *Vlok apologises for atrocities* SAPA, Aug 26, 2006; *I know who tried to kill me—Chikane* SAPA, Oct 2, 2006.

342 E-mail from Jan Wagener (Sep 13, 2007).

343 Ibid.

344 W.J. da Costa and T. Mtshali *Prosecuting apartheid's soldiers 'divisive'* Pretoria News, Feb 8, 2007.

of the Riotous Assemblies Act, and with one count of conspiracy to murder various unknown persons.[345] Both acts of conspiracy allegedly also concerned Wouter Basson and his accomplice André Immelmann from Project Coast. The indictment is based on the facts that emerged during the Basson prosecution. It was allegedly together with Basson and Immelmann from Project Coast conspired to murder Chikane. Otto, van Staden and Smith allegedly carried out the poisoning at Johannesburg airport. Vlok and van der Merwe are claimed to have been involved in the command level underlying the actual implementation of the attempted murder.[346]

It was soon seen as likely that the accused would agree on a plea and sentence agreement, a so-called plea bargain, with the PCLU.[347] Indeed in June 2007 a plea bargain was agreed upon. On the scheduled trial date on 17 August 2007, the Court only had to decide on the validity of a plea and sentence agreement concerning the charges in terms of section 105A of the Criminal Procedure Act. According to section 105A(1)(a) of the Criminal Procedure Act a plea bargain contains an agreement between the State and the accused on a plea of guilty and a just sentence. Plea-bargaining is therefore a procedure under which the accused forgoes his right to a full trial in exchange for a reduced sentence.[348] There is extensive room to negotiate the exact terms and details of the agreement.[349] However, judicial approval of the plea and sentence agreement is required and the terms must be documented and presented in court.[350] According to section 105A(8) of the Criminal Procedure Act, the court has to adjudicate on whether the agreement is just and thereafter convicts and sentences the accused in terms of the sentence agreement.

---

345 *S v Johannes Velde van der Merwe en andere*, akte van beskuldiging.

346 Ibid., opsomming van wesentlike feite.

347 E. Momberg and C. Terreblanche *Alleged NPA deal may let Vlok off the hook* The Sunday Independent, Feb 25, 2007.

348 E. Du Toit et al. *Commentary on the Criminal Procedure Act* service 35 (2006) § 105A 15–5.

349 Ibid., 15–6.

350 Ibid., 15–7.

The Court approved the plea and sentence agreement. In terms of the agreement, the five accused persons pleaded guilty to the charge of attempted murder. The charge of conspiracy to murder various other opponents of apartheid, whose identities are unknown to the State, was withdrawn by the PCLU. Vlok and van der Merwe were, according to the sentence agreement, sentenced by the Court to ten years imprisonment, wholly suspended for five years on the condition that they are not convicted of a similar crime. Otto, Smith and van Staden were sentenced to five years imprisonment, wholly suspended for five years on the same condition.[351]

9.3 *Terms of the plea bargain*

The plea and sentence agreement contains various admissions regarding the crime and lists aggravating and mitigating circumstances. Initially reference is made to the political backgrounds of the crime and the implication with the SADF project led by Basson, which allegedly had been engaged in developing toxic substances to be supplied to the various security branches.[352] It then turns to an account of the events constituting the crime of attempted murder, which confirms what had been alleged in the charges:[353] At a meeting in 1987 that had been arranged by the SADF, Johan van der Merwe 'took cognisance of an order to act against high profile members of the anti-apartheid liberation struggle in order to neutralise their influence. He also took note that, in extreme cases and only as a last resort, consideration could be given to killing them.'[354] Van der Merwe and other senior security force officials were given a list containing names of such high profile activists, among them Frank Chikane. Van der Merwe and Vlok discussed the implementation of the order and decided to set up a group of security policemen for this purpose.

[351] *S. v Johannes Velde van der Merwe en andere* (Pretoria High Court) pleit en vonnisooreenkoms, 15 August 2007.

[352] Ibid. at paras. 14–35.

[353] Ibid. at paras. 35–49.

[354] Ibid. at para. 36.

Otto and van Staden became members of this special unit and Smith later served as the unit's commander. On the orders of General Sebastiaan Smit, who had meanwhile been appointed head of the security police branch, Christoffel Smith contacted Wouter Basson for the supply of substances for the special unit's purposes 'that could be applied against the enemy'.[355] Thereafter Smith, Otto and van Staden met with André Immelmann, a scientist working for Basson's project, who had been ordered by Basson to instruct the policemen in the use of chemicals against enemies of the state. For Chikane a lethal substance was requested. Immelmann provided the three with the nerve poison Paraoxon and instructed them in how to apply it to Chikane's clothing.[356] The order to kill Frank Chikane was eventually issued by security branch head General Smit to Smith 'in terms of an order of' van der Merwe and Vlok.[357] Smith and Otto on 23 April 1989 intercepted Chikane's luggage at the airport and applied the poison to his underwear and clothing.

The plea bargain then points out various aggravating circumstances. The following are the most important:[358]

- Both van der Merwe and Vlok held high positions in the police and government.
- The only motive to kill Chikane was to prevent him from further political activities.
- None of the five accused applied for amnesty at the TRC with regard to the attempted murder of Frank Chikane.
- On 10 July 1997, van der Merwe testified before the TRC that he was not aware of a list containing names of opposition members to be targeted, which was obviously not true considering the facts of the Chikane case.
- Vlok only approached Chikane to apologise and attempt a reconciliation after it had emerged in November 2004 that the PCLU had a *prima facie* case against Smith, van Staden and Otto.

---

[355] Ibid. at para. 42.

[356] Ibid. at para. 43.

[357] Ibid. at para. 49.

[358] Ibid. at paras. 50–62.

- In the trial against Wouter Basson Smith, van Staden and Otto were approached on many occasions by the prosecutors to cooperate as state witnesses in terms of section 204 of the Criminal Procedure Act. They persistently refused to do so, gave false accounts on the events and chose instead to cooperate with Basson's legal team.
- Chikane had written to Smith, van Staden and Otto after the Basson trial, asking them to tell the full truth and to reconcile with him, which persistently was ignored by them.

However, also a number of mitigating circumstances are identified, which are apart from certain personal circumstances mainly the following:[359]

- The accused all pleaded guilty. With respect to Vlok and van der Merwe, otherwise a conviction would not have been possible, since no sufficient evidence against them was available.
- The original project to neutralise specific apartheid opposition members was not initiated by the accused but by the SADF.
- Van der Merwe and Vlok allegedly had no knowledge of the specific plan and operation to kill Chikane. Vlok was not informed, although he had given instruction to be informed should the killing of anyone on the list be considered.
- Smith and Otto were only subordinates. They later came forward to disclose their roles in the incident and have since shown remorse.
- Van der Merwe encouraged members of the security forces to apply for amnesty during the TRC process. Regarding the attempted murder of Chikane, he allegedly tried to persuade the responsible officials of the SADF to apply for amnesty together with him in this incident.
- As part of the plea bargain, the accused have undertaken to cooperate with the PCLU as witnesses in a possible prosecution of General Sebastiaan Smit.

[359] *S. v Johannes Velde van der Merwe en andere* (Pretoria High Court) pleit en vonnisooreenkoms, 15 August 2007, at paras. 63–80.

The official positions of the accused, which generally obliged them to protect the state, were obviously seen as mitigating. As such, it was emphasised that the three accused officers acted in their professional positions in defence of a 'lawfully elected government' to which they had sworn an 'oath of allegiance'.[360] It was further pointed out that the offence was committed during a period of intense political conflict in which violent acts by the liberation movement to overthrow the government were prevalent. The plea and sentence agreement took into account that the security police played a vital role in warding off the onslaught and that the distinction between lawful and unlawful means became increasingly blurred. It was further pointed out that due to his position of leadership, Chikane played a key role in causing unrest and mobilising resistance to apartheid.

9.4 *Conclusion*

The prosecution in the Chikane case is high profile and of great significance due to the rank and political position of Vlok and van der Merwe but also due to the political position of the victim, Frank Chikane, who was at the forefront of apartheid opposition and is now an influential political figure within the government. After the suspension of the arrests in 2004 it appeared as if no further progress on the matter would be made. However, after a lapse of almost three years, caused by the moratorium and various political developments,[361] the proceedings were concluded.

The eventual convictions in the case concern not only the three security police agents who were initially to be charged, but also van der Merwe, who was the highest ranking security policeman at that time and later the leading policeman of the country, and Vlok, a former minister of the apartheid government, who during the years of the most intense struggle had, by virtue of his portfolio, been politically responsible for the police's efforts to counter the apartheid opposition.

---

[360] Ibid. at para. 71.

[361] See *infra* Chapter 3(3.).

Only once before, with the former Minister of Defence Magnus Malan, had a minister of the apartheid government been charged with an apartheid crime. Vlok was the first political leader to be held accountable for the criminal practices of the apartheid state. Van der Merwe was the first high-ranking general of the security police to face charges in a court of law. Previously, charges predominantly concerned the rank and file operatives of the security police. This was the case during the 1990s and, as has been shown above, was the case after the TRC. For the first time, sentences were handed down to people who gave orders and who forged the policies under which the security forces acted. Two of the highest ranked protagonists of the apartheid state or its security forces were publicly put on trial and admitted to criminal acts, which obviously originated from specific orders given at the highest levels of the state and government. This unprecedented event alone is a very significant achievement.

Nevertheless, the plea bargain in the case was strongly criticised by victims organisations. It was rejected as being a merely symbolic public relations event, which did not reveal any substantial new information.[362] The sentences were considered to be far too mild and there has been criticism that they were agreed on behind the scenes. This practice fails to uphold the principle of restorative justice and diminishes victims' trust in a fair legal system. The critique indicates that the trial, especially regarding Vlok and van der Merwe, was seen as a broader and general reckoning with apartheid crimes. This fails to take into account that the prosecution only concerned one specific case, that of Frank Chikane, who himself was very satisfied with the plea agreement.[363]

However, the suspended sentences indeed appear lenient since the aggravating circumstances are strong. This is particularly true since Smith, Otto and van Staden, who actually carried out the poisoning, in terms of the plea bargain did not show proper remorse and rejected Chikane's requests to come forward. Another grave and aggravating

[362] Khulumani Support Group, press statement *Khulumani Support Group rejects the finding of the Pretoria High Court today* (Aug 17, 2007).

[363] *S. v Johannes Velde van der Merwe en andere* (Pretoria High Court) pleit en vonnisooreenkoms, 15 August 2007, at para. 6.

fact is that they refused to take up the offer of indemnity by cooperating with the NPA in the prosecution of Basson. Instead they chose to support the defence of Basson, who had also been implicated in the murder attempt of Chikane. Neither of them applied for amnesty. The fact that they eventually came forward to disclose the particulars of their involvement to the PCLU can certainly be attributed to their imminent prosecution. However, consideration must be given to the fact that the three operatives were only the ones who carried out orders. Those behind the crime bear greater responsibility for it. In this regard, it is an achievement that the prosecutors managed to secure convictions of members of the higher echelons of power.

The suspended sentences of Vlok and van der Merwe can probably be attributed to the nature of their involvement and the PCLU's inability to present a strong case against them. It must be borne in mind that a plea bargain essentially depends on the State's assessment of the probable outcome of the case.[364] It has been pointed out that without the admissions of Vlok and van der Merwe, it would have been impossible to prosecute them. It has also been pointed out that their involvement was allegedly confined to passing on the order in its broadest sense to act against the listed apartheid opponents and setting up a group for this purpose. The murder attempt, however, only happened years later in 1989. Allegedly, van der Merwe and Vlok did not have knowledge of the actual operation against Chikane.[365] Furthermore, the PCLU was allegedly not even aware of their involvement. Likewise, the police officers Smit, van Staden and Otto could not have had knowledge of Vlok's and van der Merwe's involvement as commanders in the background in 1987, and, thus, could not have implicated them.[366] The PCLU, thus, had two choices: first, they could pursue charges against the three officers with uncertain prospects for securing a conviction in court and without charges being brought against Vlok and van der Merwe; second, they could go with the plea and sentence agreement

[364] E. Du Toit et al. *Commentary on the Criminal Procedure Act* service 35 (2006) § 105A 15–8.

[365] E-mail from Jan Wagener (Sep 13, 2007).

[366] Ibid.

including all five. Obviously, the second choice seemed more promising. The suspended sentences of Otto, van Staden and Smith, thus, have to be seen as part of this overall agreement that included Vlok and van der Merwe. The whole plea bargain must further be seen in conjunction with the disclosure procedure in terms of the prosecution policy including all five concerned persons and the voluntary admissions of Vlok and van der Merwe.[367] Thus, on the one hand, the plea bargain was a by-product of this disclosure process and on the other hand it was a compromise since sufficient evidence was not available to sustain charges against Vlok and van der Merwe in a criminal trial.

Furthermore, there is not a compelling reason why suspended sentences should be detrimental to the principle of restorative and transitional justice. With regard to the three operatives, the prosecution of killings at the inner German border carried out by wall guards of the GDR proves that in terms of dealing with the systematic crimes of a past regime, it can be perfectly appropriate to hand down suspended sentences. 88.8% of custodial sentences that were handed down with regard to human rights violations at the border, such as manslaughter of persons illegally trying to cross the border, were covered by suspended sentences.[368] Specifically, in many manslaughter convictions, the sentence was suspended.[369] Suspended sentences were commonplace in cases where a low ranking officer was convicted. Sentences of high-ranking officers from the political and military spheres, however, were generally not suspended.[370] However, as has been pointed out, Vlok's and van der Merwe's inclusion to the plea agreement must be seen in the context of its own special circumstances.

The facts brought to bear raise the following questions: why did Vlok and van der Merwe admit to their involvement at all and why did they agree to plead guilty if there was not any solid evidence against them available to the NPA. According to their lawyer Jan Wagener, the two

---

[367] See further on the connections with the guidelines procedure *infra* Chapter 3(3.4).

[368] K. Marxen and G. Werle *Die strafrechtliche Aufarbeitung von DDR-Unrecht* (1999) 212.

[369] Ibid. 214.

[370] Ibid. 24.

took this step voluntarily and out of a moral urge to do so.[371] The police investigation only concentrated on the events of 1989. Allegedly Vlok and van der Merwe did not want to leave the three police officers to face charges alone as if there had not been any involvement in the background at the leadership level. Since they knew that there had been indications that there was involvement from those at a very high level before the murder attempt, they apparently felt it was the just thing to disclose the information, at least to a certain degree. In this regard, it is also important to note that at least van der Merwe and two of the accused former police officers are engaged together in an organisation acting on behalf of former security police members, which was also occasionally supported by Vlok.[372] This underlines the fact that it was their desire to help each other. The motivation was not to be included in a plea bargain but to support the three officers facing charges in their disclosure effort so that they would all be covered by a decision of the NDPP not to institute a prosecution as is permitted under the prosecution policy. The details of which will be dealt with below. It is difficult to see why there was not a decision against prosecution in the end since the NPA did not make any public announcements, which could have clarified the backgrounds of the proceeding. Van der Merwe and Vlok apparently had also intended and hoped for other former apartheid era security force authorities to follow their example and disclose their roles.[373] It should also be pointed out that the two were likely candidates for cooperation with the State since they were two of the very few apartheid era officials who had already cooperated during the TRC to a comparably high degree.[374] In a press statement Vlok and van der Merwe, accordingly, also announced that they had actually intended to apply for amnesty in this regard. However, since they only had limited knowledge of the incident and the main

[371] E-mail from Jan Wagener (Sep 13, 2007).

[372] See *infra* Chapter 3(1.1.2).

[373] E-mail from Jan Wagener (Sep 13, 2007).

[374] Vlok was the only apartheid minister to apply for amnesty. He applied for amnesty for the bombing of the South African Council of Churches, Khotso house and the COSATU trade unions headquarters (decisions no. AC/99/0349 and AC/99/0349).

authors of the order, authorities from the SADF, strongly refused to cooperate with the TRC, an application was not considered possible in this regard.[375]

Nevertheless, the benefits of the plea bargain are very limited with respect to its potential to reveal more information about the background of criminal activities at the governmental and military command level. The plea bargain states that an order was issued to van der Merwe to act against apartheid opponents, possibly by killing them, which emanated from the SADF, acting on higher authority. The exact terms of the order were not disclosed. Also, the specific background is in no way clarified. There is no clarification about which authorities concretely issued the order concerning the hit list or on whose higher authority the SADF officials acted. Thus, the specific political background concerning the targeting of certain prominent opposition members is only dealt with peripherally, but is not fully clarified at all and the information contained in the document, in this regard, is absolutely minimal. Furthermore, regarding Vlok's and van der Merwe's involvement, all that is stated is that the implementation of the order was discussed and a special unit was set up. There is not any mention of the exact brief of the unit and the terms for the implementation of the order, which possibly might have entailed the systematic killing and/or intimidation of those contained in the list.

In a press release issued on the day the plea agreement was presented in court, Vlok and van der Merwe indicated that they had not known who exactly worked out and issued the order to act against certain opposition members and that their limited knowledge was fully disclosed to the PCLU and completely included in the plea agreement.[376] Nevertheless, one would expect that more details could certainly have been presented in the plea bargain document since there are no particulars at all on, for instance, those who participated in the meeting of 1987. It appears strange that Vlok, who was a minister and not someone simply obeying orders, did not have further information on the real

---

[375] A. Vlok, J. van der Merwe, C. Smith, G. Otto and M. van Staden, press statement (Aug 17, 2007).

[376] Ibid.

authors of the plan. It remains unclear whether another recognisable authority transmitted it to them. All that is stated is that the initial instructions were presumably issued by the then President PW Botha. It is also claimed that no other person except Chikane was injured or killed on the basis of this order.[377]

The fact that so little information has reached the public domain certainly leaves a bitter aftertaste. It is also rather disconcerting that none of the information seems to have been tested in court. Many questions remain unanswered. The proceeding only sheds marginal light on the basic fact that systematic criminal acts were based on concrete policies and orders at the highest state levels. Since the plea bargain nevertheless clearly indicates that other people with more authority were involved in this specific matter, one must expect the PCLU to conduct further proceedings in order to deal with the case in its entirety. However, for the reasons presented above and under the circumstances, the case is at least a positive step forward in terms of establishing accountability for crimes committed during apartheid.

10. *Conclusion*

The prosecution of apartheid era political crimes after the conclusion of the TRC is characterised by delay. During the roughly eleven years that have passed from the end of the TRC in 1998 up to the time of publishing, prosecutions have been sporadic and few in number. Only seven criminal proceedings have as yet been concluded, four of which resulted in a conviction, three in an acquittal of the accused. The PEBCO case is currently pending. Its prospects for a swift continuation are bleak due to the review litigation. Considering the number of cases arising from the TRC that could potentially have been pursued in the interim period of almost a decade, the results have been minimal.[378] A

[377] Ibid.

[378] Although the circumstances are certainly not easily comparable it is nevertheless interesting to note that the process of dealing with systematic crimes after the fall of the east German GDR has led to 420 judgments, including 289 convictions and 131 acquittals. A large proportion of the convictions, at least 98 concerning the

concentrated process of prosecutions to dispose of the matter within a restricted timeframe has not taken place.

As far as the central units are concerned, structural problems and minimal funding and resources accounted for the complete lack of progress on prosecutions between 1998 and 2003. While the D'Oliveira Unit of the 1990s constituted a well equipped team of experienced prosecutors and investigators with strong political support, support for TRC-related prosecutions after 1998 declined drastically. There was also a clear lack of continuity as none of the prosecutors of the Human Rights Investigative Unit had been involved with TRC cases before and there was not any interaction with the predecessor unit. Thereafter, as outlined above, the responsibility for TRC cases was assigned to inappropriate structures in the DSO.

It was also put forward by NPA officials that the many still running amnesty proceedings prevented the prosecutors from moving ahead. This, however, does not appear compelling, since there must also have been a number of cases, which were not the subject of amnesty proceedings, such as the Basson matter. Also, as the Amnesty Committee had finished its work in 2001, there still were no trials initiated for over two years. NPA officials then maintained that they would have to wait for the political response from the President to the TRC Report of 2003. However, there was no discernable legal obligation to halt criminal proceedings pending a political announcement, especially considering that as far back as 1998, both the TRC and President Mandela had clearly recommended prosecutions to take place.

After 2003 and with the inception of the PCLU the situation indeed improved. The senior members of the unit are very experienced in prosecuting political crimes committed during apartheid and were determined to push ahead with trials. Nevertheless, investigative resources and funding remain a major obstacle. Furthermore, the promising advances made by the PCLU were halted by political interventions in

---

crimes at the inner German border, concerned gross human rights violations of state organs (See K. Marxen and G. Werle *Die strafrechtliche Aufarbeitung von DDR-Unrecht* (1999) 210).

late 2004. Thus, between its inception in 2003 and early 2008 only three cases were concluded, two of which, the Blani and Terre'Blanche cases, required very little effort.

Generally, two types of prosecutions can be identified. The first concerns those that were initiated independently by the regional prosecution offices, i.e. the Basson, Bisho-massacre, Luff and Tyani and Gumengu cases. Apart from the Basson matter, which emanated from an investigation that had been conducted by the D'Oliveira team in the 1990s, all of these trials resulted from criminal proceedings, which had already been initiated before or during the TRC and then suspended pending the disposal of amnesty applications. The proceedings were simply resumed by the regional prosecution offices at a later stage, without the involvement and sometimes even without the knowledge of the central units in Pretoria. The other set of cases was prosecuted by the PCLU. The unit initiated proceedings in the Terre'Blanche, PEBCO-Three, Blani and Chikane cases.

In fact, as far as a centralised effort to tackle post-TRC prosecutions is concerned, there have only been these four proceedings initiated by the PCLU. Thus, the assessment of prosecutions that resulted from a political or governmental effort to cope with post-TRC prosecutions through the centrally established units, is especially negative. During the interim period of almost one decade since the end of the TRC in 1998, such efforts only lead to those four proceedings being initiated, only three of which have been concluded thus far. It must also be pointed out that two of those were concluded as part of a plea and sentence agreement and a third, the Blani case, required very little effort. The achievements of the central units on post-TRC prosecutions, and thus, the achievements of the centralised approach, are therefore hardly noteworthy.

In four cases, the accused parties had not applied for amnesty for the crime in question. In all other cases amnesty had been applied for but denied. The prosecutions in the Basson, PEBCO-Three, Tyani/ Gumengu and Chikane cases are of specific significance since they concern cases of systematic state violence against opposition members.

Due to the small number of proceedings and the even smaller number of convictions, it cannot be said that accountability for apartheid era political crimes has been furthered to any significant degree. In contrast to the trials before 1998, however, proceedings overwhelmingly concerned politically motivated criminal conduct. Nevertheless, no substantial amounts of new information on systematic crimes during the apartheid era were discovered.

The Basson case was of special importance since it dealt with a wide range of exceptionally egregious, politically motivated, gross human rights violations, which emanated from a systematic SADF programme. Victims range from hundreds of SWAPO captives and Mozambican citizens to high profile ANC members in exile. From the mere scope of the charges the proceedings had the potential to mark a very significant step forward in revealing facts on systematic apartheid crimes. However, the prosecution did not secure a conviction. The validity of the accusations was not confirmed. Definite conclusions, therefore, cannot be drawn from the trial. Moreover the case certainly had a deterrent effect on the general willingness to approach more cases, since the huge amount of resources and money, which was invested, eventually proved to be futile. Nevertheless, the case was dealt with by the Constitutional Court, which, to a certain degree, set out guidelines for the prosecution of TRC-related cases and at least tentatively analysed the matter in the context of international human rights and humanitarian law.[379]

The PEBCO-Three case concerned acts of torture, abduction and murder, in many instances committed by the security police. A number of similar cases had been investigated by the TRC. Most of the facts in this case had already been revealed during amnesty hearings. The

---

[379] M. Swart 'The Wouter Basson prosecution: the closest South Africa came to Nuremberg?' (2008) 68/1 *Heidelberg Journal of International Law* 225–26, however, points out that the importance of international law in the judgment of the Constitutional Court should not be overestimated, since the legal substance of international law was still largely very foreign to the Court and to the prosecution, was in fact introduced to the litigation in a "last minute" move and handled rather awkwardly generally. Accordingly the Court has been criticised for missing a perfect opportunity to acknowledge the status of international law in South Africa and to apply it completely.

potential for new information to emerge in a trial is rather limited, should the case continue.

Although the judgment concerning the Bisho-massacre trial also resulted in an acquittal, it nevertheless dealt extensively with the facts concerning the events and made statements regarding where responsibility lay for the crimes. However, the TRC also analysed the matter intensively. The findings of the TRC and of the Court conflict strongly, especially regarding the responsibility for the massacre. Thus, although additional analysis of the events has been made in the trial, it is now even more difficult to evaluate the events and the authority of both findings is, to a certain degree, rendered compromised.

The convictions in the Chikane case, however, were highly relevant to the political backgrounds and policies formed by high-ranking state and government officials concerning the practice of combating the liberation movement by criminal means. Concrete findings on the chain of command, linking government organs to criminal acts, were hardly established by the TRC. Unfortunately, the plea bargain in the Chikane case stops short of shedding light on the exact political responsibilities concerning the order to act against liberation movement leaders. It only indicates that the command stated that consideration should also be given to killing opponents. Nevertheless, the case indicates that criminal proceedings can generally contribute to clarifying the specific chain of command behind apartheid crimes. It remains to be seen if this development is taken further in other cases in order to clarify the responsibility of those at the command level.

Chapter Three

The Politics of Prosecutions

The question of how to deal with the legacy of the TRC in terms of criminal accountability is part of the overall process of transitional justice in South Africa. The issue is, as is generally the case with matters of transitional justice, to a great extent driven by and charged with political considerations. A former minister in the ANC government even demanded that the matter should be dealt with solely through political channels and not left to the courts.[1] Obviously, the success or failure of prosecutions in the wake of the TRC depends to a large degree on the political support for such proceedings. Moreover, prosecutions have an impact on society, are perceived totally differently politically and have consequences for reconciliation. As the political factors clearly have consequences for the overall process of criminal trials, any assessment of post-TRC prosecutions has to take account of the political context within which such trials find themselves. The following chapter will do just this by touching on the discussions and players, but mainly by focussing on consultations of the government with certain groups of perpetrators and the government's decisions and general policy on the issue.

1. *Overview*

The following subchapter will describe the main political and social interest groups engaged in advocacy for or against prosecutions. Also, a cursory overview of the political discussions and public debates along

---

[1] *Apartheid crimes a political issue—Maharaj* SAPA, Aug 1, 2007.

with a collection of government's most important statements on the subject will be given.

1.1 *Interest groups*

During the operation of the TRC a wide range of NGOs, especially from the human rights sector, actively took part in the process. The number of organisations engaged with the issue of post-TRC prosecutions after 1998 is minimal compared to this. However, especially groups and networks acting on behalf of former members of the state security forces continue to exist and remain influential. The most important organisations will be described briefly to provide a background to their involvement of different forms, which will be focussed on at a later stage.

1.1.1 *Human rights organisations*

Most NGOs, which are engaged in promoting human rights in South Africa and which supported the TRC and the transition to democracy, deal only occasionally with issues of criminal accountability in the wake of the TRC.

The Khulumani Support Group[2] is the NGO most actively engaged in advocacy efforts on post-TRC prosecutions. The Khulumani group, which was founded in 1995, represents about 54,000 victims of apartheid era violence. During the work of the TRC its efforts were aimed at helping victims to take part in and benefit from the TRC process. Nowadays, the organisation seeks the implementation of proper reparations[3] for apartheid victims, the full-scale prosecution of apartheid operatives and generally the recognition of victim interests in the wake of the TRC. Khulumani calls for apartheid criminals to be held accountable since only then can victims attain justice for their endurance of gross human

---

[2] See http://www.khulumani.net.

[3] See on the reparations for apartheid victims as envisaged by the TRC scheme: K. Koppe *Wiedergutmachung für die Opfer von Menschenrechtsverletzungen in Südafrika* (2005).

rights violations.[4] Generally, the amnesty process was perceived as a very generous offer to perpetrators and they suggest that it is now time for victims to demand their share of justice. Khulumani presses for more trials and gathers affidavits of victims including accounts of the human rights violations they had to endure and information on the respective perpetrators.[5] Such affidavits are intended for possible use in criminal trials. Moreover, these efforts are aimed at conserving the records on human rights violations which have yet to be accounted for.[6]

Another significant organisation involved in advocacy on post-TRC prosecutions is the Foundation for Human Rights.[7] The Foundation for Human Rights is a grant-supplying organisation, distributing funds to various human rights and social work projects in South Africa. It is involved in funding legal actions aimed at effecting the implementation of proper trials. The executive director of the Foundation for Human Rights, former TRC commissioner Yasmin Sooka, is one of the most vocal and active advocates for the implementation of post-TRC trials.

Apart from this, there are few human rights NGOs actively involved in advocacy efforts on post-TRC prosecutions. As such, the Centre for the Study of Violence and Reconciliation in Johannesburg[8] (hereinafter CSVR) and the Cape Town-based Institute for Justice and Reconciliation[9] are worth mentioning.

1.1.2 *Security forces side*

There are two organisations or structures representing former members of the security forces. Neither group has been represented often in the media or public. However, their influence on and involvement in consultations with the government is or was significant. One organisation was an alliance engaged in support for former members of the SADF. The other organisation is acting on behalf of former members of the

---

[4] Interview with Marjorie Jobson in Pretoria (May 9, 2006).

[5] Ibid.

[6] Ibid.

[7] See http://www.fhr.org.za.

[8] See http://www.csvr.org.za.

[9] See http://www.ijr.org.za.

security police. Both groups were founded between the completion of the negotiations on the transition to democracy and the beginning of the TRC process. It was sensed that in the period of transitional justice it would be vital to form organised structures to react to prosecutions and TRC inquiries.

a. Kontak Buro

With regard to the SADF, an elite group of formerly high-ranking generals was formed to support former members of the military.[10] The group consisted of at least five to seven SADF generals, among them the former Chief of the SADF, General Jan Geldenhuys,[11] in a leading position and other prominent generals such as "Kat" Liebenberg and Georg Meiring. Also, the former Minister of Defence, General Magnus Malan and the former Chief of the SADF, General Constand Viljoen, occasionally took part in meetings of the group, apart from other former officers.

The group developed a structure to provide support for former soldiers of the SADF who, in connection with their occupation in the army, became involved with the TRC either because they were the subjects of investigations, implicated through amnesty applications, wished to apply for amnesty themselves, or were, directly or indirectly, affected by criminal investigations. The facility was called the *Kontak Buro* (Afrikaans for contact office). The *Kontak Buro* was basically a staffed office that could provide access to a certain support network, organise legal advice or counsel, provide financial support and advice SADF soldiers whether or not to apply for amnesty.[12]

The generals perceived the inquiries of the TRC into the activities of the SADF merely as a one-sided attack on the integrity of the SADF and

[10] Unless otherwise stated, the following information concerning the SADF group is taken from an interview with Jan Geldenhuys in Pretoria on 10 May 2006.

[11] General Geldenhuys was Chief of the South African army from 1980 to 1985 and of the SADF from 1985 to 1990.

[12] The organisation was criticised by the TRC of having urged SADF members not to cooperate with the TRC, thus contributing to the general lack of cooperation with the TRC on the side of the SADF (See *TRC Report*, vol. 6, s. 3, chap. 1, paras. 22–23).

its former members. The TRC was considered to be biased, unjust and untrustworthy.[13] Instead of cooperating with the process, the former SADF leadership felt responsible to defend themselves and their former colleagues against the perceived attack. Thus, apart from the initial focus on providing support to former SADF members, after the completion of the TRC in 1998 the group became involved in consultations with the government on the implementation of a further amnesty scheme in the wake of the TRC.

b. Foundation for Equality before the Law

For former members of the apartheid security police and generally for members of the police who had been involved in political conflicts, an organisation called the Foundation for Equality before the Law is actively engaged in support and advocacy efforts concerning prosecutions.[14] As the transition to democracy in South Africa was underway, and the decision had been reached to examine the atrocities of the apartheid past at the TRC, a support network was founded to react to the anticipated challenges for security force members. It contributed to this development, that the security police strongly felt that their former political superiors in the apartheid government had turned away from them and support was largely absent. Van der Merwe points out that F.W. de Klerk and Adriaan Vlok were exceptions in that they continued to support the interests of former security police operatives.

The members of the Foundation for Equality before the Law consist largely of former security police operatives.[15] It has reduced in membership size from considerably higher numbers during the TRC to about 30. Gideon Nieuwoudt, who was a main suspect in the PEBCO-Three case, was also a member of the Foundation for Equality before the Law. The management board consists mostly of formerly high-ranking

[13] See also *TRC Report*, vol. 6, s. 1, chap. 4, paras. 31–32.

[14] Unless otherwise stated, the following information on the organisation acting for former police members is taken from an interview with Johan van der Merwe in Pretoria on 5 May 2006.

[15] Yet the organisation is open to every state security force member who participated during the apartheid years in fighting the liberation struggle.

officers of the SAP, among them apparently with van Staden, Otto and van der Merwe, three of the accused in the Chikane matter.[16]

As the organisation's name suggests, according to its mission declaration, the Foundation for Equality before the Law wants to ensure equality before the law for its members.[17] More precisely, according to the constituting mission declaration, the organisation's aim is to ensure for security force members and anyone who had been involved in the counter-revolutionary struggle comprehensive protection and fair treatment in the face of the TRC and criminal trials.[18] In practical terms, this means that the organisation, similar to the *Kontak Buro*, is aimed at providing legal and financial facilities to security police members who were concerned by amnesty applications or who have to face charges for their activities in the police. Thus the Foundation for Equality before the Law was most active during the operation of the TRC, when it advised and assisted former security police members with amnesty applications. Thereafter, its activities were increasingly directed at helping those avoid prosecution who had been denied amnesty or had not applied for amnesty. Since the TRC processes, the Pretoria-based advocate and former state attorney of the apartheid government Jan Wagener has been an important supporter and advisor, both legally and politically, on the organisation's purposes.[19] The political advocacy efforts of the Foundation for Equality before the Law are directed at pressing for the permanent cessation of any TRC-related prosecutions

[16] However, the Foundation's chairperson Johan Botha comes from the civil sector. His deputy is General Johan van der Merwe. The Foundation's secretary is Major-General J.A. Steyn, formerly a high-ranking security police official in Natal. Other members of the management committee are J.H. le Roux, C. Colyn, H.D. Stadler, P.D. Uys, J.H. van Staden, D. Davidson, I.P. Minnaar, G. Otto and W.D. Pelser.

[17] That principle was unfortunately not pursued by the Foundation's members with equal vigour during the days of apartheid.

[18] Constitution and Mission Declaration of the Foundation for Equality before the Law.

[19] Jan Wagener very successfully acted as lawyer for many security police members seeking amnesty before the TRC. He continues to be the lawyer of a number of police who are in danger of being charged or who have already been charged and is politically involved to a significant extent.

and for finding a solution as to how to avoid further trials. To this end, as will later be shown, after 1998 it engaged in discussions with the government.

The motivation to avoid prosecutions also derives from the deep-rooted conviction that the crimes, which were obviously committed by the police, occurred in warlike circumstances during which it was a just obligation to defend the state against the 'terrorist onslaught' of the liberation movement. Although it is often accepted that in many instances boundaries of legality were overstepped, there is little recognition that the security forces' measures could not be justified, since their very purpose, the maintenance of a system and state based on the racist suppression of millions of people, was deeply unjust and unlawful.[20] Against this background, many aligned to the Foundation for Equality before the Law perceive the TRC and prosecutions as biased and unfair and a simple case of victor's justice.

Obviously, the viewpoints and activities of the two organisations are largely similar. Yet there was never any attempt to coordinate their efforts, although the Foundation for Equality before the Law's doors are open to former SADF members. This separation was intended by the military generals, who maintained it on the basis that different legal circumstances applied for the operations of SADF members, who mostly operated abroad in situations where rules of international conflicts and war applied, whereas the security police mostly operated under secret circumstances in South Africa and were bound by South African laws.[21] Furthermore, the military felt less vulnerable to prosecutions and accordingly did not want to side with the police.[22]

---

[20] This conclusion derives from interviews with Jan Wagener in Pretoria on 8 May 2006 and Johan van der Merwe on 5 May 2006 in Pretoria as well as from H.D. Stadler *The other side of the story* (1997).

[21] Interview with Jan Geldenhuys in Pretoria (May 10, 2006). Compare also the question whether South African courts have jurisdiction to try crimes abroad (see *supra* Chapter 2(2.3)).

[22] Interview with Jan Geldenhuys in Pretoria (May 10, 2006). This is also reflected by the fact, that far lesser SADF members applied for amnesty at the TRC than members

1.2 *Public debate*

The public discussion in the aftermath of the TRC on accountability for politically motivated human rights violations has generally been very muted and was largely confined to a few interested and concerned NGOs.[23] Public awareness of issues concerning transitional justice in South Africa has markedly declined. Some commentators suggested that after the end of the TRC, the Commission's recommendations and the tasks arising out of its work, such as prosecutions and reparations, were almost completely disregarded and largely disappeared from the political agenda.[24] In public discussions on the matter, it is necessary to distinguish generally between the conservative faction, which is opposed to prosecutions, and the human rights faction, which is calling for more trials. However, specific debate often erupted on occasions of specific prosecution events. The two factions will be discussed in turn below.

1.2.1 *The conservative spectrum and the call for even-handedness*

The conservative political spectrum and parties representing a mainly white constituency assume a generally dismissive position towards prosecutions. Many, like the right wing Afrikaner party Freedom Front Plus, reject prosecutions completely.[25] Importantly, many organisations, such as the Democratic Alliance, the conservative F.W. de Klerk Foundation or the Freedom Front Plus constantly demand that prosecutions, should they take place, be 'even-handed' and equal.[26] Prosecutions as such must not only focus on former security force members but must also include

---

of the security police, who were far more often concerned by prosecutions (V. Nerlich *Apartheidkriminalität vor Gericht* (2002) 312–14).

23 Interview with Piers Pigou in Johannesburg (May 6, 2006); N. Rousseau 'Prosecutions' in E. Doxtader (ed.) *Provoking questions* (2005) 37 at 46.

24 M. Fullard and N. Rousseau 'An imperfect past: the Truth and Reconciliation Commission in transition' in J. Daniel et al., (eds.) *State of the nation* (2003) 78 at 86.

25 Freedom Front Plus, press statement *FF Plus says NPA must prosecute Mbeki and other ANC* (Jan 25, 2006).

26 Interview with Sheila Camerer in Cape Town (March 30, 2006); Freedom Front Plus, press statement *FF Plus says NPA must prosecute Mbeki and other ANC* (Jan 25, 2006); D. Stewart *Panel presentation at the Institute for Justice and Reconciliation*

ANC and other liberation movement members, maybe even President Mbeki himself. Even-handed prosecutions and applying equal standards is allegedly demanded by the constitution's principle of equality before the law.[27] The fact that between 1984 and 1994, thousands of people were killed as a result of liberation movement activities would have to be taken into account.[28] If prosecutions are one-sided, post-TRC trials could be perceived by the white population as an act of vengeance and as being political trials. This, thus, could lead to further alienation between the ethnic groups and impact negatively on reconciliation and nation-building.[29] The NPA's list of priority cases is cited as foundation for the suspicion that prosecutions will remain one-sided, as it allegedly does not contain members of the ANC and hardly any of the liberation movement.[30]

The request to halt TRC-related prosecutions is further substantiated with the negotiations and indemnity laws in the early 1990s.[31] There, the NP representatives were convinced that legislation for a general amnesty was possible. A conditional amnesty allegedly came unexpectedly and was found to be in conflict with the Interim Constitution. Furthermore, the former NP government had conceded to far-reaching indemnity laws on the basis of which thousands of ANC members had been released from prison or were indemnified for often very serious crimes. It is argued that this should also be used as a precedent for former security force personnel. However, against this background it would now be totally unjust to prosecute former apartheid security force members on a broad basis.[32] It was also suggested that trials

---

conference 'The TRC: ten years on' (April 20, 2006); Interview with Johan van der Merwe in Pretoria (May 5, 2006).

[27] D. Stewart *Panel presentation at the Institute for Justice and Reconciliation conference 'The TRC: ten years on'* (April 20, 2006).

[28] Ibid.

[29] Ibid.; *Nieuwoudt case will drive home a message* Cape Times, Feb 13, 2004.

[30] E-mail from Sheila Camerer (June 13, 2006).

[31] F.W. de Klerk *Amnesty rules for all* Financial Mail, July 27, 2007 and D. Stewart *Panel presentation at the Institute for Justice and Reconciliation conference 'The TRC: ten years on'* (April 20, 2006).

[32] Ibid.

could impact negatively on the national project of reconciliation since it might be perceived by the white population as a one-sided process and would certainly revive the conflicts of the past.[33]

1.2.2 *Human rights and victim sector*

After 1998, a very prominent member of the human rights sector made a very controversial comment on post-TRC prosecutions. In 1999, the former chair of the South African Human Rights Commission, Reverend Barney Pityana, called for all TRC-related prosecutions to be abandoned and for legislation to be enacted to impose a moratorium on all trials.[34] He suggested that trials would be likely to fail, thus be futile, such as the Malan trial. Trials would only open up old wounds of the past and would accordingly not serve the purposes of reconciliation and nation-building and would only consume time and resources far more urgently needed to tackle the high current crime rate. Although such statements are rather rare, it is likely, nevertheless, that they express typical and widespread concerns regarding prosecutions, especially of those in political circles.

However, after 1998 the former chairperson of the TRC, Archbishop Desmond Tutu, called strongly for the institution of criminal trials. He has continuously emphasised his view that the TRC legislation requires prosecutions to go ahead and that justice must be served concerning the rights of victims, who, in accepting the amnesty scheme, accepted a significant concession and are now entitled to demand accountability.[35] He is of the opinion that failure to prosecute those who had been denied amnesty subsequently would foster a culture of impunity and undermine the rule of law.[36] In 2004, Tutu also warned against the introduction

[33] Interview with Jan Wagener in Pretoria (May 8, 2006).

[34] Comments cited in D.B. Ntsebeza 'The uses of truth commissions' in R.I. Rotberg and D. Thompson *Truth v. justice* (2000) 158 at 166 and J. Battersby *Call to stop apartheid prosecutions* The Sunday Independent, July 24, 1999.

[35] Interview with Desmond Tutu in Cape Town (March 22, 2006).

[36] Ibid.

of any kind of further indemnity or amnesty mechanism.[37] He accordingly welcomed the arrests in the PEBCO-Three case in early 2004 but, however, was critical in saying that generally, much more needed to be done on prosecutions.[38] The TRC's former deputy chairperson, Alex Boraine, in late 2006 also lamented the slow progress stating that the NPA and the government are far too slow and undedicated in their approach to post-TRC prosecutions.[39]

Generally, most organisations and people working in the human rights sector strongly call for prosecutions to take place and argue that more needs to be done to properly achieve accountability after the TRC. They are very aware of the slow and minimal progress of prosecutions and are extremely critical of the government's approach.[40] The government is often accused of being too hesitant, reluctant and unwilling to initiate prosecutions. The victim support organisation Khulumani has strongly criticised the government for utterly ignoring victims' interests in its approach to prosecutions.[41] It argues that far more criminal trials needed to be instituted[42] and that prosecutions are generally delayed too much and are taken haphazardly.[43] The Foundation for Human Right's executive director, former TRC commissioner Yasmin Sooka, has also criticised the government heavily for the delay in pushing ahead with

---

[37] C. Terreblanche *Tutu warns against blanket amnesty* The Sunday Independent, April 18, 2004.

[38] *Tutu slates SA's lack of apartheid prosecutions* SAPA, Dec 15, 2005.

[39] *SA 'should try apartheid-era torturers'* SAPA, Nov 25, 2006.

[40] A great number of the unanimous and wide-ranging points of criticism were voiced at a conference in 2006 commemorating the 10th anniversary of the first Human Rights Violations Committee hearing of the TRC (*The TRC: ten years on*, conference organised by the Institute for Justice and Reconciliation in Cape Town from 20 to 21 April 2006. See Institute for Justice and Reconciliation, *Statement: the IJR conference on the TRC: ten years on* (2006)). See for criticism of human rights organisations also: *infra* Chapter 3(3.5).

[41] Interview with Marjorie Jobson in Pretoria (May 9, 2006).

[42] M. Jobson *Panel presentation at the Institute for Justice and Reconciliation conference 'The TRC: ten years on'* (April 20, 2006).

[43] Interview with Marjorie Jobson in Pretoria (May 9, 2006).

prosecutions.[44] She has argued that the lack of prosecutions is contributing to a culture of impunity.[45] Moreover, both organisations demand that prosecutions focus to a greater extent on higher echelons of the apartheid regime, i.e. politicians and generals of the old regime, rather than ordinary rank and file activists, such as Ronnie Blani.[46] As such, the former President FW de Klerk should also be held accountable for his presumed knowledge and involvement in apartheid crimes.[47] Criticism of the government's supposedly lame response to the TRC recommendations was even voiced by international organisations, such as Amnesty International and Human Rights Watch.[48]

The request for even-handed prosecutions and the proposition that it would amount to a gross injustice should the NPA focus primarily on prosecuting former security forces and apartheid government representatives is strongly rejected by organisations and people from the human rights sector.[49] It would be totally disingenuous to lament one-sided prosecutions since liberation movement activists were prosecuted extensively during apartheid. Thousands were tried and imprisoned because they fought for their liberation, over 100 were even executed for politically motivated offences.[50] In contrast, criminal accountability for the atrocities of the apartheid state has, as yet, been absolutely

---

[44] Y. Sooka *Letter to the minister of justice and constitutional development* (Sep 8, 2005) (on file with author).

[45] Interview with Yasmin Sooka in Pretoria (May 3, 2006).

[46] Ibid.; Interview with Marjorie Jobson in Pretoria (May 9, 2006).

[47] Ibid.

[48] Amnesty International and Human Rights Watch, briefing paper *Truth and justice: unfinished business in South Africa* (Feb 2003).

[49] Interview with Madeleine Fullard in Pretoria (May 4, 2006); Interview with Yasmin Sooka in Pretoria (May 3, 2006); Interview with Piers Pigou in Johannesburg (May 6, 2006). See also C. Villa-Vicencio *The TRC still has lessons for our future* The Sunday Times, April 23, 2006.

[50] See M. Coleman (ed.) *A crime against humanity* (1998) 81–84 and *TRC Report*, vol. 2, chap. 3, paras. 21–37 on death penalty; M. Coleman (ed.) *A crime against humanity* (1998) 77–80 on political imprisonment and M. Coleman (ed.) *A crime against humanity* (1998) 43–53 on detention without trial.

minimal.[51] Against this background the priority of prosecuting crimes of the apartheid state needed to be far higher than for ANC and liberation movement members. It is also important to consider that Ronnie Blani, one of the first convictions in a post-TRC trial, was a former liberation movement member.

1.2.3 *Debate erupting on the occasion of specific prosecutions*

Public debate on the issue of post-TRC prosecutions in the media and political sphere always intensified around significant events, such as the presentation of the last TRC Report volumes in 2003 or the start of specific prosecutions. Tensions and debate at the time of prosecutions on a regional level were commonplace. For example, during the proceeding in the Luff case,[52] debates between the ethnic groups on ethnic and apartheid-related issues in the specific area were prevalent.

During the first proceedings in the PEBCO-Three case against former security police officers in 2004, some political representatives of the Afrikaner population criticised the arrests, claiming they were vindictive and could harm reconciliation.[53] Others from the victim and human rights sector welcomed them as the first major step towards post-TRC accountability.[54] However, the former head of the TRC research department and executive director of the NGO Institute for Justice and Reconciliation, Charles Villa-Vicencio, on the occasion of the PEBCO-Three prosecution also warned of certain dangers connected to prosecutions. In this regard, he was quoted as stating that the PEBCO-Three prosecution could cause unrest and could have serious implications for the process of nation-building and reconciliation.[55] As the accused persons in that case were ordinary rank and file officers, logically, the whole chain of command up to those who actually gave the orders, thus, those truly responsible, needed to be pursued in order

---

[51] See also *supra* Chapter 1(4.).

[52] See also *supra* Chapter 2(4.).

[53] *'Nieuwoudt case will drive home a message'* Cape Times, Feb 13, 2004.

[54] Ibid.

[55] J.J. Joubert and A. Muller *Versoening in gedrang* Beeld, Feb 12, 2004.

to do justice.[56] He substantiated these concerns by stating that although prosecutions were right in principle, if they failed to focus on all possible perpetrator groups and ranks, they could be regarded as one-sided and unbalanced, which could have implications for reconciliation between the ethnic groups.[57]

Ronnie Blani's trial and the judgment of April 2005 were criticised from various sides. Ackermann was heavily criticised by the relatives of the deceased for having agreed to a soft sentence.[58] The PCLU was also criticised by the ANC, former liberation movement activists and members of the human rights sector for having prosecuted Blani at all.[59] Such critics consider that Blani's prosecution should not have been a high priority. Considering his personal circumstances laid out above[60] and the fact that he was probably on the lowest tier of the liberation movement command structure, critics claim that the PCLU should make other cases a much higher priority, especially if they involve persons from the upper echelons of the security forces with far greater responsibility and individual guilt who in many cases are still not sentenced.[61]

There was also intense public scrutiny at the beginning of the court proceedings in the Chikane case in 2007. The Khulumani support group and many apartheid victims protested against the decision as being too weak and called for extended criminal trials for those responsible for the crimes committed by the apartheid security forces.[62] On the other hand, victims of ANC attacks and/or their relatives and other mem-

---

[56] C. Villa-Vicencio *Let apartheid-era perpetrators be heard* The Sunday Independent, Jan 29, 2006.

[57] E-mail from Charles Villa-Vicencio (May 31, 2006).

[58] Interview with Anton Ackermann in Pretoria (May 11, 2006).

[59] C. Terreblanche and A. Quintal *NPA feels the heat on amnesty* The Sunday Independent, Nov 28, 2004; Interview with Madeleine Fullard in Pretoria (May 4, 2006); Interview with Yasmin Sooka in Pretoria (May 3, 2006).

[60] See *supra* Chapter 2(8.).

[61] N. Rousseau 'Prosecutions' in E. Doxtader (ed.) *Provoking questions* (2005) 37 at 44–45. Interview with Madeleine Fullard in Pretoria (May 4, 2006).

[62] *Vlok trial: different conclusions drawn* SAPA, Aug 20, 2007; *Theatre of differences outside Vlok trial* SAPA, Aug 16, 2007.

bers of organisations supporting the interests of the white population protested against the trial and demanded that ANC leaders should also be held accountable.[63]

1.3 *Government and ANC statements*

The South African government and the ANC have only rarely made public statements on the issue of post-TRC prosecutions. When the TRC's operation had come to an end in 1998, President Mandela strongly emphasised that criminal trials must start within a fixed time frame[64] which

> ...needs to be realistic, taking into account how long it takes for evidence to be secured and preparations made for successful prosecution. Yet a time frame for this process is necessary; for we cannot afford as a nation and as government, to be saddled with unending judicial processes which can easily bog down our current efforts to resolve problems of the present.[65]

Mandela added that:

> These matters will of course be handled by the Office of the National Director of Prosecutions. And we believe that in discharging this responsibility the Director will take into account not only the critical need to establish accountability and the rule of law, but also to advance reconciliation and the long-term interests of our country.[66]

He further pointed out that:

> ...[W]e are not contemplating a general amnesty under any guise. Such an approach would go against the grain of the very process that we all

---

[63] Ibid.

[64] See text accompanying *supra* Chapter 1 note 58.

[65] Opening address by President Nelson Mandela in the special debate on the report of the Truth and Reconciliation Commission (National Houses of Parliament) (Feb 25, 1999).

[66] Ibid.

> agreed upon; it would undermine the culture of accountability that we seek to engender.[67]

Thereafter government politicians were rather reticent on the subject. However, the then Deputy President, Thabo Mbeki, had already indicated in early 1999 that a new amnesty could nevertheless be considered as he stated in an address to parliament his dismissive view towards prosecutions that:

> Quite a lot of people in KwaZulu-Natal did not apply [for amnesty] and with the level of violence that took place in that province, if you dig and dig and dig, you are going to have to arrest a lot of people. That can't be right. A number of generals in the SA Defence Force are very keen that this matter be dealt with, because their own sense, too, is that there may very well be significant numbers of people in the former SADF who didn't apply, and again, with regards to them, it would not be right week after week to charge people with something that happened in 1987.[68]

Moreover in May 2002, Mbeki, who had meanwhile become president, pardoned 33 prisoners who were aligned to the ANC and PAC.[69] Most of them had been sentenced for politically related offences, two-thirds had either been denied amnesty or not applied for amnesty.[70] At the ANC's national conference in December 2002[71] the discussion of guidelines for a broad national amnesty, possibly in the form of presidential pardons, was scheduled.[72] According to the head of the ANC presidency, Smuts Ngonyama, the ANC generally supported the idea to introduce a new amnesty law.[73] However the proposals on the ANC's national conference were strongly motivated by the volatile situation in KwaZulu-Natal and

---

[67] Ibid.

[68] Cited in J. Klaaren and H. Varney 'A second bite at the amnesty cherry?' in C. Villa-Vicencio and E. Doxtader (eds) *The provocations of amnesty* (2003) 265 at 265.

[69] S. Ngesi 'The presidential pardons and the media' in C. Villa-Vicencio and E. Doxtader (eds) *The provocations of amnesty* (2003) 294 at 294.

[70] Ibid.

[71] The ANC's 51st national conference took place from 16 to 20 December 2002 in Stellenbosch.

[72] P. Dickson *ANC to seek broad national amnesty* Cape Times, Dec 11, 2002.

[73] Ibid.

the fact that many IFP members did not receive amnesty.[74] Ngonyama nevertheless subsequently declared that his party was generally against running trials in the style of the Nuremberg trials, since this would occur at the cost of nation-building.[75]

Such developments and statements triggered speculation in the public that the government intended to enact another amnesty law in the wake of the TRC.[76] Some even claimed a general amnesty for the crimes relating to the apartheid conflict was considered.[77] However, in his speech at the tabling of the TRC Report in April 2003, Mbeki eventually ruled out the possibility that a general amnesty would be introduced and took up a strong and seemingly unequivocal stance for prosecutions as he stated that

> ...there shall be no general amnesty. Any such approach, whether applied to specific categories of people or regions of the country, would fly in the face of the TRC process and subtract from the principle of accountability which is vital not only in dealing with the past, but also in the creation of a new ethos within our society.[78]

He went further to stress that 'Government is of the firm conviction that we cannot resolve this matter by setting up yet another amnesty process, which in effect would mean suspending constitutional rights of those who were the receiving end of gross human right violations.'[79] He stated that it is 'in the hands of the National Directorate of Public Prosecutions, for it to pursue any cases that, as is normal practice, it

---

[74] Ibid.

[75] L. Fernandez 'Post-TRC prosecutions in South Africa' in G. Werle (ed.) *Justice in transition* (2006) 65 at 71.

[76] J. Klaaren and H. Varney 'A second bite at the amnesty cherry?' in C. Villa-Vicencio and E. Doxtader (eds) *The provocations of amnesty* (2003) 265 at 265; J. Steinberg *Amnesty quandary looms for judges* Business Day, June 8, 1999.

[77] P. Pigou *Unfinished business* Mail & Guardian, Sep 21, 2002; *Victim's to fight amnesty* Mail & Guardian, June 7, 2002.

[78] Statement by President Mbeki to the National Houses of Parliament and the Nation, at the Tabling of the Report of the Truth and Reconciliation Commission (April 15, 2003).

[79] Ibid.

believes deserve prosecution and can be prosecuted.'[80] However, he also made rather vague remarks, which indicate that other political factors will have to be considered in any approach to post-TRC prosecutions, stating that the government

> ...should continue to establish the truth about networks that operated against the people. This is an obligation that attaches to the nation's security today; for, some of these networks still pose a real or latent danger against our democracy. In some instances, caches of arms have been retained which lend themselves to employment in criminal activity.[81]

The President concluded that the NPA

> ...will leave its doors open for those who are prepared to divulge information at their disposal and to co-operate in unearthing the truth, for them to enter into arrangements that are standard in the normal execution of justice, and which are accommodated in our legislation.[82]

He further stated that 'in each instance where any legal arrangements are entered into between the NDPP and particular perpetrators as proposed above, the involvement of the victims will be crucial in determining

[80] Ibid.

[81] Ibid.

[82] Ibid. This announcement has led to considerable confusion. In its wake various media reports referred to a new deal on indemnity provisions for apartheid era perpetrators and a new mechanism of disclosure (See e.g. C. Terreblanche *New deal for apartheid abuse perpetrators* The Sunday Independent, April 20, 2003). In fact no specific arrangement had been made. Van der Merwe shortly after the speech contacted the NPA in order to find out what new process could be meant. The NPA was totally unaware of any new arrangements and what the President was actually referring to (Interview with Johan van der Merwe in Pretoria (May 5, 2006)). The NPA obviously had not been advised on the intentions behind the announcement. The arrangements Mbeki was referring to probably concern the normal instruments of plea-bargaining and state witness arrangements (see sections 105A and 204 of the Criminal Procedure Act). As such it is noteworthy that, only years later, with the Chikane case for the first time a plea bargain arrangement was entered into, which also included that the accused disclose information and cooperate in further trials (see *supra* Chapter 2(9.)).

the appropriate course of action.'[83] Such statements will later be put into context with regard to the governmental perspective concerning its actual approach towards prosecutions.

In 2007, there were announcements made regarding yet another pardon process concerning liberation movement members convicted of political crimes related to the apartheid conflict.[84]

2. *Bargaining Over the TRC's Legacy*

In 2002, rumours on secret consultations between former generals of the SADF and the government were highlighted in the media.[85] The South African government and the ANC did indeed engage in secret talks and consultations with representatives of the SADF and the security police over a long period from the end of the TRC in 1998 until about early 2004. Two separate processes of consultations concerning the two factions of the former security establishment took place.[86] Details of the secret meetings were never disclosed to the public.[87] As will later be outlined, the common denominator of the talks was that a legislative solution should be reached on how to avoid prosecutions in the wake of the TRC. The consultations are indicative of the real motivations and political considerations of the government during the years after the end of the TRC in 1998 and also provide valuable background information for the evaluation of later developments.

---

[83] Statement by President Mbeki to the National Houses of Parliament and the Nation, at the Tabling of the Report of the Truth and Reconciliation Commission (April 15, 2003).

[84] *Presidential pardons in the spotlight* SAPA, Nov 15, 2007.

[85] M. Fullard and N. Rousseau 'An imperfect past: the Truth and Reconciliation Commission in transition' in J. Daniel et al. (eds) *State of the nation* (2003) 78 at 93; P. Pigou *Unfinished business* Mail & Guardian, Sep 21, 2002.

[86] Interview with Jan Geldenhuys in Pretoria (May 10, 2006); Interview with Johan van der Merwe in Pretoria (May 5, 2006).

[87] P. Pigou *Unfinished business* Mail & Guardian, Sep 21, 2002.

2.1 *Consultations with the security police*

During and after the operation of the TRC, the Foundation for Equality before the Law occasionally conducted talks with the government concerning the amnesty proceedings and general questions of accountability.[88] Especially after the main work of the TRC was completed in 1998, consultations concerning post-TRC accountability were conducted, which mostly involved high-ranking members of the government. On behalf of the former apartheid state employees and the Foundation for Equality before the Law, former President F.W. de Klerk assumed a central role in the consultations. De Klerk often consulted with President Mbeki directly or with other high-ranking members of the government. Apart from that the organisation was in contact with various other government officials and submitted proposals.

The Foundation for Equality before the Law's aim in the consultations was to find a solution to avoid the prosecution of former members of the security police who had not received amnesty. Allegedly, legislation for a general amnesty was never requested. A general amnesty would certainly have served the organisation's purposes in avoiding trials. However, it was clear that a general amnesty was not an option since it would have seriously damaged the TRC process and its scheme of conditional amnesties and would thus not have been feasible politically. Accordingly other legislative options had to be explored. After 1998, the Foundation for Equality before the Law initially advocated a procedure, which envisaged that indemnity from prosecution could be granted, if all details regarding the crime in question were disclosed. This would therefore have reproduced the TRC's precondition of amnesty subject to a full disclosure. The proposal was later altered so that the granting of indemnity would be dependent only on the crime in question falling within the legal ambit of section 20(1) of the TRC Act. This would mean that the act was associated with a political objec-

[88] Unless otherwise stated, the information laid out in this subchapter comes from an interview with Johan van der Merwe in Pretoria on 5 May 2006. The consultations were conducted in strict confidentiality. Apart from the broad framework, details concerning negotiations with security police members could thus not be provided.

tive and was committed in the course of the conflicts of the past.[89] The proposal was quite similar to the indemnity laws of the early 1990s.[90] It was proposed that a full disclosure in terms of the TRC Act should not be required since the amnesty proceedings had shown that there were still many uncertainties as to when a full disclosure was in fact made.[91] According to the proposal, such indemnity proceedings should be conducted before a judge.[92]

Although among members of the Foundation for Equality before the Law the government had raised expectations that a solution according to the proposals was desirable, no agreement was reached. The talks continued until about 2004. The consultations had allegedly highlighted the government's lack of political will to adequately react to the TRC's recommendations on prosecutions, which also explains the huge delay in initiating trials.[93]

2.2 *Consultations with the generals*

More or less concurrently with the consultations with the police representatives, starting in 1998, the government conducted talks with a group of high-ranking former generals of the SADF.[94] Initially, the former chief of the SADF, General Constand Viljoen[95] was approached by one of the leading members of the ANC and government at that time, Jacob Zuma,[96] with the aim of consulting over questions of criminal

89 E-mail from Johan van der Merwe (May 31, 2006).

90 See *supra* Chapter 2 note 297.

91 E-mail from Johan van der Merwe (May 31, 2006).

92 Ibid.

93 Interview with Jan Wagener in Pretoria (May 16, 2006).

94 Interview with Jan Geldenhuys in Pretoria (May 10, 2006).

95 After his career in the SADF, Viljoen went into politics as the co-founder and leader of the right-wing Afrikaner party *Vryheitsfront* (the predecessor of the Freedom Front Plus) and was a member of parliament (See P. van Niekerk and B. Ludman (eds) *A-Z of South African politics 1999* (1999) 83–84 and 302–3).

96 The later deputy President of South Africa was at the time mainly involved in regional politics of his home province KwaZulu-Natal (See P. van Niekerk and B. Ludman (eds) *A-Z of South African politics 1999* (1999) 317–18).

accountability in the wake of the TRC.[97] Viljoen, however, considered that such matters were better discussed with the group of former SADF generals who had established the support network for former soldiers and the *Kontak Buro*,[98] who were, thus, already working intensely on amnesty issues and prosecutions. He immediately referred Zuma to the network group of generals around Geldenhuys.[99]

2.2.1 *The process of meetings*

General Geldenhuys agreed to meet with Zuma. A series of frequent meetings, negotiations and consultations ensued from 1998. The main process of consultations was conducted over four years until early 2003.[100] A small number of meetings, however, infrequently continued until 2004.[101] The consultations were, like the security police consultations, generally aimed at finding a mutual solution as to how to avoid trials after the TRC through new indemnity mechanisms.[102] The talks were mediated and facilitated by Johannesburg businessman Jürgen Kögl, who is closely connected to leading ANC members, especially to Jacob Zuma. All meetings took place strictly separated from the meetings with the police, which was in the interest of the generals.[103]

Zuma was asked to conduct the talks on behalf of the government or ANC.[104] Apart from him, various other high-ranking members of the ANC, such as the then Minister of Justice Penuell Maduna or Mathew Sposa, Sidney Mufamadi and Charles Nqakula also participated occasionally. On various occasions Thabo Mbeki was also present, as Vice

---

[97] Interview with Jan Geldenhuys in Pretoria (May 10, 2006).

[98] See *supra* Chapter 3(1.1.2).

[99] Interview with Jan Geldenhuys in Pretoria (May 10, 2006).

[100] Interview with Jürgen Kögl in Johannesburg (May 12, 2006).

[101] Ibid.

[102] Interview with Jürgen Kögl in Johannesburg (May 12, 2006); Interview with Jan Geldenhuys in Pretoria (May 10, 2006).

[103] Interview with Jan Geldenhuys in Pretoria (May 10, 2006).

[104] Interview with Jürgen Kögl in Johannesburg (May 12, 2006). Since in practice the distinction between ANC and government concerning the negotiations was often blurred, the two expressions will be used synonymously.

President and later in his capacity as the President.[105] On the side of the generals, Jan Geldenhuys assumed a leading role. He participated along with two to four other generals belonging to their support group. Both sides were accompanied by legal advisors. The main process of consultations came to an end in or about early 2003. Only as a matter of courtesy did a few meetings continue to take place until 2004.[106]

2.2.2 *Motivation of the government*

The main catalyst for Zuma's approach to the generals was the still very volatile political situation in KwaZulu-Natal, which was due to prolonged political tensions between supporters of the ANC and IFP during the late 1990s.[107] Zuma was at that time successfully conducting mediation and appeasement efforts between the two political factions of the ANC and IFP in order to contain possible fresh occurrences of violence.[108] The question of accountability for political crimes in the wake of the TRC was considered to be a critical issue in this regard.[109] As a great amount of politically motivated human rights violations had occurred in the conflict between IFP and ANC, especially during the negotiation period between 1990 and 1994, and considering that many IFP members accused of such crimes had not applied for amnesty, it was feared that the release of the TRC Report and prosecutions in its wake could stir up conflict again and be a constant source of unrest in the region.[110] On top of that, the second democratic elections were imminent and it was crucial to avoid new conflicts flaring up.[111] The initial intention was, thus, to create an amnesty scheme which would specifically cover the political crimes that happened between ANC and

---

105 Interview with Jan Geldenhuys in Pretoria (May 10, 2006).

106 Interview with Jürgen Kögl in Johannesburg (May 12, 2006).

107 Ibid.

108 P. van Niekerk and B. Ludman (eds) *A-Z of South African politics 1999* (1999) 317. See also *supra* Chapter 1(2.).

109 Interview with Jan Geldenhuys in Pretoria (May 10, 2006); Interview with Jürgen Kögl in Johannesburg (May 12, 2006).

110 Interview with Jürgen Kögl in Johannesburg (May 12, 2006).

111 Telephone interview with Jürgen Kögl (June 14, 2006).

IFP supporters in KwaZulu-Natal.[112] Yet it was clear that, regarding the constitutional framework and the political implications for the TRC amnesty scheme, a purely local solution would be almost impossible to implement. The generals also categorically refused to support a regionally confined amnesty process.[113]

They were contacted on this specific issue for various reasons. According to Kögl, the government intended to ensure support of other influential groups and important role-players of the apartheid regime, such as the generals, in order to put any possible solution, even if initially mainly focussing on KwaZulu-Natal, on a wider national basis.[114] The generals were already dealing with amnesty issues, had legal expertise, and as such, were relevant candidates to be canvassed for such support.

There was also a range of other specific reasons why the generals were contacted. According to Kögl, one reason for the government's initiative was the SADF's, and therefore the general's alleged involvement in the KwaZulu-Natal conflicts between the IFP and ANC.[115] During the TRC process the former top command of the SADF was accused of having fuelled the conflict between the ANC and IFP during and before the negotiations towards a transition to democracy, in order to weaken the position of the ANC. Allegations were made that weapons and expertise had been supplied to Zulu fighters. There were strong signs that a so-called "third force", established and steered by the security forces, had fuelled the atrocities committed by IFP supporters against ANC supporters, not only in Natal but also to a great extent in the Transvaal areas.[116] There were strong indications of SADF involvement in such activities, such as had been thxe case when weapons were supplied to

[112] Interview with Jan Geldenhuys in Pretoria (May 10, 2006); Interview with Jürgen Kögl in Johannesburg (May 12, 2006).

[113] Interview with Jan Geldenhuys in Pretoria (May 10, 2006).

[114] Interview with Jürgen Kögl in Johannesburg (May 12, 2006).

[115] Telephone interview with Jürgen Kögl (June 14, 2006).

[116] See *TRC Report*, vol. 6, s. 4, appendix, paras. 1–43; *TRC Report*, vol. 2, chap. 7, paras. 497–551; *TRC Report*, vol. 5, chap. 6, paras. 126–29.

the Inkatha Caprivi trainees.[117] Geldenhuys and other generals had been charged in 1995 for their alleged involvement in these Caprivi activities and the KwaMakutha massacre.[118] The government, when approaching the generals, was mindful of the fact that the SADF had supplied the Zulu fighters with weapons on a large scale and that the locations of a number of the hidden weapons caches, which had been established in the region during the last apartheid years, remain as yet unknown.[119] Government officials were wary that the generals could still possess knowledge of such still hidden and unknown weapons caches, established during the late 1980s and early 1990s, that they could, thus, still exercise negative influence on the peace process between IFP and ANC and that they could generally, through the possible third force networks, in some way thwart appeasement attempts or contribute to a re-ignition of the conflict.[120] These factors were allegedly a major reason for integrating the generals in any future approach to post-TRC accountability, to contain their potentially negative influence.[121] Such considerations are also clearly indicated in the aforementioned speech by President Mbeki.[122]

It was also considered that the TRC process suffered from a lack of sufficient findings on SADF activities, especially concerning those that took place in South Africa.[123] Very few SADF members had applied for amnesty, despite the fact that the SADF was involved in many gross human rights violations.[124] The SADF leadership practically refused

---

117 *TRC Report*, vol. 6, s. 4, appendix, para. 18.

118 See *supra* Chapter 1(4.).

119 Telephone interview with Jürgen Kögl (June 14, 2006).

120 Ibid.; Interview with Jürgen Kögl in Johannesburg (May 12, 2006).

121 Ibid. Whether the generals really had any potential to thwart the appeasement attempts in KZN remains unclear. Geldenhuys insists that the generals neither would engage in any kind of violent activity nor would they have any special knowledge of weapons caches or have the resources to exercise negative influence on mediation efforts in KwaZulu-Natal.

122 See text accompanying *supra* Chapter 3 note 81.

123 Interview with Jürgen Kögl in Johannesburg (May 12, 2006); Telephone interview with Jürgen Kögl (June 14, 2006).

124 *TRC Report*, vol. 6, s. 3, chap. 1, para. 4.

completely to cooperate with the TRC. There were no disclosures made on the involvement in violence during the negotiation period.[125] In this regard the TRC also referred to certain networks with access to weapons and resources.[126] As it was unable to establish the extent of such networks, the TRC stated that it would be essential to investigate the involvement of the police and military in third force activities more closely.[127] The government had this in mind when it approached the generals. The aim was also to work out proposals to satisfy the generals' desire to avoid prosecutions of SADF members and to create mechanisms for cooperation and disclosures on still uncovered secret SADF activities, in order to compensate for the lack of TRC findings in this regard.[128]

Another factor was the government's fear that South Africa could be exposed to claims for reparation and damages by countries, which had been attacked by the apartheid state.[129] The territorial integrity of various neighbouring countries had frequently been violated by illegal invasions of the SADF.[130] Angola, for instance, suffered enormous damages due to the war that was waged by South Africa and due to the massive support the apartheid government provided to the rebel movement UNITA.[131] Apparently, during the late 1990s neighbouring governments had discussed the issue of reparation claims against South Africa concerning the activities of the SADF. The government, thus, tried not to fuel such discussions by prosecuting SADF members for

[125] Ibid., s. 4, appendix, para. 7.

[126] Ibid., para. 33.

[127] Ibid., paras. 42–43.

[128] Interview with Jürgen Kögl in Johannesburg (May 12, 2006).

[129] The TRC found that the military strategy of South Africa during the times of Apartheid was guided by the principles of pre-emptive interventionism and counter-revolutionary warfare (*TRC Report*, vol. 2, chap. 2, para. 6). It further for instance found that the SADF committed a great amount of gross human rights violations e.g. in its war against Angola (*TRC Report*, vol. 2, chap. 2, para. 72).

[130] *TRC Report*, vol. 2, chap. 2, para. 48.

[131] Ibid., paras. 70–72.

the atrocities caused in other countries.[132] In this regard, the aim was to make sure that full-scale criminal trials did not go ahead.

Yet another aspect was that the government tried to avoid a drain of military competence and intelligence from South Africa to other African countries.[133] In the process of establishing an effective army for the new democratic South Africa, it was absolutely vital to ensure the support and expertise of former officers and generals of the apartheid state's SADF. Moreover, a number of other African countries were apparently very keen to engage officials of the SADF as advisors on improving their respective armies.[134] The South African government thus wished to avoid former SADF generals and military experts being driven away from South Africa, should SADF activities be investigated and tried on a large scale.[135]

Furthermore, the intention was to avoid setting precedents concerning criminal liability for military operations.[136] The army of the new democratic South Africa, the SANDF, at that time had increasingly become involved in peace keeping and military operations throughout Africa. The government was concerned that trials concerning military operations of the former apartheid-state's defence force, the SADF, could negatively impact on SANDF operations, in that they might lead to legal uncertainty concerning the legality of certain measures.[137] Precedents in terms of what actions by soldiers engaged in conflict situations can lead to criminal liability were to be avoided.[138] The government wanted to ensure that the effectiveness of the South African army and its capacity to act was not tainted by any kind of legal uncertainty.[139] Thus, military operations were to be generally kept out of criminal trials. However, the notion that the SADF generals would in any way be

[132] Interview with Jürgen Kögl in Johannesburg (May 12, 2006).
[133] Ibid.
[134] Ibid.
[135] Ibid.
[136] Ibid.
[137] Telephone interview with Jürgen Kögl (June 14, 2006).
[138] Ibid.
[139] Ibid.

willing and capable of instigating any kind of violent uprising against the new South African state is, allegedly, completely unfounded.[140]

The consultations generally have shown that the government is not at all keen to promote post-TRC prosecutions. Rather it has indicated its desire to leave the apartheid past behind as quickly as possible, in order to move forward towards a stable and reconciled nation and to avoid thwarting the project of nation-building by costly and extensive trials, which constantly bring up the atrocities and injustices of the past.[141] According to Geldenhuys, Zuma underlined this quite clearly when during one of the meetings he emphasised that prosecutions were not in the interest of the government as this could destroy some of the good effects the TRC had on nation-building and reconciliation. The issue needed to be dealt with in a political manner, rather than by the NPA.[142]

In summary, the government tried to work out some kind of legal mechanism, by which to generally avoid convictions, specifically concerning crimes committed in the conflict between IFP and ANC and concerning the SADF and simultaneously to create a mechanism by which to uncover more information that was not uncovered by the TRC.

2.2.3 *Interest of the generals*

Regarding the interest of the generals in the negotiations, it has often been claimed that, considering the many atrocities and criminal offences of the SADF which have not yet been dealt with properly, a general amnesty or convenient deal had been requested.[143] Yet a general amnesty was allegedly neither proposed nor discussed, especially not one that

---

[140] Ibid.; Interview with Jan Geldenhuys in Pretoria (May 15, 2006).

[141] Interview with Jürgen Kögl in Johannesburg (May 12, 2006); E-mail from Jürgen Kögl (June 26, 2006).

[142] Interview with Jan Geldenhuys in Pretoria (May 10, 2006).

[143] Interview with Yasmin Sooka in Pretoria (May 3, 2006); *Victims to fight amnesty* Mail & Guardian, June 7, 2002; P. Pigou *Unfinished business* Mail & Guardian, Sep 21, 2002; C. Carter *No truth for the thousands of apartheid dead* Cape Argus, April 8, 2006.

would only cover the generals.[144] From the outset it was rather clear that a general amnesty would not square with the TRC scheme on amnesty. A less overt and again, somehow conditional indemnity scheme was also in the generals' interest.[145] However, the generals were obviously interested in securing a convenient agreement in the interest of their former subordinates and in their own interest, which would diminish the chances that former SADF members would be charged for their involvement in SADF operations.[146] As most SADF members had been very suspicious of the TRC process, which was perceived to be biased, the generals sensed they could now take part in working out a, in their eyes, fairer procedure.[147] Furthermore, after the TRC, the general attitude towards the activities of the SADF was perceived to be unreasonably negative and hostile. The TRC's findings in its report were perceived to be an unjustified attack on the SADF's integrity.[148] When entering into consultations with the government the generals were motivated by the opportunity to correct the perceived wrong image of their activities in another forum.[149]

2.2.4 *Results*

The aim of the government was to take the amnesty legislation of the TRC as a reference point and try to establish a new mechanism adapted to the previous amnesty legislation.[150] The mechanism had to apply to the whole of the country and could not be limited to the province of

---

144 Interview with Jürgen Kögl in Johannesburg (May 12, 2006); Interview with Jan Geldenhuys in Pretoria (May 15, 2006).

145 Telephone interview with Jürgen Kögl (June 14, 2006).

146 Interview with Jan Geldenhuys in Pretoria (May 10, 2006).

147 Interview with Jan Geldenhuys in Pretoria (May 15, 2006).

148 Interview with Jan Geldenhuys in Pretoria (May 10, 2006). The top commanders never made an effort to acknowledge the brutal atrocities which had been caused by the SADF. It also never properly participated in TRC hearings which would have given the SADF command an occasion to defend against perceived unjustified allegations.

149 Interview with Jan Geldenhuys in Pretoria (May 15, 2006); Interview with Jürgen Kögl in Johannesburg (May 12, 2006).

150 Interview with Jürgen Kögl in Johannesburg (May 12, 2006).

KwaZulu-Natal. By the end of 2002, the consulting parties had agreed on a detailed proposal for the enactment of a legal mechanism practically amounting to a new amnesty law.[151] It envisaged a legal concept according to which a special plea on amnesty would be introduced as an amendment to the Criminal Procedures Act.[152] The solution on how to deal with criminal accountability in the wake of the TRC should, thus, be embedded in the normal court procedures. After the agreement was reached, the consultations were practically concluded and only continued with the participation of Zuma and Minister of Justice, Maduna, on an infrequent basis as a matter of courtesy and to conduct a rather general exchange of thoughts on the topic until 2004.[153]

The solution provided that perpetrators of politically motivated offences falling within the ambit of the TRC Act should not principally be exempted from criminal liability.[154] In case they are criminally charged, an alleged perpetrator who had not received amnesty by the TRC could then in the criminal trial launch a special plea on amnesty. Once such a plea was launched, a special inquiry by the judge embedded in the normal public criminal trial should ensue. Should the plea for amnesty succeed, the trial needed to result in an acquittal of the accused.[155] The envisaged preconditions for a successful plea on amnesty were that the criminal offence in question needed to satisfy exactly the same test which was outlined as a precondition to the granting of amnesty according to the TRC Act. It, thus, had to be committed within the fixed time frame applicable for the TRC Act and had to be connected with a political objective and committed in the course of the conflicts of the past etc.[156] Furthermore, the alleged perpetrator would then have to make a full disclosure before the court in order to succeed with the plea.[157] Whether the criteria are satisfied should be

[151] Ibid.; Interview with Jan Geldenhuys in Pretoria (May 10, 2006).
[152] Ibid.
[153] Interview with Jürgen Kögl in Johannesburg (May 12, 2006).
[154] Ibid.; Interview with Jan Geldenhuys in Pretoria (May 10, 2006).
[155] Ibid.
[156] Ibid.
[157] Telephone Interview with Jürgen Kögl (June 14, 2006).

subject to the scrutiny of the judge and other participants as is normal procedure in a criminal trial.[158] If the plea would not succeed, the trial would resume.[159]

The solution that was agreed upon at the consultations of the generals and the government, thus, embodied an exact replication of the TRC amnesty scheme. The only difference was that the competence to decide on the granting of indemnity would rest with an ordinary criminal court and not with a special committee such as the Amnesty Committee of the TRC. The idea to introduce a special plea on amnesty to criminal procedure law was not at all new. Before the TRC process began, the NP launched a similar proposal aimed at extending the amnesty regime by the same means.[160]

By late 2002 the proposal had been worked out in great detail by the Justice Department and was practically ready to be presented to Parliament for enactment.[161] The public was neither informed of the existence of the proposal nor of details thereof. By the end of 2002, it was first put forward for the consideration of President Thabo Mbeki. The implementation of the proposal depended on the decision of President Mbeki.[162] In early 2003 it was eventually rejected by President Mbeki.[163] The President apparently did not expressly communicate to the consultation group of generals and ANC government representatives that he rejected the draft law. However, his announcements in the speech at the tabling of the TRC Report in Parliament in April 2003 effectively and unmistakably signalled to the consulting parties a rejection of their proposal on another round of indemnity legislation.[164] As mentioned above,[165] Mbeki had announced that it would be up to

[158] Interview with Jürgen Kögl in Johannesburg (May 12, 2006); Interview with Jan Geldenhuys in Pretoria (May 10, 2006).

[159] Ibid.

[160] F. Kutz *Amnestie für politische Straftäter in Südafrika* (2001) 143.

[161] Interview with Jürgen Kögl in Johannesburg (May 12, 2006).

[162] Ibid.

[163] Ibid.

[164] Ibid.

[165] See *supra* Chapter 3(1.3).

the NPA to pursue post-TRC prosecutions according to its normal procedures and that any approach such as general amnesty will not be considered, which of course means that the specific indemnity procedure proposed would, at least at the beginning, not be implemented. What exactly motivated Mbeki to turn away from the proposal at that stage cannot be established. However, it is implicit from his speech that he apparently did not consider such an obvious legislative introduction of another amnesty mechanism similar to that of the TRC as appropriate, since he expressly stated that any new amnesty approach, whether applied regionally or nationally, would harm the TRC process. However, elements of the consultations did, as will be shown below, reappear in later policy decisions.

3. *A Prosecution Policy for TRC-Related Cases*

It becomes clear from the consultations with the security forces that the government attempted to introduce new legal mechanisms aimed at avoiding trials directly after 1998. As has been outlined in the preceding paragraphs, the solution, which had been reached by late 2002, was in early 2003 not found fit by the President to provide a sufficient new indemnity mechanism. However, the urge to introduce a satisfactory mechanism persisted. It took until late 2004 for the government to start a new process of developing a solution. Eventually in early 2006, a new legal approach to post-TRC prosecutions was introduced. On 24 January 2006 the NPA presented a set of new guidelines to the public, which were supposed to apply specifically to prosecutions of political crimes connected with the conflicts of the apartheid past.[166] The so-called 'prosecution policy and directives relating to the prosecution of offences emanating from the conflicts of the past and which were

[166] See NPA, press statement *Amended prosecution policy and directives relating to prosecution of criminal matters arising from the conflicts of the past* (Jan 24, 2006).

committed before 11 May 1994' were an amendment to the general prosecution policy of the NPA.[167]

Traditionally, prosecutors in South Africa have wide discretion on the decision on whether or not to initiate a prosecution.[168] According to section 179(5)(a) and (b) of the Constitution and 21 of the NPA Act, the NDPP, with the concurrence of the Minister of Justice, has to determine and issue policy directives, which have to be observed by the prosecutors in the prosecution process.[169] In guiding the prosecutors' discretion, this generally tries to achieve fair, transparent, consistent and predictable processes.[170] The directives are not a statute but outline binding guidelines for the exercise of the prosecutors' discretion. As section 21(2) of the NPA Act states, they have to be tabled in parliament. According to sections 179(5)(a) of the Constitution and 21 of the NPA Act, the prosecution policy is drafted by the NDPP. However, in this case it was in fact not the NDPP but the government, more precisely the Department of Justice, which entirely drafted the guidelines and only formally were they issued by the NDPP.[171] Although the policy amendment was only presented to the public in January 2006, it had already come into effect on 1 December 2005.[172] It has given rise to

---

167 Prosecution Policy, appendix A.

168 M. Schönteich *Lawyers for the people* (2001) 19–20; F.G. Richings 'The prosecutor's discretion: a plea for circumspection' (1977) 1 no. 2 *South African Journal of Criminal Law and Criminology* 143 at 143–44.

169 The section reads:

(5) The National Director of Public Prosecutions

(a) must determine, with the concurrence of the Cabinet member responsible for the administration of justice, and after consulting the Directors of Public Prosecutions, prosecution policy, which must be observed in the prosecution process;

(b) must issue policy directives which must be observed in the prosecution process.

Section 21 (1) of the NPA Act repeats this instruction.

170 M. Schönteich *Lawyers for the people* (2001) 52.

171 Interview with Jan Wagener in Pretoria (May 8, 2006); Interview with Torie Pretorius and others in Pretoria (May 2, 2006).

172 NPA, press statement *Amended prosecution policy and directives relating to prosecution of criminal matters arising from the conflicts of the past* (Jan 24, 2006).

considerable controversy and was suspended by the High Court of Pretoria in December 2008.

3.1 *Previous history*

After the conclusion of the consultation processes and the establishment of the PCLU in early 2003, no political interventions occurred for over one year. This situation changed significantly in late 2004, when the first prosecutions were initiated by the PCLU. The PEBCO-Three prosecution had been initiated in early 2004, Ronnie Blani had been charged in October 2004 and in November 2004 the PCLU was ready to effect arrests in the Chikane case.

The events in the Blani and Chikane cases had triggered the decision to develop specific guidelines. With regard to the indictment of Ronnie Blani, many criticised that priority was put on such a case, considering that apartheid officials were rarely forced to account for their crimes.[173] This decision to prosecute a former liberation force cadre raised concerns and unease in high echelons of the government and in ANC circles as well as in local ANC structures.[174] In addition to this, the arrests in the Chikane case were imminent. As outlined above, the accused' attorney Jan Wagener immediately intervened politically and apparently put great pressure on the government to stop the proceedings.[175] Following this and in an extraordinarily swift move, the NPA was advised on behalf of President Mbeki to suspend the arrests,[176] which it did. The NPA's official explanation for its action was that it had realised that there was no strategic plan as to how to deal with TRC-related cases and that it was necessary to approach them on a

---

[173] See *supra* Chapter 2(8.).

[174] C. Terreblanche and A. Quintal *NPA feels the heat on amnesty* The Sunday Independent, Nov 28, 2004.

[175] See *supra* Chapter 2(9.1). The imminent arrests according to Ackermann decisively contributed to the decision to work out guidelines (E-mail from Anton Ackermann (Oct 18, 2005)).

[176] Interview with Jan Wagener in Pretoria (May 8, 2006).

holistic and uniform basis.[177] The events reportedly prompted meetings of the Minister for Justice and the Minister of Safety and Security with high-ranking NPA and police officials, at which appropriate political and policy approaches to post-TRC prosecutions were discussed.[178] In November 2004, they eventually resolved to impose a moratorium on all TRC-related prosecutions and investigations pending the composition and approval of guidelines.[179]

It took more than a year until the moratorium was resolved in January 2006. During the presentation of the completed prosecution guidelines, the NPA announced that prosecutions would go ahead.[180] On 17 January 2006, representatives of the NPA tabled the guidelines in Parliament's portfolio Committee on Justice and Constitutional Development.[181] The portfolio committee was given only short notice on the scheduled presentation and was convened for an ad hoc meeting.[182] Although the guidelines are of great significance for the further conduct of post-TRC prosecutions, there was no parliamentary participation in their drafting and proper parliamentary discussion at their presentation was also impossible due to the ad hoc nature of the presentation.[183]

During the process of drafting the guidelines it was also not possible for the public and civil sector to participate in any way. None of the major South African NGOs, such as the victim organisation Khulumani,

---

177 S. Adams *Drama in Chikane's poison case* The Star, Nov 11, 2004.

178 C. Terreblanche and A. Quintal *NPA feels the heat on amnesty* The Sunday Independent, Nov 28, 2004.

179 E-mail from Anton Ackermann (Oct 21, 2005). The acting NDPP Bulelani Ngcuka had advised the PCLU to stop all further investigations and prosecutions (E-mail from Anton Ackermann (Oct 18, 2005)).

180 *NPA apartheid-era prosecutions to start* SAPA, Jan 24, 2006.

181 See Justice and Constitutional Development Portfolio Committee *Briefing and deliberation on the amendment of the prosecuting policy to provide for directives for the prosecution of matters before 11 May 1994*, Jan 17, 2006 (protocol of minutes available at http://www.pmg.org.za).

182 Interview with Sheila Camerer in Cape Town (March 30, 2006).

183 Ibid. However, sections 179(5) of the Constitution and 21 of the NPA Act do not provide for parliamentary participation apart from the mere tabling of the completed policy.

could give any input or were in any way consulted on the contents of the document.[184] Moreover, although the Foundation for Human Rights and Khulumani had constantly requested that the Department of Justice issues information about the guidelines and eventually furnishes a copy thereof, they were not heard or adhered to.[185] The government was generally extraordinarily reluctant to issue information.[186] More precise details on the contents were only reported in the media shortly before the guidelines came into effect.[187] The former security force members were also allegedly not properly involved in the process of developing the guidelines.[188] However, according to the attorney Jan Wagener on a very occasional and infrequent basis representatives of this side were consulted informally.[189]

3.2 *Contents*

The amendments to the prosecution policy shall be applicable to the prosecution of crimes arising out of the conflicts of the past, which

---

[184] Interview with Marjorie Jobson in Pretoria (May 9, 2006); Interview with Yasmin Sooka in Pretoria (May 3, 2006).

[185] Ibid.

[186] The Foundation for Human Rights and Khulumani learned only in late 2004 from a journalist that a policy amendment was drafted at all. There were signs that the guidelines would reintroduce an amnesty scheme similar to that of the TRC. A coalition of human rights and victim NGOs then in December 2004 and September 2005 wrote letters to the NDPP and Minister of Justice requesting further information and cautioning against the repetition of the TRC amnesty scheme. All requests remained unanswered. Again only through hints of a journalist did the NGOs learn in December 2005, that the policy amendment had been completed (Interview with Yasmin Sooka in Pretoria (May 3, 2006)). Moreover, the victim organisation Khulumani, although having contacted the NPA continuously for information, was not even informed of the scheduled press conference in January 2006, on which the guidelines were presented. Only through journalists was the organisation informed of the presentation shortly beforehand.

[187] C. Terreblanche *Back door amnesty plan revealed* The Sunday Independent, Nov 27, 2005.

[188] Interview with Jan Wagener in Pretoria (May 8, 2006); Interview with Johan van der Merwe in Pretoria (May 5, 2006).

[189] Interview with Jan Wagener in Pretoria (May 8, 2006).

were committed before 11 May 1994, i.e. crimes that also fell within the jurisdiction of the Amnesty Committee.[190] On the one hand, the document lays out a procedure that must be strictly adhered to regarding persons who want to make representations to the NDPP in relation to TRC crimes.[191] On the other hand side, the amendment lays out a catalogue of material criteria which, in addition to the general criteria outlined in the normal prosecution policy, govern the discretionary decision of the prosecutors on whether or not to prosecute a case.[192] It was further determined that the regional Directors of Public Prosecutions must refer all post-TRC prosecutions to the NPA, thus, all TRC-related cases are centralised in the office of the PCLU.[193]

The procedural part of the policy amendment determined, apart from a number of negligible formal requirements, that any person possibly facing prosecution may submit an affidavit containing representations on the alleged criminal offence, if he wished to enter into arrangements with the NPA.[194] Such affidavit must contain

> ...a full disclosure of all the facts, factors or circumstances surrounding the commission of the alleged offence, including all information which may uncover any network, person or thing, which posed a threat to our security at any stage or may pose a threat to our current security.[195]

The material criteria governing the prosecutor's decision to take a case to trial are of critical importance. There are basically three sets of criteria. The first set is based on the preconditions for granting amnesty as stated in the TRC Act.[196] First, it must be taken into account 'whether the alleged offender has made a full disclosure of all relevant facts, factors or circumstances' concerning the alleged offence.[197] The next

---

190 Prosecution Policy, appendix A.

191 Ibid., para. B.

192 Ibid., para. C. The criteria expressly shall be applicable besides the general criteria governing the discretion of the NDPP set out in paragraph 4 of the general prosecution policy.

193 Prosecution Policy, appendix A, para. B.5.

194 Ibid., para. B.3.

195 Ibid.

196 See section 20 of the TRC Act.

197 Prosecution Policy, appendix A, para. C.3.(a).

factor is whether the offence was associated with a political objective and committed in the course of the conflicts of the past, which needs to be determined on the basis of a number of factors: the motive; the object or objective; whether the offence was committed in furtherance of an order or with the approval of an organisation, institution or liberation movement of which the accused offender was a supporter, agent or member; and finally, the relationship between the offence and the objective pursued and the proportionality in respect thereof, which does not include objectives of personal gain and personal malice, ill-will or spite.[198]

The second set of criteria encompasses factors relating to the personal circumstances and behaviour of the alleged offender:[199]

- the degree of cooperation of the alleged offender, including his endeavours to disclose 'the truth of the conflicts of the past, including the remains of victims; or possible clandestine operations [...] including the exposure of networks that operated or are operating against the people, especially if such networks still pose a real or latent danger against our democracy.'
- the health of the alleged offender and other humanitarian considerations;
- 'the credibility of the alleged offender';
- the offender's 'sensitivity towards the need for restitution';
- 'the degree of remorse shown by the alleged offender and his or her attitude towards reconciliation';
- the 'renunciation of violence and willingness to abide by the Constitution on the part of the alleged offender'; and
- 'the degree of indoctrination to which the alleged offender was subjected'.

---

198 Ibid., para. C.3.(b).

199 Ibid., paras. C.3.(c) and (d).

The final set of criteria contains a range of rather general factors:[200]

- 'whether the offence is serious';
- the extent to which the prosecution or non-prosecution may positively or negatively affect the national project of nation-building through transformation, reconciliation, development and reconstruction;
- 'whether the prosecution may lead to the further or renewed traumatisation of victims and conflicts in areas where reconciliation has already taken place';
- 'if relevant, the alleged offender's role during the TRC process, namely, in respect of co-operation, full disclosure and assisting the process in general';
- 'considerations of any views obtained for purposes of reaching a decision' and any other criteria deemed relevant.

The NDPP must obtain the views of concerned victims before reaching a decision and consult with victims in any further process concerning the perpetrator.[201] Any decision to continue or discontinue investigations or proceed with prosecutions must be approved by the NDPP.[202] Furthermore, the Minister of Justice must be informed of all decisions taken or imminent in respect of procedures under the amendment.[203] A decision not to prosecute and the reasons thereof must be made public.[204] The NPA and other agencies shall not use any information obtained from the alleged offender in the procedure in any possible subsequent criminal proceeding against the person who made the disclosure.[205]

---

200 Ibid., paras. C.3.(e)–(j).
201 Ibid., para. B.9. and 13.
202 Ibid., para. B.7.
203 Ibid., para. B.11.
204 Ibid., para. B.10.
205 Ibid., para. B.15.

3.3 *Rationales*

The policy amendment was intended to give effect to the aforementioned announcements of the President from 2003.[206] Generally, it was stated that it was necessary to standardise the dealings with all post-TRC cases in terms of specifically defined criteria, and that the normal policy would not have sufficed for this purpose.[207] As such, to ensure consistency and also considering the complexities of the cases, the amendment determined that all post-TRC prosecutions are centralised at the PCLU. Consistency was especially necessary to avoid undermining the project of nation-building. Thus, the guidelines were designed to provide a uniform, rational, effective and reconciliatory basis on which the cases will be dealt with in the future.[208] A more detailed justification for the guidelines was not provided. Another motive underlying the guidelines, however, seems to be the perceived sensitivity that such cases require in terms of reconciliation and nation-building.[209] Apparently, the guidelines were generally designed to allow the NDPP to stop a prosecution wherever it is deemed detrimental for the overall progress of reconciliation and nation-building.

3.4 *Practical implementation*

Soon after the policy amendment was introduced, the Foundation for Equality before the Law approached the NPA attempting to discover

---

[206] NPA, press statement *Amended prosecution policy and directives relating to prosecution of criminal matters arising from the conflicts of the past* (Jan 24, 2006). See also Prosecution Policy, appendix A, para. A.1.

[207] Ibid.; Presentation at the tabling of the prosecution policy amendment in the Justice Portfolio Committee, Jan 17, 2006, para. 5.3 (available at http://www.pmg.org.za); Justice and Constitutional Development Portfolio Committee *Briefing and deliberation on the amendment of the prosecuting policy to provide for directives for the prosecution of matters before 11 May 1994* Jan 17, 2006 (protocol of minutes available at http://www.pmg.org.za).

[208] Prosecution Policy, appendix A, para. A.5.

[209] Ibid., paras. C.3.(f) and (g).

how the guidelines would be implemented in practice.[210] Various clients of the organisation's attorney, Jan Wagener, were willing to launch an application with the NPA under the policy procedure, should a prosecution target them.[211] Apparently, a satisfactory answer could not be given, which indicates that the practical scope and implementation had yet to be worked out.

As far as the records show, up to the completion of this research in April 2009, only one set of proceedings had been completed under the guidelines. As has already been outlined above, soon after the guidelines came into effect, applications according to the policy amendment were tendered by the three former security police officers, Otto, van Staden and Smit, accused of having attempted to murder Frank Chikane.[212] Shortly thereafter, Vlok and van der Merwe also entered into a disclosure proceeding in terms of the guidelines.[213] The five subsequently made representations during September 2006 and possibly thereafter concerning the crime as required by the policy. In January 2007, the NPA announced that it would push ahead with the charges against the three accused,[214] which obviously meant that it had not decided against initiating a prosecution after conclusion of the guidelines procedure.

For the attorney of the accused, Jan Wagener, the decision to proceed with the charges came unexpectedly.[215] The attorney was absolutely adamant that his clients made full disclosure of their knowledge of the events as required by the guidelines.[216] Vlok, van der Merwe and Smith even submitted themselves to a polygraph test that allegedly proved they had told the full truth.[217] Indeed it is expressly pointed out in the plea

---

210 Interview with Johan van der Merwe in Pretoria (May 5, 2006).

211 Interview with Jan Wagener in Pretoria (May 16, 2006).

212 See *supra* Chapter 2(9.2).

213 E-mail from Jan Wagener (Sep 13, 2007).

214 J.J. Joubert and W. Jordaan *Cops up for apartheid crimes* Beeld, Feb 7, 2007; W.J. da Costa and T. Mtshali *Prosecuting apartheid's soldiers 'divisive'* Pretoria News, Feb 8, 2007.

215 E-mail from Jan Wagener (Feb 12, 2007).

216 E-mail from Jan Wagener (Sep 13, 2007).

217 A. Vlok, J. van der Merwe, C. Smith, G. Otto and M. van Staden, press statement (Aug 17, 2007).

agreement that the accused approached the NPA immediately to take part in the procedure under the guidelines and made disclosure. The plea bargain ambiguously states in Afrikaans that the accused have '*oop kaarte gespeel*', which means that they have played with their cards on the table.[218] Although it is not expressly stated that there was full disclosure, the expression nevertheless logically indicates that the accused did not hide anything. Furthermore, the accused eventually asked for forgiveness and showed remorse. Chikane had previously indicated that he is not really interested in their prosecution.[219] In a spectacular symbolic act of repentance Vlok publicly washed Chikane's feet in August 2006 at the Union Buildings in Pretoria,[220] which coincided with and was certainly connected with the guidelines procedure. Vlok and van der Merwe cooperated with the TRC to a considerably higher degree than other leading apartheid officials. All of these factors are explicit criteria of the guidelines, which logically can only lead to one decision: not to prosecute. This is especially true for Vlok and van der Merwe who came forward voluntarily. On the basis of the guidelines, it is therefore not clear why the NDPP nevertheless decided to prosecute. The decision might have been taken for obscure political reasons.

However, the NPA refused to furnish reasons for its decision to the public or the accused and did not provide any information whatsoever on the proceedings.[221] On the occasion of the presentation of the plea bargain arrangement, the guidelines proceeding was also not properly investigated, although it was obviously closely connected to the plea agreement.

---

[218] *S v Johannes Velde van der Merwe en andere* (Pretoria High Court) pleit en vonnisooreenkoms 15 August 2007 at para. 80.

[219] E. Naidoo *No general amnesty for apartheid crimes* The Sunday Independent, July 3, 2005.

[220] M. Swart 'Sorry seems to be the hardest word: apology as a form of symbolic reparation' (2008) 1 *South African Journal on Human Rights* 50 at 64.

[221] E-mail from Jan Wagener (Feb 16, 2007).

3.5 *Reactions to the guidelines*

The reactions from within the sector of human rights, victim organisations and activists to the guidelines and the process of their drafting were overwhelmingly critical. As the criticisms have common features, the main points can be summarised here:[222]

- The guidelines effectively amount to a replica of the amnesty procedure as was laid out in the TRC Act. As the NDPP is entitled to decide against an indictment if the perpetrator makes a full disclosure, the policy confers powers on the NPA, which were formerly exercised by the Amnesty Committee. This continuation of the TRC's legal regime on amnesty is unacceptable since the amnesty process had taken place in a carefully confined and negotiated framework, which was not meant to be extended.
- Perpetrators were deliberately given a second chance to achieve impunity, although many shunned the TRC process in the first place by rejecting the very generous offer of amnesty or presented untruthful versions of their crimes. This is totally unacceptable considering the great concession the amnesty scheme demanded of victims.
- The process outlined by the policy amendment totally lacks transparency. In stark contrast to the TRC legislation, the new guidelines do not make provision for the publication of information deriving from perpetrator testimonies or the records thereof. The procedures will be carried out *in camera*. The public does not even have to be informed if a procedure according to the guidelines is taking place.

---

[222] Interview with Marjorie Jobson in Pretoria (May 9, 2006); Interview with Yasmin Sooka in Pretoria (May 3, 2006); Memorandum of Howard Varney on discussion concerning the prosecution policy amendment attended by Yasmin Sooka, Marjorie Jobson, Howard Varney, Ahmed Motala (executive director of the CSVR), Jody Kollapen (chair of the South African Human Rights Commission) (Dec 9, 2005) (on file with author); Y. Sooka *Panel presentation at the Institute for Justice and Reconciliation conference 'the TRC: ten years on'* (April 20, 2006); M. Jobson *Panel presentation at the Institute for Justice and Reconciliation conference 'The TRC: ten years on'* (April 20, 2006); Institute for Justice and Reconciliation *Statement: the IJR conference on the TRC: ten years on* (2006).

- Sufficient provision is not made for a satisfactory involvement of victims in the process. There are not even provisions for concerned victims to be given an exact record of the representations made by the relevant perpetrator.
- Although the policy amendment fundamentally concerns the rights and interests of many victims of apartheid era crimes, there was regrettably no consultation or cooperation with victim organisations in their drafting. While the TRC process was always accompanied by extensive public participation and discussion, the drafting of the guidelines took place entirely behind closed doors. This contravenes the spirit of openness and democratic debate, which had been established during the TRC process.
- The centralisation of all TRC cases in the office of the PCLU needs to be accompanied by a huge increase in the provision of resources, if the unit is to be capable at all of dealing with all possible cases. Otherwise the result would be a de facto amnesty for most cases.
- The NPA's contention that victims should not feel aggrieved if a prosecution is not pursued, since they can seek civil redress or prosecute privately,[223] is utterly disingenuous.[224] It is absolutely clear that neither private prosecutions nor civil claims are a realistic option. Generally, according to section 7 of the Criminal Procedures Act anyone with a substantial interest in a case can institute a private prosecution, in the event that the NDPP has issued a certificate stating that the State declines to prosecute the matter.[225] The privately prosecuting party must carry out the complete investigation for the case.[226] The NPA is not even obliged to hand over evidence and incriminating material it has already prepared.[227] The private litigant is also without investigative

223 NPA, press statement *Amended prosecution policy and directives relating to prosecution of criminal matters arising from the conflicts of the past* (Jan 24, 2006). See also Prosecution Policy, appendix A, paras. A.3.(d) and A.4.

224 Interview with Howard Varney in Johannesburg (May 6, 2006).

225 *Nolle prosequi* certificate. See sections 7–16 of the Criminal Procedure Act.

226 V. Nerlich *Apartheidkriminalität vor Gericht* (2002) 218.

227 Ibid.

> rights similar to those of the NPA and police.[228] Furthermore a private prosecution imposes a great financial onus and risk on the litigant, since they must finance the investigation and, in the event of an acquittal, not only incur their own legal costs but also those of the accused's defence team.[229] Victims and NGOs certainly cannot meet these demands.[230] Furthermore, the time limit to pursue civil claims has lapsed in most cases and is thus also not a realistic option.[231]

Right after the amendments entered into force a number of human rights organisations have asked the government to set the guidelines aside.[232] Various international NGOs have also joined in criticising the guidelines. For example, the International Bar Association expressed deep concern over the policy, since it replicates the TRC amnesty legislation, seriously violates victims' rights and could foster a culture of impunity for the human rights violations committed under apartheid.[233] A number of African human rights organisations, the International Centre for Transitional Justice and former Constitutional Court Judge Richard Goldstone voiced similar concerns in a letter to the President.[234] It is also noteworthy that the policy was also rejected by senior members of the PCLU.[235] Some prosecutors requested civil society to

[228] Ibid., 46.

[229] Ibid.

[230] Interview with Howard Varney in Johannesburg (May 6, 2006); Interview with Marjorie Jobson in Pretoria (May 9, 2006).

[231] Interview with Howard Varney in Johannesburg (May 6, 2006).

[232] Y. Sooka *Panel presentation at the Institute for Justice and Reconciliation conference 'The TRC: ten years on'* (April 20, 2006).

[233] Letter from Mark S. Ellis, executive director International Bar Association, to Brigitte Mabandla, Minister of Justice and Constitutional Development (March 14, 2006) (on file with author). See also International Bar Association, press statement *IBA critical of amendments to South Africa's prosecution policy* (March 29, 2006). The International Bar Association is a leading international organisation of legal practitioners, bar associations and law societies.

[234] Letter to President Thabo Mbeki, President of South Africa (April 7, 2006).

[235] T. Pretorius *Panel presentation at the Institute for Justice and Reconciliation conference 'The TRC: ten years on'* (April 20, 2006).

monitor the processes carefully to see that the guidelines are not being misused.[236] They argued that the guidelines did not add any practical value to their work and are simply not necessary to conduct effective and successful prosecutions.[237]

Considering the strong rejection of the amendments by human rights and victim groups, it is rather surprising that the representative of perpetrators, the Foundation for Equality before the Law, also strongly rejected the guidelines. They believed that the criteria's vagueness and obscurity make them highly unpredictable.[238] They also suggested that prosecutors will not be able to conduct the procedure in an impartial way, since they will have already investigated the case and have prepared an indictment.[239] They, thus, will have reached specific conclusions on the course of events in the specific case. Regardless of whether such conclusions are correct or not, the prosecutors will inevitably judge the credibility of a perpetrator's 'full disclosure' on the basis thereof. It would have been important and far better, if such a procedure had been placed before an independent forum, such as a court, as had previously been suggested in the consultations with the government.[240] Some have nevertheless identified positive potential for the guidelines' procedure, as perpetrators who had been denied amnesty unjustly at the TRC would get a second chance and generally the probability of criminal trials would be diminished.[241] However, representatives of perpetrators had expected, on the basis of the apparently promising negotiations with the government, a clear legislative solution providing for an independent and foreseeable indemnity mechanism, which would lay out clear preconditions and a strict obligation to grant indemnity. However, the guidelines did not meet this expectation. Against this

236 Ibid.

237 Interview with Anton Ackermann in Pretoria (May 11, 2006).

238 Interview with Jan Wagener in Pretoria (May 8, 2006); Interview with Johan van der Merwe in Pretoria (May 5, 2006).

239 E-mail from Johan van der Merwe (May 31, 2006); E-mail from Johan van der Merwe (June 4, 2006).

240 Ibid.

241 Interview with Jan Wagener in Pretoria (May 8, 2006).

background, to some in the Foundation for Equality before the Law the guidelines were rather unexpected.[242]

3.6 *Court challenge of the guidelines*

In July 2007, various relatives of victims of crimes committed by the apartheid security forces as well as human rights NGOs launched an application at the Pretoria High Court against the amendment of prosecution policy. The application sought an order of the High Court to suspend and stay the operation of the prosecution guidelines and to eventually declare the policy amendments to be inconsistent with the South African Constitution, and therefore unlawful and invalid.[243]

The applicants were Thembisile Nkadimeng, the sister of MK activist Nokuthula Simelane, who was abducted, tortured and probably murdered by the security police in 1983,[244] Nyameka Goniwe, Nombuyiselo Mhlauli, Sindiswa Mkhonto and Nomonde Calata, the widows of the four liberation movement activists known as the Cradock-Four, who were murdered by members of the Eastern Cape security police in 1985[245] as well as three human rights organisations, the Khulumani Support Group, the CSVR and the International Centre for Transitional Justice in New York.[246] The respondents were the NDPP, the Minister of Justice, the alleged perpetrators in the Cradock-Four murder case, Eric

---

242 Interview with Johan van der Merwe in Pretoria (May 5, 2006).

243 *Thembisile Nkadimeng and others v National Director of Public Prosecutions and others*, Notice of Motion, Case no. 32709/07 (T) July 2007 (on file with author).

244 See *infra* Chapter 4(5.1.1).

245 See *infra* Chapter 4(5.2).

246 The applicants were represented by lawyers from the Legal Resources Centre in Johannesburg and the Foundation for Human Rights has contributed to the funding (Interview with Howard Varney in Johannesburg (May 6, 2006)). The victims' relatives brought the application in their own interest as family members of the deceased persons in terms of section 38(a) of the Constitution, the organisations' application was based on their own interest and the representation of the public interest in terms of section 38(d) of the Constitution. All applicants also based their interest on the overall interest of the group of all apartheid victims possibly concerned by the Prosecution Policy in terms of section 38(c) of the Constitution.

Taylor, Johannes Lotz, Johannes van Zyl and Hermanus du Plessis as well as the alleged perpetrators in the Simelane case, Willem Coetzee, Anton Pretorius, Frederick Mong and Msebenzi Radebe.

The applicants expect the prosecution of the alleged perpetrators, since they were refused amnesty either completely, as in the Cradock-Four case, or for parts of the crimes, as in the Simelane case. They argue that the prosecution policy potentially prevents this from happening, should the alleged perpetrators successfully apply for indemnity under the procedure, a result that they seek to prevent.[247] It is submitted that the policy amendment allows for the NDPP to grant de facto indemnity to perpetrators and thereby infringes the right to dignity according to section 10 of the Constitution, as the protection of perpetrators from prosecution is at the expense of victims and victims' families who are thereby denied justice and whose quest for closure is prevented. Their respect, dignity and value in the wider community is undermined and the constitutional pact underlying the agreement on amnesty, on which many victims relied, is demeaned. The right to life according to section 11 of the Constitution would be violated, as murderers remain unpunished. As the impunity mechanism also encompasses acts of torture and abduction, the right of an individual to his/her freedom and security, as stated under section 12 of the Constitution, would also be violated. Moreover, there would also be a violation of section 9 of the Constitution, the right to equal protection and equality before the law, since the policy discriminates against victims of a crime committed with a political objective before 11 May 1994 and perpetrators who participated in the amnesty process in good faith and were granted amnesty as well as those who did not participate at all or were refused amnesty but who now get a second offer of indemnity. The unlawfulness of the policy is further highlighted in two ways: first, by the fact that it is not a law of general application, which is required by section 36(1) of the Constitution for any limitation of the Bill of Rights; and second, by the rule of law as enshrined in section 1 of the Constitution, since the

[247] *Thembisile Nkadimeng and others v National Director of Public Prosecutions and others*, Founding Affidavit, Case no. 32709/07 (T) July 2007 (on file with author).

policy grants selective impunity in a manner that lacks transparency and prevents sufficient participation of interested parties. The policy guidelines would also constitute an infringement of South Africa's international law obligations as it violates the International Covenant for Civil and Political Rights and the Convention against Torture and Other Cruel, Inhuman or Degrading Treatment or Punishment.

The respondents answered the criticism that the policy amendments would not allow for decisions not to prosecute in cases where there is sufficient evidence. Furthermore, it could not amount to effective indemnity in any event, because perpetrators would still be exposed to private prosecutions and civil claims. During the court hearings, the NDPP counsel submitted that representations in terms of the amendments would have no other purpose than to be used for plea and sentence or state witness arrangements in terms of sections 105A and 204 of the Criminal Procedure Act.

With the judgment on 12 December 2008 of judge Legodi, the High Court of Pretoria declared the policy amendments to the National Prosecution Policy to be inconsistent with the Constitution, unlawful and invalid and therefore suspended them.[248] The Court found that representations by perpetrators as envisaged by the policy amendment are not sanctioned by the Constitution. Section 179(5)(d) of the Constitution only provides for representations in cases where a decision to institute a prosecution has already been taken. However, in the view of the Court, representations in terms of the amendments apply to persons who are still facing possible prosecution.[249] The Court went on to point out that representations in terms of the guidelines cannot be the representations which are required in terms of sections 105A (plea bargaining) or 204 (state witnesses) of the Criminal Procedure Act, because both provisions apply only to situations where a prosecution has already been initiated. Furthermore, in terms of section 204

[248] *Nkadimeng and others v The National Director of Public Prosecutions and others* (Transvaal Provincial Division) Case no 32709/07, unreported, at para. 18.1.

[249] Ibid., at para. 15.3.1.1 and 15.3.1.2.

of the Criminal Procedure Act, indemnity is granted by a court and not by the NDPP.[250]

The Court accordingly concluded that the policy amendments could only mean that perpetrators be granted indemnity in cases of full disclosure, because otherwise the making of representations would not make sense. There would also be no incentive for perpetrators to come forward and make representations on their deed, if they would not afterwards be rewarded with a decision by the NDPP not to prosecute.[251] Consequentially, there would be simply no need for the disclosure procedure if it was not intended to result in indemnity.[252] Against this background the Court labelled the amendments in drastic terms as a "recipe for conflict and absurdity".[253] Accordingly, the Court confirmed the position of the applicants in that it views the amended guidelines as a copy of the TRC amnesty mechanism. It also pointed out that there cannot be any systematic connection between criteria such as the degree of remorse, the effects on reconciliation etc and a decision whether to prosecute or not.[254] The Court considered that the NPA has to prosecute where there is sufficient evidence to secure a conviction and a decision not to do so under such circumstances would be unconstitutional.[255] In this context it referred to a constitutional obligation of the NPA to prosecute.[256] The Court stated that it is not for victims to investigate crimes but much rather the responsibility of police and prosecutors to do so.[257] The making of representations directed at allowing for decisions

---

[250] Ibid., at para. 15.3.1.4.

[251] Ibid., at para. 15.5.3.1. The court apparently presumed that there is no protection mechanism for self-incriminating disclosures. It either did not consider paragraph B.15. of the amendment, where it is stated that no state agencies shall use information stemming from perpetrator disclosures in any proceedings against the person at a later stage, or did not consider that provision to sufficiently rule out the use of self-incriminating evidence, since it is not a law.

[252] Ibid., at para. 15.5.4.

[253] Ibid., at para. 15.5.3.

[254] Ibid., at para. 15.14.3.

[255] Ibid., at para. 15.4.4.

[256] Ibid., at para. 15.5.2.1.

[257] Ibid., at para. 16.2.3.3.

not to prosecute would accordingly be unlawful but in light of sections 105A and 204 of the Criminal Procedure Act also totally unnecessary. The normal prosecution policy is sufficient to provide guidelines for the decision whether to prosecute or not.[258]

Thus, in strong terms the Court declared the amendments to be unconstitutional. However, the judgment lacks supportive legal analysis. The Court did not base the conclusions it reached on a systematic legal interpretation and application of the respective explicit or implicit constitutional provisions at all. The NPA has lodged an appeal against the High Court ruling at the Supreme Court of Appeal, which had still not been heard or concluded upon the publication of this book.

3.7 *Evaluation*

The amendment of the prosecution policy reveals a great deal on the political viewpoints of the government and the developments on post-TRC prosecutions behind the scenes. They will therefore be evaluated in the following paragraphs.

3.7.1 *The guidelines criteria*

The criteria are rather vague. This is especially the case with respect to those criteria relating to a perpetrator's personal circumstances, such as the degree of remorse and his/her attitude towards reconciliation, the willingness to abide by the Constitution, etc. The same is true for criteria concerning the possible impact of a trial on society such as its effect on nation-building and reconciliation. It appears very unlikely that prosecutors will be in a position to determine such implications properly and with certainty so as to be able to apply the criteria in a consistent manner. Furthermore, the policy document does not specify how the individual preconditions that make up the criteria relate to each other in practical application. According to the NPA, there is no

[258] Ibid., at para. 15.3 and 15.4.

hierarchy in the catalogue.[259] Thus, what if the accused makes a full disclosure before the NDPP, yet shows no inclination to effect restitution? What if a victim demands prosecution, but the perpetrator has complied with all other criteria? The policy amendment does not even outline what the specific result of the process must be, if the alleged perpetrator has complied with most criteria. It is only stated that the criteria must be applied in a balanced way before reaching a decision on whether or not to prosecute.[260] The final decision remains in the NDPP's discretion.

However, even though the implementation in the Chikane case provided a different example, in theory, regarding the logic of the guidelines, one would expect that the satisfaction of the disclosure and political offence requirements in particular were intended to lead to a decision to preclude prosecution. Also, should the NDPP be convinced that a specific prosecution will have a negative impact on reconciliation, lead to renewed trauma or that the perpetrator cooperated satisfactorily, such circumstances were also meant to lead to a non-prosecution. What sense would it, in terms of the guidelines, make to press for a prosecution, if such a case would obviously harm the reconciliation effort in a specific case? Or why should one decide to prosecute an alleged perpetrator if he came forward and made a full disclosure and cooperated with the authorities in unearthing the truth? Thus, in theory the catalogue of criteria essentially outlines a whole range of reasons on which a decision not to prosecute can be based.

Furthermore, most criteria seem rather out of place for that particular stage of a criminal procedure. For one, with regard to the general prosecution policy, it is incomprehensible why factors like the accused's willingness to abide by the Constitution should contribute to a decision to forego prosecution, especially in the context of such serious crimes as murder or torture. Secondly, personal factors, such as the degree of indoctrination, should be considered by the trial court in handing

---

[259] *Presentation at the tabling of the prosecution policy amendment in the Justice Portfolio Committee*, Jan 17, 2006, para. 5.3 (available at http://www.pmg.org.za).

[260] Prosecution Policy, appendix A, para. C.3.

down a just sentence but should not have a connection to the question of whether a trial should be initiated in the first place.

It also seems inappropriate to place such a procedure before the NDPP. The NDPP's sole purpose in terms of section 179(2) of the Constitution is to hold perpetrators of crimes accountable. However, prosecutors would be required by the guidelines to consider a range of criteria on behalf of the perpetrator, which are outside the normal criteria outlined in the general prosecution policy. A conflict of interest between exercising the duty to prosecute and assessing wide-ranging factors for the perpetrators is inevitable. Obviously, a court would have been better charged with conducting such a process, as it would resemble more closely its usual tasks in a criminal trial of assessing mitigating and aggravating circumstances on the side of the accused.

3.7.2 *A copy of the amnesty process?*

The policy amendment more or less repeats verbatim the preconditions for granting amnesty through the Amnesty Committee according to the TRC Act. As such, the requirement for the crime to be associated with a political objective and to be committed in the course of the conflicts of the past,[261] including the catalogue of factors determining this,[262] is repeated, as well as the requirement to make a full disclosure of all relevant facts, factors and circumstances concerning the crime.[263] The major difference to the TRC Act is that the policy amendment does not provide an outline for attaining a strict resolution. Whereas the Amnesty Committee was legally obliged to grant amnesty once it was satisfied that the preconditions had been met, the decision in terms of the guidelines still remains at the discretion of the NDPP. However, it is clear that under the terms of the amendment the NDPP may refuse to prosecute once a full disclosure has been made and the offence can be deemed political. As also the High Court of Pretoria has pointed out, this might logically even be a decision intended for such cases by

[261] See section 20(1)(b) of the TRC Act.

[262] See section 20(3) of the TRC Act.

[263] See section 20(1)(c) of the TRC Act.

the authors of the prosecution policy guidelines. Also, since private prosecutions are not a realistic option, a decision by the NDPP not to prosecute grants the perpetrator a *de facto* indemnity or amnesty. Thus, in essence the amendments repeat the basic TRC amnesty scheme of a trade-off of impunity for a full disclosure, yet at the full discretion of the NDPP. The NPA was, however, at pains to stress that the guidelines were not meant to be a rerun of the TRC amnesty process, which is also emphasised in the policy amendment.[264] The strong resemblance of the guidelines to the TRC Act suggests otherwise.

However, there are major differences between the policy process and the TRC amnesty process with regard to victim and public participation. While the Amnesty Committee hearings relating to gross human rights violations took place in public,[265] and the records of hearings and decisions were published, the process outlined by the policy amendment could take place completely *in camera*. Confessions made on a specific crime could not necessarily be published. Also, while at TRC amnesty hearings concerned victims could be present, testify, adduce evidence or submit other relevant material,[266] no such provisions were made in the policy amendment. Obviously the interest was to ensure the procedures received as little public attention as possible. Moreover, there are other fundamental differences. While the run-up to the amnesty legislation was accompanied by large-scale public participation and gave ample opportunities for victim interest groups to give their input, the drafting process for the guidelines did not involve public participation at all and numerous demands of the major victims organisation, Khulumani, for information were simply totally ignored.

These facts contradict the President's statements, in which he maintained that the involvement of victims would be crucial in determining the future course of action and specific agreements between perpetrators and the NPA. He also stated that the matter could not be dealt with

---

[264] NPA, press statement *Amended prosecution policy and directives relating to prosecution of criminal matters arising from the conflicts of the past* (Jan 24, 2006); Prosecution Policy, appendix A, para. A.3.

[265] See section 33(1)(a) of the TRC Act.

[266] See section 19(4)(b) of the TRC Act.

by another amnesty process as this would fly in the face of victims, considering their concessions made in the first amnesty process.

3.7.3 *A political instrument and product of the consultations?*

The political consultations with representatives of the former security forces, which preceded the enactment of the guidelines, indicate that the amendment of the prosecution policy was designed merely to meet the political concerns, highlighted at the meetings. Any discernable similarity between the two processes would underline this perception that the guidelines were intended to be a tool to pursue a political agenda driven by the concerns and motivations, which surfaced at the talks.

However, there was not a direct continuity between the drafting of the guidelines and the consultations, which came to an end by 2004. The meetings with the generals resulted in a specific legislative proposal, which was not enacted in the form agreed upon. Thereafter, the process of drafting the policy amendment was conducted without the proper involvement of the former security forces. The generals were not even involved.[267] Thus, the policy amendment was not a direct product of the consultation processes. Nevertheless, it was certainly influenced by it to a great extent, since there are significant similarities between what was discussed or agreed upon in the consultations and what was incorporated in the policy. The policy amendment reproduces the basic scheme, which already formed the core of the draft legislation worked out in the SADF consultations, i.e., that a full disclosure of a political crime can result in non-prosecution. Equally, the negotiations with former police members envisaged the granting of indemnity, if some kind of disclosure was made and if the crime satisfied the political offence requirement according to the TRC Act criteria. Accordingly those who participated in the consultations or had insight into their operation, maintain that the guidelines contain a number of central features from the negotiations on how to avoid full-scale prosecutions

---

[267] Interview with Jan Geldenhuys in Pretoria (May 10, 2006).

in the wake of the TRC.[268] Thus, although the guidelines even go beyond that, the repetition of central preconditions for the granting of amnesty contained in the TRC Act is a feature, which emanates from and was worked out in the consultations with perpetrator groups. One must therefore conclude that the guidelines' enactment was obviously part of, and was in a way the conclusion of a broader political process that was characterised by the secret consultations with the perpetrator groups, which were already underway in 1998.

There are, however, two major differences. While both proposals of the security forces envisaged that any further indemnity process should be outlined by specific legislation, the guidelines are not a law but merely a directive for prosecutorial practice. Secondly, while the proposals envisaged that the indemnity process must take place before a court or in the course of a trial and must be conducted by a judge, the policy amendment places the decision concerning a non-prosecution in the discretion of the prosecutor. This point in particular makes the guidelines, in terms of how the public can benefit from further perpetrator disclosures and in terms of what should be required for a consistent and reliable process of post-TRC prosecutions, even less attractive than the proposals from the consultations. The proposals would have guaranteed public transparency as the process would have taken place in a criminal trial or at least before a court. Through the court records and possibly the reasons given by the judge for his decision, the information deriving from the perpetrator testimonies would have been retained and could have contributed to the compilation of a public record on apartheid atrocities. Furthermore, if indemnity had been granted in the course of an ordinary criminal trial, there would have been fixed rules for victim participation according to the normal provisions of criminal trials. Accordingly the solutions would have ensured more reliability and independence since indemnity would have been granted by a judge and in the course of a criminal trial. Thus, the

[268] Interview with Jürgen Kögl in Johannesburg (May 12, 2006); Interview with Jan Wagener in Pretoria (May 8, 2006); Interview with Johan van der Merwe in Pretoria (May 5, 2006).

proposals from the consultations clearly had some significant advantages over the guidelines.

The decision to turn away from these specific features of the proposals was certainly for concrete reasons. By not enacting the indemnity scheme as a law, the intention may have been to shield the guidelines, to a certain degree, from scrutiny according to the constitutional principles outlined by the Constitutional Court concerning the constitutionality of the TRC Act's amnesty legislation, which had also set out guidelines for the validity of any future legislation on amnesty.[269] This speculated goal was not reached, at least in the High Court litigation. Furthermore, placing the decision to prosecute at the discretion of the NDPP retains a much greater degree of influence for the government on criminal proceedings. The events in the Chikane case have clearly shown that the government is in a position to influence decisions of the NDPP and that its position is not entirely independent from political influence. The NDPP followed the instructions of the government to revoke a specific prosecutorial decision, although the preconditions for a prosecution of the accused had certainly been fulfilled. Although the Minister of Justice has final word on the NPA in terms of section 179(6) of the Constitution, the government is by no means entitled to interfere with the actual conduct of specific prosecutions and may not influence a specific discretional decision to prosecute. The NDPP is also by no means obliged to obey instructions by the government in respect thereof.[270] However, with regard to post-TRC prosecutions, the situation is obviously different. This was shown by the imposition of the moratorium on all post-TRC prosecutions and the political intervention in the scheduled arrests of the three security police officers in the Chikane case.

Also, it was often suggested that the position of the NDPP was generally strongly exposed to political influence and that the NDPP

---

[269] See *The Azanian Peoples Organisation and others v The President of South Africa and others* (CC) Case no. CCT 17/96 25 July 1996. See also infra Chapter 4(1.1.1).

[270] J. de Waal and I. Currie *The new constitutional and administrative law* vol. 1 (2001) 313.

had thus far been very loyal to the government.[271] The legislative setup of the restructured prosecution authority has given rise to criticisms concerning the position of the NDPP in conjunction with politics. On the one hand, it provides for the appointment of the NPA's head by a totally independent decision of the President,[272] and on the other hand it gives the NDPP a very powerful position; it can review any decision to prosecute and has generally great influence on practically all prosecutors and criminal proceedings[273].[274] Considering the appointment process of the NDPP, which is entirely in the discretion of the President, there were doubts that the NDPP would be sufficiently independent and thus subject to politics.[275] The appointment of a highly political figure as the first NDPP has further fuelled such apprehensions.[276]

The policy amendment foresees that the decision-making process as to whether to prosecute a post-TRC case is entirely up to the NDPP since it is empowered to make any final decision. Due to this, and the fact the policy is, to a certain degree, the conclusion of the political process of consultations it is probable that the guidelines were meant to serve as a political instrument. One can assume that the process was drafted to give the government a tool to exercise political influence in situations where it is deemed necessary, such as in the Chikane case and eventually to pursue the agenda discussed at the consultations of keeping the number of trials to a minimum.

3.7.4 *Conclusion*

The prosecution policy amendment for TRC-related cases was certainly driven by the government's motivations arising out of the consulta-

---

271 Interview with Yasmin Sooka in Pretoria (May 3, 2006); Interview with Jan Wagener in Pretoria (May 8, 2006).

272 See section 179(1)(a) of the Constitution and section 10 of the NPA Act.

273 See section 179(5)(d) of the Constitution and section 22 of the NPA Act.

274 D. van Zyl Smit and E. Steyn 'Prosecuting authority in the new South Africa' in *Centre for the Independence of Judges and Lawyers Yearbook* vol. 8 (2000) 137 at 146.

275 Ibid., 151 and 153; M. Schönteich *Lawyers for the people* (2001) 44 and 46.

276 Ibid.

tions with various representatives of the former apartheid security forces, which were aimed at finding solutions to keep the number of post-TRC trials as low as possible. The guidelines for their setup and criteria create wide-ranging opportunities to forego prosecuting the crimes of apartheid and had the potential to easily prevent a number of cases from reaching the stage of indictment.

The first case considered under the guidelines did not lead to impunity. Although *prima facie* a number of the most important criteria were complied with, the NDPP decided to prosecute. However, it cannot be determined with certainty what the NPA's reasons were for deciding to lay charges in the Chikane case after all, since no information was made public on the guidelines procedure preceding the plea and sentence agreement. It also cannot be ruled out that the decision was essentially political and thus not representative. The Chikane procedure at least shows that the guidelines are a highly flexible means according to which arbitrary decisions can be made without any public participation or reasoning. It also shows that, contrary to what one would expect on the basis of the theoretical setup of the policy amendment, one cannot assume with certainty that the guidelines procedure automatically resulted in a *de facto* indemnity of the alleged perpetrators, in cases where its criteria were complied with.

Since the concept of the process is lacking transparency and public participation, neither victims nor the public could be certain to benefit in terms of publishing more information regarding the truth about apartheid era atrocities. Generally, the practical value of the procedure would be very limited. The main reasons for the guidelines put forward by government officials were that a holistic approach was necessary and that effect should be given to the President's speech to reveal more information on possibly dangerous networks.[277] However, in terms of

[277] The proposition that secret networks at all still pose a latent danger to the state is strongly rejected by many but cannot be answered conclusively in this book (Interview with Jan Geldenhuys in Pretoria (May 15, 2006); Interview with Johan van der Merwe in Pretoria (May 5, 2006); Interview with Jürgen Kögl in Johannesburg (May 12, 2006); Interview with Yasmin Sooka in Pretoria (May 3, 2006)). The existence of a range of weapons caches which are still hidden is, however, not doubted.

giving incentives to perpetrators to reveal more information, it would also be possible to use the two legal mechanisms of plea and sentence and state witness agreements according to sections 105A and 204(2)(a) of the Criminal Procedure Act. Both mechanisms encourage perpetrators to come forward and disclose in exchange for a complete or partial indemnity.[278] Since it is unlikely that perpetrators who thus far deliberately refused to cooperate will now come forward voluntarily, the basic precondition of the threat of an imminent prosecution is the same. Moreover, plea-bargaining and state witness arrangements, which take place within a clear legislative framework and are independently adjudicated by a court, might also be far more convenient for perpetrators, especially considering the Foundation for Equality before the Law's strong critique concerning the vagueness and unpredictable nature of the guidelines. The proceedings in the Chikane case are also indicative with regard to the apparent lack of practical necessity, since it is not comprehensible why the accused first underwent the new procedure and apparently made extensive disclosures, if they were eventually convicted via a plea and sentence agreement.

By enacting the guidelines, which could potentially prevent further trials, the government contradicted the recommendations of the TRC and the overall scheme of conditional amnesties, which foresaw prosecutions in cases where amnesty was not granted. Furthermore, a setup which allows for the granting of *de facto* indemnity on a regular basis in cases where a full disclosure is made, as the High Court asserts the function of this amendment to be, is an essential reproduction of the amnesty process, which would have grave consequences for the legitimacy and reputation of the TRC's amnesty process and for the interests of victims in the amnesty process. The TRC Act provided for a definite and specified time frame for the amnesty process. This was the result of extensive discussions and part of a broad consensus. It was never meant to be extended in any form. This would be totally unacceptable for victims who relied on the fixed framework of the

[278] See for both mechanisms also *infra* Chapter 4(3.3).

amnesty legislation.[279] Furthermore, the drafting process has led to further alienation of official politics from the civil sector, human rights and victim organisations.

As a result, one must conclude that the guidelines marked a grave step backwards in the process of establishing accountability for apartheid era crimes after the conclusion of the TRC; a step which has been reversed by the High Court in Pretoria. However, the great delay and uncertainty in prosecuting apartheid era crimes which has been caused by the enactment is irreversible.

4. *Conclusion on Government's Political Considerations*

As shown above, the issue of criminal accountability in the wake of the TRC is, to a large extent, charged with political influences and considerations. In the following subchapter the political motivations and considerations on the part of the government will be summarised and evaluated. New aspects will be highlighted.[280]

Although in 1998 President Mandela called for trials within a fixed timeframe, the subsequent government under President Mbeki was clearly reluctant to create the appropriate conditions to institute trials on a general basis. Instead it engaged in working out solutions on how to avoid further trials and on how to enact new indemnity legislation, stopped a promising prosecution and imposed a moratorium, which further delayed the proper start of trials for more than one year. The approach indicates a clear lack of political will.

Key reasons for the government's generally dismissive attitude towards prosecutions lie in the motivations for entering into consultations with

---

[279] Interview with Marjorie Jobson in Pretoria (May 9, 2006); Interview with Desmond Tutu in Cape Town (March 22, 2006).

[280] It is important to mention that no comment or statement was made by government officials. The deputy Minister of Justice, Johnny de Lange and the Director-General of the President's office, Frank Chikane, were both unsuccessfully approached for comment by the author. The government's approach therefore had to be determined on the basis of the information laid out in the subchapters above.

the SADF generals, which have been laid out above.[281] However, there are other factors that contribute to the generally dismissive attitude towards trials. Commentators and experts on the issue of post-TRC prosecutions see as a central factor the fact that former liberation fighters can also become the focus of the prosecution authorities.[282] Former liberation movement cadres who were not granted amnesty are legally as exposed to criminal liability as former security forces operatives. The trial of former activist Ronnie Blani highlighted discomfort among ANC and government members concerning the prosecution of liberation activists. Of course, not only ordinary rank and file but also members of the higher echelons of the ANC and government could be vulnerable to prosecution. A number of leading ANC members submitted 'collective' amnesty applications, which had been refused.[283]

In November 1997, 37 high-ranking members of the ANC submitted applications for amnesty. Among them were current President Thabo Mbeki,[284] former Deputy President Jacob Zuma and ministers such as Charles Nqakula or the National Commissioner of Police Jackie Selebi. In support of their application, all commonly referred to a declaration of the ANC formulated for this purpose.[285] As such the applications

---

[281] See *supra* Chapter 3(2.2.2).

[282] Interview with Yasmin Sooka in Pretoria (May 3, 2006); Interview with Desmond Tutu in Cape Town (March 22, 2006); Interview with Charles Villa-Vicencio in Cape Town (March 29, 2006); J. Klaaren and H. Varney 'A second bite at the amnesty cherry?' in C. Villa-Vicencio and E. Doxtader (eds) *The provocations of amnesty* (2003) 265 at 265–66. Klaaren and Varney also suggested that the prospects of huge delictual claims against the state or political organisations such as the ANC following a conviction in a criminal trial could be a factor. However, since no further signs indicating the relevance of this issue could be made out and thus far no claims have been lodged, this issue can be left aside.

[283] See further L. McGregor 'Individual accountability in South Africa: cultural optimum or political facade?' (2001) 95 *American Journal of International Law* 32 at 39–44; J. Sarkin *Carrots and sticks: the TRC and the South African amnesty process* (2004) 15 and 214; F. Kutz *Amnestie für politische Straftäter in Südafrika* (2001) 140; *TRC Report*, vol. 1, chap. 7, para. 95 (Practically all sources only deal with the political and legal implications of the applications and not with the contents thereof.).

[284] Application no. AM/5506/97.

[285] Decision no. AC/99/0046.

stated that collective responsibility was assumed for all criminal acts committed by ANC members in the execution of the ANC's strategic and policy decisions during the struggle against apartheid.[286] It was further stated that none of the applicants had been aware of or involved in any crimes and could not have knowledge of all particular acts committed on the basis of their policy directives. Accordingly no particular acts or specified incidents were mentioned in the applications.[287] Although they obviously contravened section 20(1) of the TRC Act, which requires that a particular crime should be disclosed in any application for amnesty, the Amnesty Committee granted amnesty for the 37 applications.[288] The decision was challenged by both the TRC and the NP.[289] The Cape Town High Court in May 1998 reversed the decision to grant amnesty and ordered that the applications be considered anew.[290] Meanwhile, over 70 other applications by high-ranking ANC members had been tendered, which were also based on the common declaration.[291] Eventually, in the second run, the Amnesty Committee refused to grant amnesty in any of the applications since no specific conduct, which could constitute a crime, had been disclosed.[292]

However, since no particular acts were disclosed in the applications it does not automatically mean that a prosecution concerning the application has to follow. Nevertheless, the mere fact that top ANC members had been denied amnesty was politically exploited

---

[286] *TRC Report*, vol. 1, chap. 7, para. 95.

[287] Decision no. AC/99/0046; J. Sarkin *Carrots and sticks: the TRC and the South African amnesty process* (2004) 16.

[288] *TRC Report*, vol. 1, chap. 7, para. 95.

[289] See L. McGregor 'Individual accountability in South Africa: cultural optimum or political facade?' (2001) 95 *American Journal of International Law* 32 at 41. Due to section 5(e) of the TRC Act, the TRC could not instruct the Amnesty Committee to withdraw its decision. The NP accused the Amnesty Committee of bias.

[290] *The National Party of South Africa and James Marren Simpson v The Chairperson; Committee on Amnesty of the Truth and Reconciliation Commission and 38 others* (C) Cases no 3626/98, 3859/98, 3729/98 8 May 1998, unreported.

[291] Decision no. AC/99/0046; J. Sarkin *Carrots and sticks: the TRC and the South African amnesty process* (2004) 276.

[292] Decision no. AC/99/0046.

and used to pressure the government. As mentioned above, various political parties and organisations called for 'even-handed' prosecutions, 'equally' targeting ANC members.[293] As most of the advocates of such calls rejected the idea of prosecutions and preferred the concept of a general amnesty, it is obvious that the call is intended to pressure the government into stopping further trials. The Foundation for Equality before the Law, represented by its attorney, Wagener, even went so far as to compile complete dockets supporting the prosecution of top ANC members, including about five of the top ANC leadership, among them President Mbeki.[294] An attorney, Jaap Cilliers, who had also been the attorney of Wouter Basson, had been approached to evaluate the dockets. It was claimed the dockets contained sufficient evidence to support charges.[295]

The PCLU even requested the Foundation for Equality before the Law to hand over the dockets since it intended to investigate the matters and evaluate the possibility of pressing charges.[296] The organisation refused. It of course had no interest in the conviction of top ANC members, since its preference was for the preclusion of all prosecutions.[297] Only in the event of further trials, especially if such prosecutions focused only on the former apartheid side and not on liberation movement crimes, was there an intention to use the gathered information as a means to exercise political pressure and to publish the information and, only theoretically, to eventually engage in private prosecutions, all with the aim of preventing any further trials.[298] In 2004, when the arrests in the Chikane case were suddenly suspended on the directions of the President, the issue apparently played an influential role. According to Wagener, he used the matter successfully to pressure the govern-

293 See *supra* Chapter 3(1.2.1).

294 Interview with Johan van der Merwe in Pretoria (May 5, 2006).

295 Ibid.

296 L. Fernandez 'Post-TRC prosecutions in South Africa' in G. Werle (ed.) *Justice in transition* (2006) 65 at 75.

297 Interview with Johan van der Merwe in Pretoria (May 5, 2006).

298 Ibid.

ment to stop the arrests.[299] Thus obviously the matter weighs heavily in the government's considerations. In July 2008 representatives of the Foundation for Equality before the Law publicly reiterated their willingness to act against leading ANC officials by instituting private prosecutions, should the state move ahead with criminal proceedings against their members.[300]

The former SADF generals also view the issue of potential criminal liability of ANC members as a major consideration for the government. Moreover, if any of the generals had been charged after the TRC, they were willing to pressure the government with exactly the same means, politically exploiting the issue by calling for the prosecution of ANC members.[301]

Advocates of even-handed prosecutions suggest that criminal liability could concern various orders given through the specific direct command structure of the ANC in exile.[302] During the apartheid years the ANC directed violent struggles against the South African state from abroad. The top command structure of the ANC at the time was the National Executive Committee (hereinafter NEC), which exercised direct responsibility over any sizeable militant ANC organisation or cell operating in South Africa.[303] The NEC also directed the ANC's armed wing, MK. Most of the 37 ANC amnesty applicants who were denied amnesty are former members of the NEC.[304] The past conduct of the ANC and its organs was also subject to investigations and hearings by the TRC. The TRC later in its report emphasised that the ANC was an internationally recognised liberation movement involved in a just war against apartheid, which was considered a crime against humanity.[305] Nevertheless, it found that ANC organs at times used means that resulted in unjustifiable

299 Interview with Jan Wagener in Pretoria (May 8, 2006).

300 B. Webb *Tit-for-tat threat by apartheid generals* Sunday Tribune, July 20, 2008.

301 Interview with Jan Geldenhuys in Pretoria (May 15, 2006).

302 Interview with Jan Wagener in Pretoria (May 16, 2006).

303 *TRC Report*, vol. 2, chap. 4, appendix, page 393.

304 Ibid.

305 *TRC Report*, vol. 2, chap. 4, para. 2.

gross human rights violations.[306] These conclusions were drawn especially with regard to the bombing and the landmine campaigns, both of which were launched by the ANC to target state facilities and security force personnel and equipment in South Africa.

Now, advocates of even-handed prosecutions claim that these campaigns, especially the landmine campaign, which was instructed by the NEC and carried out by MK, could form the basis for a criminal liability of former NEC members.[307] The TRC pointed out that it had been the declared aim not to harm civilians in such campaigns[308] but that inevitably and foreseeably bombs directed at other targets also killed civilians.[309] The landmine campaign was also designed and ordered by the NEC. During the mid-1980s, MK was given the task of planting landmines in rural areas of northern South Africa and other border regions to target military patrols.[310] According to the TRC this inevitably led to many civilian casualties, which was also the reason that the ANC quickly abandoned the campaign.[311] From the findings of the TRC it is clear that bomb attacks, such as the Church Street bomb, and the landmine campaign were directly attributable to orders given by the NEC. It is further clear that in many cases it was obvious and foreseeable, even though clearly not intended, that civilians would be harmed by such actions.[312] These circumstances might potentially provide the basis to

---

306 Ibid. See further *TRC Report*, vol. 3, chap. 6, paras. 500–12; *TRC Report*, vol. 2, chap. 4, paras. 13–45.

307 Interview with Jan Wagener in Pretoria (May 16, 2006).

308 *TRC Report*, vol. 6, s. 5, chap. 3, para. 30.

309 *TRC Report*, vol. 2, chap. 4, para. 37. The most prominent of such bomb attacks was the explosion of a car bomb in front of the South African Air Force headquarters in Church Street, Pretoria, in 1983, which killed 21 people, 10 of whom were civilians. Another prominent attack was that in 1986 on the Magoo's Bar/'Why Not' Bar, a bar in Durban popular among security force members. It resulted in three deaths (see *TRC Report*, vol. 2, chap. 4, paras. 13–37).

310 *TRC Report*, vol. 2, chap. 4, para. 38.

311 Ibid., para. 45.

312 *TRC Report*, vol. 6, s. 5, chap. 3, paras. 30, 39, 40, 42–43. See also *TRC Report*, vol. 2, chap. 7. The TRC report illustrates that lower and local ANC parts of the organisation also account for numerous deaths in the course of the struggle. Equally

establish the criminal liability of high-ranking ANC and government members who were involved in the NEC or other command structures at that time and who had been refused amnesty.

The NPA had, however, announced in 2004 that there was not sufficient evidence warranting criminal investigations against the 37 ANC members who had been refused amnesty.[313] Regardless, it seems highly unlikely that it would be easy for the PCLU to institute criminal proceedings against leading politicians of the ANC, such as former President Thabo Mbeki. Nevertheless, the more crucial factor is that the side of the security forces, police and military alike, can use their influence to exercise political pressure, stir up significant political conflict and unrest and to damage the reputation of leading ANC officials by publicly linking them to criminal acts and claiming they could be charged for murder or other crimes. This would of course affect the stability of the government. Furthermore, the opponents of prosecutions will continue to claim that post-TRC prosecutions are unjust and harm reconciliation if they only concentrate on former security force members. These circumstances must certainly contribute to the government's reluctance to promote post-TRC prosecutions and to their desire to consult with the perpetrator groups.

A range of other factors certainly also contribute to the lack of political will to pursue post-TRC prosecutions. It has been mentioned above that one of the ANC leaders stated that prosecutions were not in the country's interest.[314] It is likely that this represents a common position among many government members. As such, sources from the Justice Ministry were reported in the media as mentioning that the government had no interest in South African politics being dominated and disrupted by a series of spectacular trials relating to the apartheid era.[315]

Underlying this are probably concerns, which were also voiced in the public debate on post-TRC prosecutions. Post-TRC trials would

---

many gross human rights violations resulted from decisions of MK operatives, taken independently from any official command structures.

313 *NPA won't prosecute ANC 37* SAPA, June 2, 2004.

314 See text accompanying *supra* Chapter 3 note 75.

315 J. Steinberg *Juggling justice, practically* Business Day, June 21, 2001.

constantly highlight accounts of the injustices, atrocities and crimes of the apartheid past over a period of several years. It is most probably feared that this could result in the recurrence of rifts between the ethnic groups and fuel alienation and accusations concerning the apartheid past.[316] As mentioned above, compared to the period when the TRC was in session, during which the media reported almost daily on the TRC and its revelations and findings on the violent conflicts of the past, public debate has generally become rather quiet and sporadic. The government probably welcomes this since it indicates that the ethnic groups might have left the conflicts of the past behind. The government certainly fears that this quiet could be changed by a row of TRC-related trials.[317] The recent prosecutions, especially that in the Chikane case, the PEBCO-Three and Ronnie Blani cases, have shown that such occasions inevitably also give rise to renewed public discussion and conflicts based on ethnic grounds. The Afrikaans speaking white population in particular might perceive prosecutions as part of an overall attack on their ethnic group and might therefore further feel alienated from the new South African state.[318] The concern is, thus, that old wounds might be opened up and that some of the good effects the TRC had on nation-building might be tainted. Thus, as far as South African society is concerned, the government is surely anxious that prosecutions will be a serious obstacle in the process of leaving the past behind and moving forward towards a reconciled nation with harmony reigning between the various ethnic groups. The government's sensitivity towards such issues is also obvious from the amended policy guidelines, as it is stated there that the NDPP needs to take into account how a prosecution could impact on the 'national project of nation-building through transformation, reconciliation, development and reconstruction within and of our society' and whether the prosecution could cause renewed trauma and conflict where reconciliation has already taken place.[319]

---

[316] Interview with Desmond Tutu in Cape Town (March 22, 2006); Interview with Charles Villa-Vicencio in Cape Town (March 29, 2006).

[317] Interview with Desmond Tutu in Cape Town (March 22, 2006).

[318] Ibid.

[319] See *supra* Chapter 3(3.2).

Simple issues of governance thereby also come into play as any government is interested in heading a stable society and not one constantly shaken by ethnic conflicts or alienation. There may also be an economic dimension as it is certainly more advantageous in this regard to signal to the international community that the conflicts of the past have ceased indefinitely and the multi-ethnic society and country have stabilised for good.

Apart from these general considerations, concrete practical factors also militate against further wide scale prosecutions. The process of post-TRC prosecutions starts with a legacy of failure.[320] At least as far as the high profile cases are concerned, two very extensive, costly and time consuming trials, the trial of former Minister of Defence Magnus Malan and others, and the Wouter Basson trial ended with acquittals. TRC cases have proved to be very arduous, time-consuming and expensive. The current government has to face an extremely high crime rate[321] and has limited resources for the police and prosecutors.[322] In this regard it is probably reluctant to assign sufficient resources to the prosecution of apartheid crimes, considering the pressing need to deal with current crime and the past examples of failed TRC prosecutions attempts.

On the other hand, the government is aware that the TRC amnesty scheme unequivocally demands prosecutions. It had been commonly acknowledged in the consultations with the apartheid security forces after 1998 that due to this a general amnesty would not be feasible politically.[323] It is clear that abstaining completely from pursuing prosecutions, which would, according to the above findings, suit the government,

---

320 Interview with Yasmin Sooka in Pretoria (May 3, 2006).

321 In 2006 18,500 cases of murder, 55,000 of rape and 119,000 of armed robbery were recorded (crime statistics available at http://www.saps.gov.za).

322 See L. Fernandez 'Post-TRC prosecutions in South Africa' in G. Werle (ed.) *Justice in transition* (2006) 65 at 77–79. The later constitutional court judge Richard Goldstone had already in 1994 pointed out that the justice system of the new South Africa would simply not be capable to cope with all crimes committed during apartheid (P. Parker 'The politics of indemnities, truth telling and reconciliation in South Africa' (1996) 17 1–2 *Human Rights Law Journal* 1 at 9).

323 Interview with Johan van der Merwe in Pretoria (May 5, 2006); Interview with Jan Geldenhuys in Pretoria (May 10, 2006).

could seriously damage the legitimacy and the reputation of the TRC. Harming the TRC and its beneficial effects for the country is not in the government's interest. Thus, the government faces a dilemma regarding its obvious reluctance to foster prosecutions.

The guidelines were certainly intended to balance these conflicting factors. With them, the government decided that prosecutions would go ahead, turned away from strict indemnity procedures in a court, *prima facie* leaving it in the hands of the NDPP to decide whether to prosecute. At first glance, this satisfies the TRC's requirement for trials to go ahead. Nevertheless, the intention of the government to restrict the scope of prosecutions could also easily be satisfied by the policy amendment, since it provided for ample and flexible measures to influence any specific criminal proceeding. According to the design of the policy amendment, a prosecution, for example, may be rejected if it is deemed detrimental for reconciliation and nation-building, which is the factor that most obviously introduces political considerations into the prosecution process.

As a result of the considerations outlined above, one must conclude that the government had a tendency to prefer a course of partial and controlled forgetting about the past over comprehensively and unequivocally dealing with past political crimes through criminal proceedings.

Chapter Four

Normative Standards and Practical Prospects for Further Prosecutions

The process of initiating and conducting criminal trials in the wake of the TRC for those who committed politically motivated gross human rights violations during the apartheid conflict has certainly not been dealt with exhaustively. During the decade succeeding the official end of the TRC in 1998, very few trials were initiated. The task to conduct post-TRC prosecutions is, thus, far from conclusion.

The following chapter will highlight the features of the applicable legal framework which must guide the official approach to establishing criminal accountability for politically motivated human rights violations in South Africa. This also includes dealing with statutory limitations and legally consistent prioritisation criteria. Concurrently, the practical prospects for further trials and the question of whether we may expect a significant number of further proceedings will be examined. Although it is not possible to assess here which cases could still be prosecuted, a short collection of cases will be presented, which were either announced by the NPA as exhibiting sufficient prospects for a successful prosecution, or which due to certain specific features are of extraordinary or exemplary relevance for victims and the issue of post-TRC criminal accountability as a whole.

1. *Constitutional and International Law Requirements*

Criminal proceedings concerning the politically motivated gross human rights violations of the apartheid era are invariably embedded in a legal framework. As such, norms and legal standards from both constitutional as well as international law place specific obligations on the government and also determine the legality of the current official approach and the actual conduct of prosecutions through the NPA. The South African government and the NPA must consider this legal framework and fulfil any legal requirements. The extent to which the State continues to fail to conduct a significant number of criminal trials and its policy of trying to prevent trials on a large scale might be seen as conflicting with such requirements. However, any possible legal obligations and South Africa's compliance therewith will be outlined in the following paragraphs.

1.1 *Constitutional law obligations*

The politically motivated crimes which were committed in the course of the apartheid conflict violated a range of fundamental human rights, which are meanwhile explicitly protected in the Constitution of democratic South Africa. Many apartheid opponents were abducted, tortured and killed by the security forces simply for their resistance to the inhumane regime. Many civilians also died through activities of the liberation movement. The relevant rights of the Constitution's Bill of Rights[1] concerned by such conduct are the right to the respect of human dignity of every human being, as enshrined in section 10 of the Constitution, the right to life, according to section 11 of the Constitution and the fundamental rights of freedom and security emanating from section 12 of the Constitution. Section 12 contains the rights not to be arbitrarily deprived of personal freedom, not to be detained without trial, to be free from all forms of violence regardless whether public or private, not to be tortured and not to be treated in a cruel, inhuman or degrading way, as well as the right to bodily and psychological integrity.

According to section 7(2) of the Constitution the state is obliged to protect, respect, promote and fulfil the Bill of Rights. This obligation is not confined to preventive measures but extends to punitive measures

[1] See sections 7 to 39 of the Constitution.

if there has been a serious violation of a right contained in the Bill of Rights. Impunity for such serious violations would effectively render the rights meaningless. The prosecution of murder, thus, is a central means to protect the right to life and the prosecution of assault likewise is a central means to protect the right to bodily integrity.[2] The state is accordingly obliged to protect the life of its citizens through the enforcement of the criminal law to the best of the state's abilities.[3] The obligation arises, to the same extent, also for violations of other fundamental rights such as the right not to be subjected to violence and torture.[4] As a result, the state has a constitutional obligation to prosecute offences that threaten or violate the rights of citizens, and this obligation is of central importance in the overall constitutional framework.[5]

The importance of the institution of criminal proceedings where rights are violated is further underlined through section 179 of the Constitution, which establishes the prosecution service and outlines that it needs to exercise its functions without fear, favour or prejudice.[6] It is of specific relevance in the present context, that the prosecution service's obligations apply not only to violations of rights that occurred after the Constitution came into force but also to offences committed beforehand.[7]

1.1.1 *The AZAPO rationale*

However, according to section 7(3) of the Constitution, constitutional rights can be subject to limitations. The Constitutional Court has elaborated extensively on the limitation of rights in cases of indemnity from prosecution for politically motivated crimes committed in the course of the apartheid conflict. In 1996, the Court dealt with the constitu-

---

[2] *S. v Basson* (CC) Case no. CCT 30/03 10 March 2004 at para. 31.

[3] J. de Waal et al., *The Bill of Rights handbook* 4ed (2001) 242.

[4] Ibid., 259.

[5] *S. v Basson* (CC) Case no. CCT 30/03 10 March 2004 at paras. 31–32; *S. v Basson* (CC) Case no. CCT 30/03 9 September 2005 at para. 144.

[6] *S. v Basson* (CC) Case no. CCT 30/03 10 March 2004 at para. 33; *S. v Basson* (CC) Case no. CCT 30/03 9 September 2005 at para. 144.

[7] *S. v Basson* (CC) Case no. CCT 30/03 10 March 2004 at para. 37.

tionality of the amnesty legislation contained in the TRC Act in what commonly became known as the "AZAPO case".[8] The decision is of great significance for the general constitutional principles applicable to prosecuting past human rights violations.

The Court had to decide whether section 20(7) of the TRC Act, which exempts perpetrators who were granted amnesty from criminal and civil liability, contravened the Interim Constitution. It, thus, had to decide under which circumstances the non-prosecution of politically motivated human rights offenders of the apartheid era was constitutionally justified. The applicants in the case[9] argued that the relevant amnesty regulations of the TRC Act were unconstitutional since the state would thereby violate its constitutional duty to prosecute crimes committed during the apartheid regime.[10] Specifically, the applicants claimed that section 20 of the TRC Act would violate section 22 of the Interim Constitution, according to which '[e]very person shall have the right to have justiciable disputes settled by a court of law or, where appropriate, another independent and impartial forum.' The respective provision is now enshrined in section 34 of the Constitution.

From the outset, the Constitutional Court made it clear that an amnesty, that is, the official granting of indemnity or factual impunity,[11]

---

[8] *The Azanian Peoples Organisation and others v The President of South Africa and others* (CC) Case no. CCT 17/96 25 July 1996. See on the judgment C. Braude and D. Spitz 'Memory and the spectre of international justice: a comment on AZAPO' (1997) *South African Journal on Human Rights* 269–82; J. Dugard 'Is the truth and reconciliation process compatible with international law? An unanswered question' (1997) *South African Journal on Human Rights* 258–68; F. Kutz *Amnestie für politische Straftäter in Südafrika* (2001) 105–32; Z. Motala 'The Promotion of National Unity and Reconciliation Act, the constitution and international law' (1995) 28 *Comparative and International Law Journal of Southern Africa* 338–62; J. Sarkin 'The trials and tribunals of South Africa's Truth and Reconciliation Commission' *South African Journal on Human Rights* (1996) 617 at 625–39.

[9] The challenge was brought by the AZAPO, the widow of Steve Biko and relatives of Griffith Mxenge and Florence and Fabian Ribeiro who were murdered by the security police.

[10] F. Kutz *Amnestie für politische Straftäter in Südafrika* (2001) 106.

[11] Ibid., 7–9.

impacts on fundamental rights since all persons are entitled to the protection of the law against unlawful invasions of the right to life, respect for and protection of their dignity and the right not to be subjected to torture.[12] The Court pointed out that in case rights are invaded, the victims must have the right to obtain redress before ordinary civil or criminal courts and that the perpetrators must account before such courts for the crimes they commit. The Court was obviously also then of the conviction that, although the Constitution only came into force at a later stage, it nevertheless demands redress for the crimes committed during apartheid. The Court stated that an amnesty effectively obliterates such rights.[13] In the Court's view therefore, the submission that an amnesty constitutes a violation of section 22 of the Interim Constitution, had considerable merits.[14] Accordingly the Constitution needed to authorise such a violation.[15]

In clarifying whether this was the case, the Court mainly focussed on a provision in the epilogue of the Interim Constitution. The part in question is the passage which provides for the enactment of a law on amnesty. As pointed out above, it says that 'amnesty shall be granted in respect of acts, omissions and offences associated with political objectives and committed in the course of the conflicts of the past.'[16] The Court found the epilogue to be of no lesser status than any other provi-

---

[12] *The Azanian Peoples Organisation and others v The President of South Africa and others* (CC) Case no. CCT 17/96 25 July 1996 at para. 9.

[13] Ibid.

[14] Ibid., at para. 10. In this regard the decision contradicts with later decisions of the Constitutional Court where it explicitly ruled that section 34 of the Constitution, formerly section 22 of the Interim Constitution, only applies to non-criminal disputes (*S. v Pennington and Summerley* (CC) Case no. CCT 14/97 18 September 1997 at para. 46). Yet the Court in the AZAPO case obviously applied section 22 also to criminal disputes. See also M.E. Bennun 'Amnesty and international law' in C. Villa-Vicencio and E. Doxtader (eds) *The provocations of amnesty* (2003) 92 at 106 and J. de Waal et al., *The Bill of Rights handbook* 4ed (2001) 555.

[15] *The Azanian Peoples Organisation and others v The President of South Africa and others* (CC) Case no. CCT 17/96 25 July 1996 at para. 10. See section 33 of the Interim Constitution and 36 of the Constitution.

[16] See text accompanying *supra* Chapter 1 note 41.

sion of the Interim Constitution and found that this section not only permitted the granting of amnesty but even obliged the legislature to pass an appropriate law on amnesty.[17] The Court found two subsequent reasons supporting the constitutionality of the amnesty provision.

First, the special political circumstances of the negotiation and transition period of the early to mid 1990s were taken into account.[18] The Court pointed out that the crucial factor for upholding the amnesty provisions was that without amnesty the 'historic bridge', as outlined in the epilogue, might never have been successfully erected.[19] Amnesty in this sense was, according to the Court, a vital means of effecting a successful and peaceful transition to a democratic society.[20] It stated that the negotiated hand-over of power to a democratically elected government with the full support of the former state forces and the agreement on a democratic constitution might not have been reached, was it not for the epilogue's provision on amnesty as a means to promote nation-building and reconciliation.[21]

Secondly, the Court took into account the fact that it would be of overwhelming importance for the victims of political violence, the nation as a whole as well as the project of nation-building to uncover the truth about the apartheid crimes in order to establish a better public record of the past atrocities. To achieve this only by means of criminal investigation would, due to the secretive methods involved, widespread cover-ups and the dearth of investigations during the apartheid era, be very difficult. Accordingly, it would be necessary to offer incentives

---

[17] *The Azanian Peoples Organisation and others v The President of South Africa and others* (CC) Case no. CCT 17/96 25 July 1996 at para. 14.

[18] The Court made extensive reference at various points to the difficult task of negotiation, transition and the spirit of reconciliation encapsulated in the Interim Constitution (*The Azanian Peoples Organisation and others v The President of South Africa and others* (CC) Case no. CCT 17/96 25 July 1996 at paras. 2–4, 17, 21, 48).

[19] *The Azanian Peoples Organisation and others v The President of South Africa and others* (CC) Case no. CCT 17/96 25 July 1996 at para. 19.

[20] Ibid., at para. 32.

[21] Ibid., at para. 19.

to those who are aware of the information by means of amnesty to uncover the truth about past human rights abuses.[22]

The reasons can be summarised to the effect that amnesty was justified on the basis of the epilogue and was required by the objectives of effecting a peaceful transition to democracy and uncovering the truth about criminal acts committed during the apartheid era.

1.1.2 *The present approach and the constitutional framework*

In examining whether the State's present approach to post-TRC criminal accountability does justice to these constitutional requirements or to what extent it might be unconstitutional, we must recall once again two features which characterise this present approach.

For one, there have been very few criminal proceedings in TRC-related cases after 1998. After 2003, when proceedings were actually meant to be pursued by the centrally located PCLU, the number of proceedings declined even further. Only two significant prosecutions, those in the Blani and Chikane cases, have been concluded by the PCLU between 2003 and 2008. Only the prosecution in the PEBCO-Three case is currently pending. It has been pointed out that there are many practical restrictions that bar the PCLU from making greater progress in terms of the number of prosecutions. However, there have certainly not been as many prosecutions as were potentially possible,[23] even when the significant constraints on resources are taken into account. Thus, the NPA is, to a certain degree, simply refraining from investigating and prosecuting cases, thereby, to a certain extent, creating a state of *de facto* indemnity. The government contributes significantly to this state of impunity by not giving the NPA the support it would need to go further. Instead it has, as shown above, attempted to restrict prosecutions from progressing further. Although the NPA is independent under the terms of section 179 of the Constitution, the government restricted potential criminal proceedings and sought to put in place measures to further limit their potential.

---

[22] Ibid., at para. 17.

[23] See for concrete practical prospects *infra* Chapter 4(5).

It is certainly possible that the constitutional obligation to prosecute only extends to that which is reasonably and practically possible, and, thus, must also take account of the very limited resources available to the NPA and other pressing needs of the state. However, to the extent that the NPA deliberately refrains from instituting criminal proceedings in cases exhibiting sufficient prospects of success, it violates this constitutional obligation. The minimal progress in reaching anywhere near the maximum capacity for prosecutions does not do justice to these constitutional requirements and the NPA and the government are obliged to do more.

The other critical circumstances are discretionary decisions of the NDPP not to prosecute, either based on the ordinary prosecution policy of the NPA or on any possible amendment of the policy applicable to TRC-related cases. It has already been pointed out that, unlike countries that adopted the so-called Principle of Legality which obliges prosecutors to pursue every crime, in South Africa prosecutors generally have a wide discretion as to whether to indict a perpetrator or not.[24]

As already mentioned above, the High Court of Pretoria abstained from analysing the underlying constitutional provisions when coming to the conclusion that the policy amendment, which was intended to guide the use of discretion, is unconstitutional. However, the government's intended policy approach needs to be examined on a basis similar to the amnesty law during the 1990s. The fact that the amendments were not introduced as a law, that they do not outline a legally binding concrete result and that the NDPP's generally prosecutorial decisions according to the general prosecution policy neither effect criminal nor civil liability does not exempt them from constitutional muster similar to that of the TRC Act in the AZAPO litigation before the Constitutional Court. Once again without systematic constitutional law analysis, the High Court concluded accordingly when adjudicating the amendments. It confirmed that the guidelines create the possibility for the prosecutors to grant perpetrators *de facto* indemnity. What is generally crucial in this regard is that decisions of the NDPP not to institute a prosecution are

---

[24] M. Schönteich *Lawyers for the people* (2001) 19–20.

tantamount to legal amnesty, as perpetrators would effectively receive impunity. It has already been pointed out that private prosecutions are simply not a realistic option for apartheid era victims.[25]

Moreover, according to section 8(1) of the Constitution, the Bill of Rights binds all state organs. Generally therefore, it cannot make a difference whether perpetrators are not prosecuted on the basis of a law or an administrative policy, as long as this results from a decision of a state organ and effectively grants the perpetrator immunity from criminal accountability. It also flows from section 179(2) of the Constitution, which states that '[t]he prosecuting authority has the power to institute criminal proceedings on behalf of the state, and to carry out any necessary functions incidental to instituting criminal proceedings', that the institution of criminal proceedings is a matter of importance to the state. Indeed, it is one of the primary tasks of the state connected to its constitutional duty to protect the Bill of Rights.[26] Thus, it is clear that the NDPP cannot simply justify a decision not to prosecute by referring to the possibility to prosecute privately. The High Court strongly confirmed this trite perception, when plainly stating that it is not for victims to investigate crimes.[27] Accordingly, it would be inappropriate to evaluate discretionary decisions not to prosecute differently to the amnesty law simply with reference to the fact that criminal and civil liabilities legally remain intact.

Decisions of the NDPP to preclude prosecution, whether based on specific guidelines or on the general prosecution policy, effectively obliterate the victims' rights to judicial redress and their human rights in the Bill of Rights in the same way recognised by the Constitutional Court in the AZAPO decision on the amnesty law.[28] Yet there is no constitutional provision in the current constitution which, like the epi-

[25] See text accompanying *supra* Chapter 3 note 230.

[26] *S. v Basson* (CC) Case no. CCT 30/03 10 March 2004 at para. 33; *S. v Basson* (CC) Case no. CCT 30/03 9 September 2005 at para. 144.

[27] *Nkadimeng and others v The National Director of Public Prosecutions and others* (Transvaal Provincial Division) Case no. 32709/07, unreported, at para. 16.2.3.3.

[28] *The Azanian Peoples Organisation and others v The President of South Africa and others* (CC) Case no. CCT 17/96 25 July 1996 at paras. 9–10.

logue of the Interim Constitution, authorises the state not to prosecute gross human rights violations which occurred under apartheid.

However, item 22 of schedule 6 of the Constitution extends the provisions of the Interim Constitution's epilogue to the present constitution as it provides that:

> Notwithstanding the other provisions of the new Constitution and despite the repeal of the previous Constitution, all the provisions relating to amnesty contained in the previous Constitution under the heading 'National Unity and Reconciliation' are deemed to be part of the new Constitution for the purposes of the Promotion of National Unity and Reconciliation Act, 1995 (Act 34 of 1995), as amended, including for the purposes of its validity.

However, commentators have pointed out that this section is only applicable to maintain the purposes of the TRC Act, thus, providing for the option of amending it only in terms of its defined scope and ambit.[29] Undoubtedly the section does not constitute a general extension of the epilogue's broad requirement to grant amnesty into the future. Thus, it is not possible to base a completely new process of indemnity on it. It is clear that it was not the intention of the legislator to provide for any new and separate indemnity process in the new Constitution.

Apart from the epilogue, the Constitutional Court's other main consideration in upholding the amnesty law were the necessities of the political situation during the negotiation period. The situation was very unstable and the country found itself on the brink of open civil war. The support of the security forces for the transition needed to be assured. Commentators consequently pointed out that an expiry of the transition period alters the evaluation of any further amnesty mechanism drastically.[30] There can be no doubt that at present the South African state has stabilised significantly and the new democratic order is well established. There are certainly no forces in the country, which are willing or capable of threatening the stability of South Africa

[29] J. Klaaren and H. Varney 'A second bite at the amnesty cherry?' in C. Villa-Vicencio and E. Doxtader (eds) *The provocations of amnesty* (2003) 265 at 281.

[30] Ibid., 279.

in any significant way.[31] Thus, there is no constitutional authority, which could now, some 13 years after the first democratic elections, justify the extended non-prosecution or indemnification of apartheid era political crimes.

However, the general prosecution policy concerning the prosecutor's conduct with regard to the exercise of prosecutorial discretion states in paragraph 4.(c), that in cases where a reasonable prospect for a successful prosecution was established, a decision not to prosecute might nevertheless be taken by the prosecutor if the public interest so demands. This test needs of course to be applied on a case by case basis, but nevertheless indicates that with regard to TRC-related cases the public interest might be used to justify non-prosecution in terms of the general prosecution policy in certain cases. Constitutional considerations must certainly be taken into account when applying the general prosecution policy, as a decision that is in blatant opposition to important constitutional principles can hardly be claimed to be in the public interest. The benefit of enhancing the public knowledge on past atrocities by offering perpetrators incentives to disclose was identified by the Constitutional Court as a major aspect of the public interest when upholding the legality of the amnesty legislation.

However, this factor was only one of many in the Court's considerations. When considered alone, it is clearly outweighed by the following considerations: the public interest in prosecution is strengthened by the mere gravity of the crimes in question. According to section 7(1) of the Constitution, the Bill of Rights is considered a cornerstone of South Africa's new democracy. Accordingly, it hardly seems possible, in general terms, to declare the non-prosecution of violations of its central values, such as the right to life, to be in the public interest. Furthermore, as made clear at the outset, the TRC's legal scheme on amnesty demands the prosecution of those who were not granted amnesty. Not only might the legitimacy of the whole mechanism be seriously harmed should prosecutions not follow, but victims who relied on the central proposition of post-TRC prosecutions when accepting

[31] Interview with Charles Villa-Vicencio in Cape Town (March 29, 2006).

the indemnification of perpetrators might justifiably feel betrayed. Furthermore, a central statement of the Constitution is, according to its section 1(a), that South African democracy is based on the values of the advancement of human rights, freedom and equality to which the Bill of Rights gives specific expression. Constitutional Court judge Albie Sachs has pointed out that:

> Nothing shows greater disrespect for the principles of equality, human dignity and freedom than the clandestine use of state power to murder and dispose of opponents. It follows that any exercise of judicial power which has the effect of directly inhibiting the capacity of the state subsequently to secure accountability for such conduct goes to the heart of South Africa's new constitutional order.[32]

This statement forcefully demonstrates how important it is for the public interest to prosecute the crimes committed by the apartheid security forces. To do otherwise would be in blatant opposition to these principles, undermine the rule of law according to section 1(c) of the Constitution and would do nothing to promote a human rights culture. Any decision not to prosecute that is not prompted by practical realities, such as availability of evidence, thus, cannot be justified. Moreover, due to the aforementioned forceful assertion of constitutional rights and values, the Constitution implicitly prohibits the use of discretion in this regard altogether, as it would subtract from these fundamental legal pillars. In a legal sense and in the public interest the Constitution even obliges the NPA to prosecute violations of the Bill of Rights wherever possible.

The High Court of Pretoria accordingly and correctly declared the policy amendment unconstitutional. The government is barred from introducing a similar indemnity process in the future. Any discretionary decision of the NPA not to prosecute gross human rights violations, although there is sufficient evidence and a prospect of success is therefore unconstitutional. Furthermore, the lack of progress on criminal

[32] *S. v Basson* (CC) Case no. CCT 30/03 10 March 2004 at para. 112 (separate opinion of Sachs J.).

proceedings does not do justice to the Constitution's general requirement to protect the Bill of Rights by applying the criminal law. Thus, the government is obliged to provide more support and must refrain from restrictive interference.

1.2 *International law obligations*

The question whether the South African state's present conduct of criminal investigations and prosecutions of politically motivated human rights violations satisfies legal requirements also has implications under international law, as many of the crimes might constitute international crimes. The litigation at the Constitutional Court in the Basson case already highlighted that international law places obligations on the NPA and national courts regarding criminal accountability for past human rights abuses, which must certainly be considered to a far higher degree in the future than has thus far been the case.[33] The following subchapter seeks to outline in broad terms whether the South African state is obliged, under international law, to institute criminal proceedings when there is evidence supporting charges in cases of political human rights violations during the apartheid era, and likewise whether refraining from instituting criminal proceedings under such conditions violates international law. 'Prosecution' in this context refers to the criminal investigation, charging and possible sentencing of perpetrators alleged to have committed the type of crimes referred to previously, if there is sufficient evidence that there is a reasonable prospect of a successful conviction.[34]

In the South African context, academic research has focussed largely on the question of whether the TRC amnesty programme violated international obligations.[35] Although the question of whether states

[33] See *supra* Chapter 2(2.3).

[34] See K. Ambos *Straflosigkeit von Menschenrechtsverletzungen* (1997) 163.

[35] J. Dugard 'Dealing with crimes of a past regime. Is amnesty still an option?' (1999) 12 *Leiden Journal of International Law* 1001–15; J. Dugard 'Is the truth and reconciliation process compatible with international law? An unanswered question' (1997)

have a duty under international law to prosecute must be assessed under the same premises, determining the legality of an amnesty under international law must be done in a particular way. While a general and unconditional amnesty would not be acceptable under international law, the South African scheme on conditional amnesty needed to be judged in a differentiated manner.[36] A restricted amnesty was inevitably necessary and legally permissible for the restoration of peace in the transitional society.[37] As has already been outlined above, the TRC Act fulfilled these conditions. However, the same circumstances no longer apply with the passage of time. These specific national features which were considered with respect to amnesty laws, thus, cannot be considered when determining whether South Africa has a duty under international law to prosecute.

It is clear that under certain circumstances international law imposes an obligation on states to prosecute international crimes, such as crimes against humanity or war crimes.[38] Duties to prosecute derive first and foremost from international covenants but might also derive from customary international law.[39] It is necessary to consider whether the criminal acts of the apartheid forces committed abroad or in South Africa by SADF or police members constitute crimes under international law covered by international law obligations.

South African Journal on Human Rights 258–68; A. du Bois-Pedain *Transitional amnesty in South Africa* (2007) 300–35; G. Werle *Principles of international criminal law* (2005) paras. 188–92; M.E. Bennun 'Amnesty and international law' in C. Villa-Vicencio and E. Doxtader (eds) *The provocations of amnesty* (2003) 92–114. See also *The Azanian Peoples Organisation and others v The President of South Africa and others* (CC) Case no. CCT 17/96 25 July 1996.

36 G. Werle *Principles of international criminal law* (2005) paras. 190–91; J. Dugard 'Dealing with crimes of a past regime. Is amnesty still an option?' (1999) 12 *Leiden Journal of International Law* 1001 at 1009–13; C. Kress 'War crimes committed in non-international armed conflicts and the emerging system of international criminal justice' (2000) 30 *Israel yearbook on human rights* 103 at 167–68.

37 Ibid.

38 G. Werle *Principles of international criminal law* (2005) para. 177.

39 Ibid., para. 179.

1.2.1 *Treaty law*

Various statutory sources of international law impose specific duties on states to institute criminal proceedings if treaty obligations are breached. As such, the four Geneva Conventions of 1949[40] and the Convention against Torture and other Cruel, Inhuman or Degrading Treatment or Punishment of 26 June 1987 (hereinafter "Torture Convention") are of particular relevance.

Each of the four Geneva Conventions outlines a catalogue of prohibited grave breaches of prohibitions of the Conventions.[41] Common to them all are, *inter alia*, any wilful act of killing, torture or inhuman treatment including biological experiments, wilfully causing great suffering or serious injury to body or health, unlawful deportation or transfer or unlawful confinement of a protected person. Apart from defining the breaches, each Convention explicitly obliges signatory states to provide for effective legal sanctions to prohibit grave breaches and 'to search for persons alleged to have committed, or to have ordered to be committed, such grave breaches' and to 'bring such persons, regardless of their nationality, before its own courts'.[42] These provisions undoubtedly convey a duty to prosecute perpetrators of grave beaches.[43] South Africa acceded to the Geneva Conventions in 1952.[44] The Conventions' application is, however, according to Article 2 common to the four Conventions (hereinafter "Article 2"), primarily confined to international armed conflicts. Purely internal conflicts are generally excluded from the Conventions' ambit.

---

40 Convention I for the Amelioration of the Condition of the Wounded and Sick in Armed Forces in the Field; Convention II for the Amelioration of the Condition of Wounded, Sick and Shipwrecked Members of Armed Forces at Sea; Convention III relative to the Treatment of Prisoners of War; Convention IV relative to the Protection of Civilian Persons in Time of War; Geneva 12 August 1949.

41 Article 50 Convention I, art. 51 Convention II, art. 130 Convention III, art. 147 Convention IV.

42 Article 49 Convention I, art. 50 Convention II, art. 129 Convention III and art. 146 Convention IV.

43 M. Scharf 'The letter of the law: the scope of the international legal obligation to prosecute human rights crimes' (1996) 59 *Law & Contemporary Problems* 41 at 44.

44 J. Dugard *International law* (1994) 56.

With regard to the South African context, three major fields of operation of the apartheid security forces need to be distinguished: first, the security police's activities in resisting the liberation movement's opposition efforts inside South Africa; second the state's actions against the guerrilla activities of the Namibian liberation movement SWAPO; and finally, the military operations conducted by the SADF in Angola, the war against the Angolan army and Cuban forces.

The South African conflict between the security forces and the national liberation movements is of a genuinely internal character, notwithstanding the fact that on various occasions the ANC was attacked outside South Africa's borders. The character of the conflict with SWAPO in Namibia is less obvious.[45] South-West Africa was, at the time, *de facto*, a part of South Africa. In 1920 the territory was entrusted to South Africa by the League of Nations and, although the United Nations (hereinafter UN) subsequently revoked the mandate, South Africa remained entirely in charge of the political and administrative instruments of the territory.[46] The country only gained independence in 1990. It is, thus, not possible to characterise Namibia of the time as a sovereign state.[47] Thus, the conditions of this conflict do not qualify it as an international conflict. The war fought against Angola, which was started during the 1970s and drastically intensified during the 1980s, however, must certainly be classified as an international armed conflict in terms of Article 2 of the Conventions. South Africa is under an obligation in terms of the four Geneva Conventions to prosecute possible grave breaches which occurred during this war.[48]

An obligation to prosecute human rights violations committed in Namibia and South Africa might, however, be established under article

---

45 See for human rights violations committed during security force operations in Namibia: *TRC Report*, vol. 2, chap. 2, paras. 73–157.

46 *S. v Basson* (CC) Case no. CCT 30/03 9 September 2005 at paras. 194–196.

47 The Constitutional Court in the Basson matter explicitly refrained from exploring the precise characterisation of the conflict with SWAPO (*S. v Basson* (CC) Case no. CCT 30/03 9 September 2005 at para. 179).

48 See for human rights violations committed by the SADF in Angola: *TRC Report*, vol. 2, chap. 2, paras. 10–72.

3 common to the Geneva Conventions (hereinafter "Article 3"), which lays down minimum standards, which must be fulfilled in non-international armed conflicts. According to Article 3, persons not actively taking part in the armed conflict shall not be subjected to *inter alia* violence to life and bodily integrity, in particular, murder of all kinds, mutilation, cruel treatment and torture. The application of Article 3 to the conflict in South Africa and the SWAPO conflict would, however, mean that the threshold of an 'armed conflict' was reached. This is the case in protracted states of armed violence between governmental authorities and organised armed groups.[49] The fight against SWAPO guerrilla activities, which took place mainly in the northern border regions of Namibia's Owamboland but also in Angola, was conducted primarily by military means and certainly reached high levels of prolonged armed violence.[50] It has also been classified as an armed conflict by the Constitutional Court, which stated in the Basson judgment that, regardless of whether the conflict in Namibia was international or not, the minimum standard of Article 3 would apply.[51]

Whether the same can be concluded with regard to the conflict with the liberation movement, mainly ANC and PAC, in South Africa is rather doubtful. In contrast to riots and occasional disruptions and clashes, an armed conflict requires high levels of protracted violent conflict.[52] The apartheid conflict, however, never reached the stage of full-scale civil or guerrilla warfare. Although political unrest climaxed during the 1980s, it was largely confined to township areas and the liberation movement never seriously threatened the apartheid state by military means.[53] The Constitutional Court consequentially stated in its AZAPO decision of 1996 that it was not convinced that the conflict

[49] C. Kress 'War crimes committed in non-international armed conflicts and the emerging system of international criminal justice' (2000) 30 *Israel yearbook on human rights* 103 at 117.

[50] See *TRC Report*, vol. 2, chap. 2, paras. 1–157.

[51] *S. v Basson* (CC) Case no. CCT 30/03 9 September 2005 at para. 179.

[52] M. Scharf 'The letter of the law: the scope of the international legal obligation to prosecute human rights crimes' (1996) 59 *Law & Contemporary Problems* 41 at 44.

[53] See also A. du Bois-Pedain *Transitional amnesty in South Africa* (2007) 323–24.

reached levels required for an armed conflict in terms of Article 3.[54] Thus, Article 3 applies in the Namibian context but does not apply to the conflict within South Africa.

However, does this mean that South Africa has an obligation under the Geneva Conventions to prosecute the political crimes committed during the Namibian conflict? The Convention's formulation of an obligation to prosecute extends explicitly to cases of grave breaches and does not deal with Article 3. It is nevertheless pointed out by legal scholars that the prohibitions of Article 3 must be viewed as included in the grave breaches doctrine, since only such an interpretation would do justice to the development of human rights protection mechanisms during the preceding decades.[55] Such an approach seems questionable, considering the conscious separation of Article 3 and the grave breaches doctrine in terms of the state's duty to prosecute. However, it must be borne in mind that this differentiation stems from a conviction to maintain a strict separation of internal and international conflicts. This approach has become increasingly blurred in international law, especially since the ruling of the International Court of Justice in the Nicaragua case.[56] With regard to such developments, there is in fact no justification to treat breaches of Article 3, which occurred in internal conflicts, different from those that occurred in international conflicts. Civilians must, therefore, also be treated as protected persons. The Constitutional Court has also strongly expressed its willingness to accept an overlap of internal and international conflicts in analysing the application of Article 3 in the framework of the overall protection regime of the Geneva Conventions.[57] Thus, breaches of Article 3 must be interpreted as constituting grave breaches in terms of the Conven-

---

[54] *The Azanian Peoples Organisation and others v The President of South Africa and others* (CC) Case no. CCT 17/96 25 July 1996 at para. 29.

[55] G. Werle *Principles of international criminal law* (2005) para. 180.

[56] K. Ambos *Straflosigkeit von Menschenrechtsverletzungen* (1997) 185.

[57] *S. v Basson* (CC) Case no. CCT 30/03 9 September 2005 at para. 179.

tions.[58] The duty to prosecute as outlined in the Geneva Conventions, thus, extends to violations of the rules for internal armed conflicts.

The effect of this interpretation is that South Africa has an obligation under the Geneva Conventions to prosecute any breach of Article 3 that occurred in the conflict with the SWAPO liberation movement in Namibia.

Further obligations regarding the internal conflicts might derive from the two additional 1977 Protocols to the Geneva Conventions. Article 1(4) of Protocol I[59] supplements Article 2 of the Geneva Conventions so that jurisdiction is extended to armed conflicts fought against colonial domination and alien occupation and against racist regimes in the exercise of the right of self-determination.[60] Thus, the full application of the Geneva Conventions according to Article 2 is extended to the situations outlined in Protocol I. The Protocol was apparently motivated to a large degree by the apartheid conflict in South Africa.[61] The outlined situations clearly fit the Namibian conflict. Protocol II[62] supplements Article 3 of the Geneva Conventions to the effect that it shall include

---

58 G. Werle *Principles of international criminal law* (2005) para. 180; K. Ambos *Straflosigkeit von Menschenrechtsverletzungen* (1997) 186; A. du Bois-Pedain *Transitional amnesty in South Africa* (2007) 306. See further on the distinction between international and non-international conflict C. Kress 'War crimes committed in non-international armed conflicts and the emerging system of international criminal justice' (2000) 30 *Israel yearbook on human rights* 103 at 114–23; T. Meron 'International criminalisation of internal atrocities' (1995) 89 *AmJIntL* 554–77; *Prosecutor v Dusko Tadic*, Decision on the defence motion for interlocutory appeal on jurisdiction (AC) Case no. IT-94-1-AR72 2 October 1995 para. 83.

59 Protocol Additional to the Geneva Conventions of 12 August 1949, and Relating to the Protection of Victims of International Armed Conflicts (Protocol I), 8 June 1977.

60 The right is enshrined in the Charter of the United Nations and the Declaration on Principles of International Law concerning Friendly Relations and Co-operation among States in accordance with the Charter of the United Nations.

61 J. Dugard *International law* (1994) 334.

62 Protocol Additional to the Geneva Conventions of 12 August 1949, and Relating to the Protection of Victims of Non-International Armed Conflicts (Protocol II), 8 June 1977.

armed conflicts that take place in the territory of a High Contracting Party between its armed forces and dissident armed forces or other organised armed groups, which under responsible command, exercise such control over a part of its territory as to enable them to carry out sustained and concerted military operations.

Both Protocols, however, again require an armed conflict, which did not exist for the internal South African conflict. Furthermore, the requirements of Protocol II were clearly not met by the expansion of militant opposition activities in South Africa, which were far from being able to exercise sustained military operations in apartheid South Africa. Moreover, South Africa only became party to the Protocols in November 1995, which, thus, have no application for state sponsored crimes committed during the apartheid era.[63] Whether the Protocol I in that exact form codified customary international law, which was already applicable during the period in question, is rather doubtful.[64] This is especially so for South Africa, which specifically refrained from acceding to the Protocols to avoid their possible application to the state's fight against liberation movement activities.[65]

A further treaty source establishing an obligation to investigate and charge perpetrators of gross human rights violations is the Torture Convention. The covenant, which entered into force in 1987, requires each signatory state to ensure that acts of torture are investigated, charged and sentenced.[66] Torture in terms of the Convention is, according to Article 1(1), defined as any act by which severe pain or suffering, whether physical or mental, is intentionally inflicted on a person for such purposes as obtaining from him or a third person information or a confession, punishing him for an act he or a third person has committed or is suspected of having committed, or intimidating or coercing

---

[63] *The Azanian Peoples Organisation and others v The President of South Africa and others* (CC) Case no. CCT 17/96 25 July 1996 at para. 29.

[64] A. du Bois-Pedain *Transitional amnesty in South Africa* (2007) 323.

[65] J. Dugard 'Is the truth and reconciliation process compatible with international law? An unanswered question' (1997) *South African Journal on Human Rights* 258 at 265.

[66] See articles 4–7 Torture Convention.

him or a third person, or for any reason based on discrimination of any kind, when such pain or suffering is inflicted by or at the instigation of or with the consent or acquiescence of a public official or other person acting in an official capacity.

The TRC found that the South African police systematically used torture against the liberation movement for political and often arbitrary reasons, but mostly to force them to cooperate or disclose information about underground activities.[67] There can be no doubt that this practice constitutes torture in terms of the Convention. Yet South Africa only ratified the Torture Convention on 10 December 1998. Moreover, according to a decision of the Committee Against Torture, a treaty body established under Article 17 of the Torture Convention, the Convention only covers incidents, which took place after its entry into force in 1987.[68] It is also not possible to sustain the proposition that South Africa might nevertheless, by acceding to the Convention, have accepted a duty to prosecute all as yet unpunished acts of torture that took place after 1987. Article 28 of the 1969 Vienna Convention on the Law of Treaties, to which South Africa is a party, makes it clear that a convention only is applicable to situations which occurred after the entry into force of the convention for the signatory state in question. According to Article 27(2) Torture Convention, it only enters into force 30 days after ratification by acceding states. Thus, no duty to prosecute arises from the Convention for South Africa.

Eventually it is necessary to address the question of whether South Africa is obliged under international conventions to prosecute the racial segregation and discrimination of apartheid as such.[69] According to Article I.1 of the International Convention on the Suppression and Punishment of the Crime of Apartheid of 1973 (hereinafter Apartheid

[67] *TRC Report*, vol. 6, s. 5, chap. 2, para. 16.

[68] Report of the Committee Against Torture to the General Assembly on its 45th session on 21 June 1990, supplement No. 44 (A/45/44), Annex V, para. 7.5.

[69] See generally on apartheid as a crime against humanity R.C. Slye 'Apartheid as a crime against humanity: a submission to the South African Truth and Reconciliation Commission' (1998–1999) 20 *Michigan Journal of International Law* 267–300.

Convention)[70] signatory states declare apartheid to be a crime against humanity and all racist and discriminatory acts flowing from the apartheid policies as crimes violating the principles of international law. Article II of the Convention outlines policies and practices of racial segregation and discrimination, which typically occurred during the apartheid era, as criminal conduct in terms of the Convention. According to Article IV of the Convention, signatory states are obliged to prosecute persons accused of acts which constitute crimes of apartheid under the Convention.

However, South Africa never became a party to the Apartheid Convention, not even today.[71] The Convention, thus, only establishes an obligation to prosecute the discriminatory policies of apartheid for the present government, if the Convention became part of customary international law. Although the Apartheid Convention was not unanimously adopted by states[72] some commentators have contended that the Apartheid Convention's definition of apartheid as a crime against humanity has meanwhile found expression as customary international law.[73] Also the Rome Statute for the International Criminal Court has incorporated in its Article 7(1)(j) the crime of apartheid as a crime against humanity.[74] Nevertheless, considering the limited international

---

70 International Convention on the Suppression and Punishment of the Crime of Apartheid, ratification by General Assembly resolution 3068 (XXVIII) of 30 December 1973, entry into force 18 July 1976.

71 J. Dugard 'Is the truth and reconciliation process compatible with international law? An unanswered question' (1997) *South African Journal on Human Rights* 258 at 262; A. du Bois-Pedain *Transitional amnesty in South Africa* (2007) 325.

72 R.C. Slye 'Apartheid as a crime against humanity: a submission to the South African Truth and Reconciliation Commission' (1998–1999) 20 *Michigan Journal of International Law* 267 at 293.

73 J. Dugard 'Is the truth and reconciliation process compatible with international law? An unanswered question' (1997) *South African Journal on Human Rights* 258 at 263; R.C. Slye 'Apartheid as a crime against humanity: a submission to the South African Truth and Reconciliation Commission' (1998–1999) 20 *Michigan Journal of International Law* 267 at 300.

74 The Rome Statute, however, only concerns crimes falling in the ambit of the Statute, thus only those committed after its entry into force in 2002 (A. du Bois-Pedain

support of the Apartheid Convention's obligation to prosecute,[75] it cannot be said that a specific obligation under customary international law has developed that conveys a specific duty on the South African state to prosecute the politics of apartheid as such. Furthermore, there would be no grounds in South African law to prosecute the political acts of apartheid. The acts of designing and executing the policies of apartheid were not penalised at the time. Within its own system, the legality of apartheid for the past remained intact, even under the new dispensation.[76] This follows from the Interim Constitution,[77] in which the apartheid laws were repealed, but which did not abolish the legality of apartheid retroactively.[78]

1.2.2 *Customary international law*

Apart from these limited sources in statutory international law, obligations for South Africa to prosecute might also arise out of customary international law.[79] The preamble of the Statute of the International Criminal Court (hereinafter "Rome Statute"), to which South Africa is also a party, states that 'the most serious crimes of concern to the international community as a whole must not go unpunished and that their effective prosecution must be ensured', as well as 'that it is

Transitional amnesty in South Africa (2007) 326).

75 R.C. Slye 'Apartheid as a crime against humanity: a submission to the South African Truth and Reconciliation Commission' (1998–1999) 20 *Michigan Journal of International Law* 267 at 293–95; A. du Bois-Pedain *Transitional amnesty in South Africa* (2007) 307–8.

76 G. Werle 'Without truth no reconciliation' (1996) 29 *Verfassung und Recht in Übersee—Law and politics in Africa, Asia and Latin America* 58 at 63.

77 Ibid. See section 229 on the continuation of existing laws. See generally H. Corder 'Towards a South African constitution' (1994) 57 4 *The Modern Law Review* 491–533.

78 See also M.R. Rwelamira 'Punishing past human rights violations: considerations in the South African context' in M.R. Rwelamira and G. Werle (eds) *Confronting past injustices* (1996) 3 at 7.

79 See on the forming of customary international law: J. Dugard *International law* (1994) 24–32.

the duty of every State to exercise its criminal jurisdiction over those responsible for international crimes'.[80]

Today, there is overwhelming scholarly support for the contention that customary international law has indeed developed after the second world war so that it places states under a duty to prosecute certain serious crimes under international law.[81] Although it is rather doubtful that this also obliges third party states, regardless of where the crime was committed, it is strongly supported with regard to the state of commission.[82] The progress of human rights protection mechanisms and treaties are cited as support for this contention. These include the International Law Commissions Draft Code of Crimes against the Peace

---

80 It needs to be pointed out that this passage alone does not constitute a specific obligation (C. Tomuschat 'The duty to prosecute international crimes committed by individuals' in H.J. Cremer et al., (eds) *Tradition und Weltoffenheit des Rechts* (2002) 315 at 338). Also, the wording 'jurisdiction' might be ambiguous regarding the interpretation of the precise scope of the statement (C. Kress 'War crimes committed in non-international armed conflicts and the emerging system of international criminal justice' (2000) 30 *Israel yearbook on human rights* 103 at 163).

81 K. Ambos *Straflosigkeit von Menschenrechtsverletzungen* (1997) 203; J. Dugard 'Is the truth and reconciliation process compatible with international law? An unanswered question' (1997) *South African Journal on Human Rights* 258 at 262; D.F. Orentlicher 'Settling accounts: the duty to prosecute human rights violations of a prior regime' (1991) 100 *The Yale Law Journal* 2537 at 2582–94; C. Tomuschat 'The duty to prosecute international crimes committed by individuals' in H.J. Cremer et al., (eds) *Tradition und Weltoffenheit des Rechts* (2002) 315 at 342–43; G. Werle *Principles of international criminal law* (2005) para. 179. C. Kress 'War crimes committed in non-international armed conflicts and the emerging system of international criminal justice' (2000) 30 *Israel yearbook on human rights* 103 at 162–63 cautions that whether a duty can be established in this regards depends on the methodological approach to determining customary international law. M. Scharf 'The letter of the law: the scope of the international legal obligation to prosecute human rights crimes' (1996) 59 *Law & Contemporary Problems* 41 at 59 rejects the notion of a customary law duty to prosecute since multiple examples of amnesty laws adopted by states in transition indicate that no consistent state practice in this regard exists.

82 G. Werle *Principles of international criminal law* (2005) para. 179; C. Tomuschat 'The duty to prosecute international crimes committed by individuals' in H.J. Cremer et al., (eds) *Tradition und Weltoffenheit des Rechts* (2002) 315 at 343.

and Security of Mankind; several declarations and resolutions of the UN General Assembly, such as the adopting of the Principles of International Cooperation in the Detection, Arrest, Extradition and Punishment of Persons Guilty of War Crimes and Crimes Against Humanity;[83] and the great progress made in trying crimes under international law since the Nuremberg trials, i.e. the International Criminal Tribunal for the Former Yugoslavia, the International Criminal Tribunal for Rwanda and the International Criminal Court.[84]

Basically, crimes under international law concern acts that involve direct and individual criminal responsibility as laid out by statutory or customary rules of international criminal law.[85] The core crimes under international law are war crimes, crimes against humanity, genocide and the crime of aggression.[86] The international element of crimes under international law is established through the scope and gravity of the acts in question, such as the systematic and large-scale use of force typically by state organs, suggesting that important values of the international community are concerned.[87] Such an international link exists, for instance, in cases of systematic violations of basic human rights.[88] Given the fact that during the apartheid conflict grave human rights violations occurred on a regular and widespread basis over decades, the relevance of international law is obvious.

War crimes are to a large extent covered by the codification of international humanitarian law, which has been referred to above. However, the international law duty to prosecute crimes against humanity as separate crimes under international law is of specific interest in the South African context. Crimes against humanity generally require a

[83] General Assembly resolution 3074 (XXVIII) of 3 December 1973.

[84] J. Dugard 'Dealing with crimes of a past regime. Is amnesty still an option?' (1999) 12 *Leiden Journal of International Law* 1001 at 1003; D.F. Orentlicher 'Settling accounts: the duty to prosecute human rights violations of a prior regime' (1991) 100 *The Yale Law Journal* 2537 at 2593.

[85] G. Werle *Principles of international criminal law* (2005) para. 72.

[86] Ibid., para. 74.

[87] Ibid., para. 81.

[88] Ibid., para. 102.

widespread or large-scale and systematic attack on a population or parts of a population or large groups of civilians.[89] The attack needs to target a specific group, a civilian population or also a political group.[90] The specific disruption of values of the international community in cases of crimes against humanity occurs by systematic or large-scale violations of fundamental human rights of the civilian population.[91] Recent developments mean that crimes against humanity are no longer required to take place in the context of an armed or international conflict.[92]

Torture on a widespread and systematic scale is, on this basis, typically considered to be a crime against humanity.[93] As such, under customary international law torture is understood to be the infliction of severe pain or suffering by a person acting in an official capacity especially if this is part of a widespread or systematic practice.[94] Widespread and systematic use of extrajudicial killings and abductions or enforced disappearance of persons are also typically considered to be crimes against humanity, if such conduct was authorised, supported or acquiesced in by the state or a political organisation.[95]

Of the criminal acts committed by the state security forces during the conflict in South Africa, murder, kidnapping and abduction are some of the most prominent.[96] As has already been pointed out in this book,

[89] G. Werle *Principles of international criminal law* (2005) paras. 82 and 666; C. Tomuschat 'The duty to prosecute international crimes committed by individuals' in H.J. Cremer et al., (eds) *Tradition und Weltoffenheit des Rechts* (2002) 315 at 340; K. Ambos *Straflosigkeit von Menschenrechtsverletzungen* (1997) 187–88.

[90] G. Werle *Principles of international criminal law* (2005) para. 633.

[91] Ibid., para. 84.

[92] K. Ambos *Straflosigkeit von Menschenrechtsverletzungen* (1997) 188; C. Kress 'War crimes committed in non-international armed conflicts and the emerging system of international criminal justice' (2000) 30 *Israel yearbook on human rights* 103 at 127; R.C. Slye 'Apartheid as a crime against humanity: a submission to the South African Truth and Reconciliation Commission' (1998–1999) 20 *Michigan Journal of International Law* 267 at 286.

[93] G. Werle *Principles of international criminal law* (2005) para. 710.

[94] A. Cassese *International criminal law* (2003) 119.

[95] Ibid., 74 and 80; G. Werle *Principles of international criminal law* (2005) paras. 675–77 and 752–57.

[96] See on the use of the security forces of such practices *supra* Chapters 1 and 2.

acts of torture were committed by the security forces on a widespread basis. In fact torture of prisoners was a very common tool to get information. Political prisoners were commonly subjected to often severe torture in order to move them to work for the police as informants or to extract information on their colleagues. Torture was so common that thousands of prisoners became victim of such conduct. What in many cases preceded the torture of political captives was the kidnapping of the opposition activist and what usually followed such conduct in cases of denied cooperation was the elimination of the liberation activist. Extrajudicial killings and abductions of apartheid opponents increased significantly from the early 1980s onwards and were a means often used to combat political resistance. It is clear from this that there was a systematic pattern in the state security force's use of torture and, to a lesser but still very significant degree, of kidnapping and murder of political opponents in the quest to quell resistance to apartheid. In terms of the aforementioned definition of crimes against humanity, state organs committed such acts on a large scale and widespread basis. The acts were directed at a political group—the opponents to apartheid.

However, a legal evaluation of this subject denied that the high threshold required for actions to constitute crimes against humanity was met in the South African context.[97] With regard to torture, it is referred specifically to Article 7(2) of the Rome Statute, which requires the crime against humanity to be committed in the furtherance of a state policy to commit such violations. As such, it is pointed out that many of the criminal acts were committed on an operational level only and, though they were certainly accepted or even welcomed by superior authorities as they contributed to the purpose of quashing the resistance, there is not sufficient proof that torture was part of a state policy or even ordered by figures at the highest political levels.[98] The crimes were not committed in a holistic and concentrated effort to violate rights but rather on a case by case basis.

This view, however, is not convincing. The definition of torture in the Rome Statute does not necessarily conform to the understanding

---

[97] A. du Bois-Pedain *Transitional amnesty in South Africa* (2007) 326–27.

[98] Ibid.

of torture as a crime against humanity in terms of customary international law. In fact, the customary international law definition of crimes against humanity does not require a policy element.[99] Since the Nuremberg trials, most definitions of crimes against humanity did not encompass a policy element.[100] The policy element in the Rome Statute can be interpreted as a mere reference to the requirements of a widespread and systematic attack.[101] The systematic and widespread nature of the crimes has already been pointed out. Furthermore, the TRC found sufficient indicators that the criminal conduct in question was not something developed solely on an operational level but clearly resulted, at least indirectly, from policy guidelines of the highest state levels demanding a violent, if not even criminal conduct.[102]

Even if one opts for requiring a policy element in terms of persecution on political, ethnic or religious grounds,[103] which it has been pointed out is not required by the customary law definition, the crimes of the South African security forces committed in quashing the resistance to apartheid can be defined as crimes against humanity. The definition employed by the French *Cour de Cassation* for instance held that crimes against humanity are

> ...inhumane acts and persecution committed in a systematic manner in the name of a State practising a policy of ideological supremacy, not only against persons by reason of their membership of a racial or religious community, but also against the opponents of that policy whatever the form of their opposition.[104]

---

[99] G. Werle *Principles of international criminal law* (2005) para. 666.

[100] Ibid.

[101] Ibid., para. 667.

[102] See *TRC Report*, vol. 5, chap. 6, paras. 84–99.

[103] See J. Dugard 'Is the truth and reconciliation process compatible with international law? An unanswered question' (1997) *South African Journal on Human Rights* 258 at 263.

[104] *Fédération Nationale des Déportés et Internés Résistants et Patriotes and Others v Barbie* (France, Cour de Cassation) [1984] 78 ILR 125 at 137.

It is clear that the human rights violations were committed by the security forces in the course of furthering and protecting the racist and oppressive apartheid state policy of ideological supremacy. The crimes were committed on racial grounds but mainly against opponents for their political opposition, which underlines that the crimes in question must be seen as crimes against humanity. The South African Constitutional Court on occasion of the Basson case also stated that it was firmly convinced that apartheid led to the commission of crimes against humanity, though it did so in rather general terms without explaining whether this held true only for the situation in Namibia or also for the conflict in South Africa.[105]

As a result, the systematic and large-scale use of kidnapping, extra-judicial killings and torture by the apartheid security forces, which was committed to protect the apartheid regime against political opposition, qualifies as crimes against humanity in terms of the above mentioned definitions. Thus, on the basis of the customary international law duty to prosecute crimes against humanity, South Africa is obliged to investigate and prosecute such acts of murder, abduction and torture committed by the apartheid state security forces.[106]

---

105 *S. v Basson* (CC) Case no. CCT 30/03 10 March 2004 at para. 37.

106 Some even argue for a rule under customary international law imposing a duty on states to prosecute every human rights violation committed by organs of a prior regime, even in cases where they occur on an occasional basis without constituting crimes against humanity (D.F. Orentlicher 'Settling accounts: the duty to prosecute human rights violations of a prior regime' (1991) 100 *The Yale Law Journal* 2537 at 2583–85). In support of this notion reference is made to a wide range of United Nations and intergovernmental organisations' practices and activities with regard to the prohibition of certain human rights violations as well as the incorporation of such a duty in various international instruments such as the Inter-American Convention to Prevent and Punish Torture or the Draft Declaration on the Protection of Persons from Enforced Disappearance prepared under UN auspices. Above the International Covenant on Civil and Political Rights is cited for support. It is, however, rather doubtful whether such a rule under customary international law has indeed already developed.

1.2.3 *Conclusion*

South Africa is obliged under international law to prosecute any crime constituting a grave breach in terms of the four Geneva Conventions, violations of common Article 3 and acts of the security forces as far as they constitute crimes against humanity under customary international law. The Constitutional Court has pointed out in the Basson judgment the circumstances in which South African courts have jurisdiction to try crimes which were committed in Namibia and abroad.[107]

Any of the international law obligations outlined only concern acts, which are attributable to the state and committed by state organs. If the NPA refrains from investigating and prosecuting members of the apartheid security police, SADF or other state employees who are alleged to have committed political crimes, which constitute grave breaches or breaches of Article 3 or crimes against humanity, despite evidence that there are sufficient prospects of a successful prosecution, South Africa will violate international law. Any legal setup providing for extended non-prosecution of apartheid era human rights offenders would equally constitute a violation of international law.

The government must further, as also explicitly required by the Geneva Conventions, undertake to enact appropriate legislation to provide for criminal proceedings to take place. In this regard it must refrain from enacting restrictive measures since otherwise it would breach its obligations under international law. The reluctant and restrictive approach of the South African government towards criminal proceedings equally does not do justice to the requirements of international law.

2. *The Prosecution of Torture and Statutes of Limitation*

In the preceding subchapters, it has been shown that under certain circumstances South Africa is obliged to prosecute acts of torture committed during the apartheid conflict, should those acts constitute crimes against humanity. However, there is one major obstacle for the

[107] See *supra* Chapter 2(2.3 and 2.5).

NPA to comply with this obligation. According to the limitation period in section 18 of the Criminal Procedure Act, the right to lay criminal charges, except for *inter alia* cases of murder and kidnapping as well as the crime of genocide, crimes against humanity and war crimes, as contemplated in section 4 of the Implementation of the Rome Statute of the International Criminal Court Act, lapses after 20 years from the point of time the crime was committed.[108] The prosecution of offences listed in section 18 never becomes statute barred. The 20 year limit is not absolute since prescription is interrupted by the institution of a prosecution.[109]

Concerning the prosecution of the most serious crimes relevant for post-TRC prosecutions, murder, kidnapping and torture, the statute of limitation has the effect that murder and kidnapping are not subject to any time limitation. Torture, however, is prosecuted as assault or assault causing grievous bodily harm, which is covered by the statute of limitation and cannot be prosecuted after 20 years from the time the offence was committed. Thus, section 18 of the Criminal Procedure Act currently precludes the NPA from prosecuting any acts of torture that were committed before 1988. This is especially serious considering the fact that the mid- to late 1980s witnessed a climax in violence in South Africa, which resulted in increased incidents of torture. The massive delay in instituting criminal proceedings in a significant number of post-TRC cases has, therefore, led and continues to lead to many cases of torture being time-barred from prosecution. However, the following subchapter seeks to outline the possibility to argue that under

---

108 Section 18 of the Criminal Procedure Act ('Prescription of right to institute prosecution') reads:
The right to institute a prosecution for any offence, other than the offences of- (*a*) murder; (*b*) treason committed when the Republic is in a state of war; (*c*) robbery, if aggravating circumstances were present; (*d*) kidnapping; (*e*) child-stealing; or (*f*) rape; (*g*) the crime of genocide, crimes against humanity and war crimes, as contemplated in section 4 of the Implementation of the Rome Statute of the International Criminal Court Act, 2002, shall, unless some other period is expressly provided by law, lapse after the expiration of a period of 20 years from the time when the offence was committed.

109 See *R. v Magcayi* 1951 (4) SA 356 (O) and *R. v Friedman* 1948 (2) SA 1034 (C).

international law the statute of limitation of section 18 of the Criminal Procedure Act does not apply to torture. It also seeks to point out ways under constitutional law to neutralise the statute of limitation.

Section 18(g) of the Criminal Procedure Act itself exempts certain international crimes from the statute of limitation. It provides that the crime of genocide, crimes against humanity and war crimes, as contemplated in section 4 of the Implementation of the Rome Statute of the International Criminal Court Act no. 27 of 2002, are not covered by the statute of limitation. This exemption, however, is only applicable from the point of its introduction in 2002 and is obviously only related to the crimes contemplated in the Rome Statute. Article 29 Rome Statute determines that statutes of limitation are not applicable to crimes within the jurisdiction of the court. This provision required implementation in the national law of signatory states.[110] In South Africa, this was done with the introduction of section 18(g) of the Criminal Procedure Act, which is designed to implement only the Rome Statute, from 2002 forward, and not to apply to all past circumstances of international crimes.

The UN Convention on the Non-Applicability of Statutory Limitations to War Crimes and Crimes Against Humanity of 16 November 1968 also constitutes an attempt to rule out any obstacles in national law to the prosecution of serious international crimes. According to Article 1 of the Convention, national statutes of limitation shall not be applicable to war crimes and crimes against humanity. However, thus far only 50 states have signed the treaty[111] and South Africa has never been party to it. The rules outlined therein are, thus, not applicable.

It has been argued, however, that there is also a rule under customary international law that precludes the application of national statutes of limitation at least with regard to the most egregious of international crimes, such as genocide, crimes against humanity and torture.[112] Statutes of limitation would contradict the rules penalising such crimes. It is submitted that these crimes are so abhorrent that their authors

[110] W.A. Schabas *An introduction to the International Criminal Court* 3ed (2007) 233.
[111] See http://www.ohchr.org/english/countries/ratification/6.htm.
[112] A. Cassese *International criminal law* (2003) 319.

must be invariably punished, otherwise the important deterrent effect of preventing future reoccurrences could be undermined. Furthermore, the universal nature of international crimes is in conflict with various national statutes of limitations.[113] The French *Cour de Cassation* took a similar view as it ruled that crimes against humanity, in that case the murder of thousands of Jews during World War II, could not be subject to the French statute of limitation.[114] Other commentators have pointed out that whether and to what extent such a rule has become part of customary international law is far from being clear.[115] The moral and technical desirability for the non-application of statutory limitations to serious international crimes, which are the aspects mainly cited in support of a customary rule, is certainly not matched by a consistent state practice and *opinio juris* in this regard, as necessary for customary international law.[116]

Calls by states in support of a respective rule under international law have largely been made through resolutions of the UN General Assembly, which are not binding.[117] Moreover, the highly limited acceptance of the relevant UN convention and the lack of a consistent widespread practice in national approaches to the issue indicate that a state practice, in terms of customary international law, has yet to be established.[118] The European Convention on the Non-Applicability of Statutory Limitations to Crimes Against Humanity and War Crimes of 1974 has equally only been met with minimal support and has not

---

113 Ibid., 318.

114 *Fédération Nationale des Déportés et Internés Résistants et Patriotes and Others v Barbie* (France, Cour de Cassation) [1984] 78 ILR 125 at 315.

115 G. Werle *Principles of international criminal law* (2005) para. 553.

116 C. Kress 'War crimes committed in non-international armed conflicts and the emerging system of international criminal justice' (2000) 30 *Israel yearbook on human rights* 103 at 164–65.

117 W.A. Schabas *An introduction to the International Criminal Court* 3ed (2007) 233–34. See General Assembly resolutions 3(I); 170(II); 2583(XXIV); 2712(XXV); 2840(XXVI); 3020(XXVII); 3074(XXVIII).

118 S.R. Ratner and J.S. Abrams *Accountability for human rights atrocities in international law* (2001) 143–44; H. Kreicker 'Die völkerstrafrechtliche Unverjährbarkeit und die Regelung im Völkerstrafgesetzbuch' (2002) *Neue Justiz* 281 at 285.

entered into force yet.[119] Moreover, the process of drafting the Rome Statute for the International Criminal Court highlighted that the various delegations were clearly not in agreement as to the acceptance of rules under international law concerning statutes of limitation.[120] Furthermore, in the South African context, the most serious crimes of concern, such as murder, are, unlike the regulation of the respective legislation in France, which was examined by the *Cour de Cassation*,[121] exempted from the South African statute of limitation. Thus, a rule does not exist under customary international law that precludes the applicability of section 18 of the Criminal Procedure Act with regard to torture.

However, the non-applicability of the provision with regard to torture might also be argued under South African constitutional law.[122] During apartheid, the crimes of the security forces were virtually never prosecuted and operatives were protected by a system and policy of non-prosecution.[123] This practice of impunity is contrary to the values of human rights and the rule of law according to the democratic constitution. Thus, it might be argued that compelling constitutional implications require an interpretation of the statute of limitation to the effect that the limitation period is interrupted during the apartheid period when there was not a prospect of prosecution.[124] In the preceding subchapters it was pointed out that deliberate impunity for state sponsored, political and gross human rights violations is in stark conflict with fundamental constitutional values and international law. The state of impunity for state sponsored political crimes during the apartheid era is, thus, absolutely incompatible with the present constitutional order. The Constitutional Court found that the duty to prosecute extends to

[119] Ibid.

[120] Ibid.

[121] See W.A. Schabas *An introduction to the International Criminal Court* 3ed (2007) 233.

[122] See V. Nerlich *Apartheidkriminalität vor Gericht* (2002) 67–69.

[123] K. Koppe *Wiedergutmachung für die Opfer von Menschenrechtsverletzungen in Südafrika* (2005) 26.

[124] V. Nerlich *Apartheidkriminalität vor Gericht* (2002) 69. Nerlich, however, rejects this proposition considering that with murder and kidnapping the most serious crimes of apartheid remain prosecutable.

crimes committed before the Constitution came into effect. The same should be true concerning a possible interruption of the statute of limitation during times before its entry into force. These circumstances indeed provide good grounds to assume that compelling constitutional circumstances mean that the statute of limitation was interrupted during the state of systematic impunity for security force violence. Only from 1994 and more specifically from the coming into force of the Interim Constitution on 27 April 1994 onwards was there a realistic prospect and possibility for apartheid crimes to be prosecuted.

German courts took a similar view in the prosecution of political crimes committed under the Nazi regime and in the former socialist GDR. According to the *Bundesgerichtshof*, the German Federal Supreme Court, the German statute of limitation's limitation period was suspended until the capitulation of the German army in May 1945 if the crimes in question were condoned or ordered by the former regime and not prosecuted due to an unlawful policy of impunity for politically motivated gross human rights violations.[125] Similar findings were made with respect to certain crimes of state forces of the GDR and legislation was enacted accordingly after 1990.[126]

Academics have pointed out yet another way of neutralising the statute of limitation. It has been argued that the crimes of the security forces could be prosecuted directly as international crimes which, according to section 232 of the Constitution, would be directly applicable in South Africa as international law and not only under national South African law.[127] Section 18 of the Criminal Procedure Act would then have no application, as it is confined to South African crimes, such as assault.

It remains to be seen how, if at all, South African courts will be willing in potential future trials to interrogate and possibly follow such arguments. First, the NPA would be required to adopt a more open attitude to such approaches and not to strictly rely on the statute of limitation.

---

125 BGHSt 18, 367 (368–369).

126 BGHSt 40, 48–59; K. Marxen and G. Werle *Die strafrechtliche Aufarbeitung von DDR-Unrecht* (1999) 5–7.

127 See V. Nerlich *Apartheidkriminalität vor Gericht* (2002) 81–96.

3. *Strategies and Priorities*

The issue of strategy has proved to be of major concern in considering the approach towards post-TRC prosecutions. In the face of highly limited resources and considering the large number of *prima facie* politically motivated crimes for which amnesty was not granted, choices invariably have to be made regarding which cases to concentrate on with criminal proceedings.

However, the most important consideration regarding prosecution prioritisation is whether there is sufficient evidence available to prosecute or whether there is a sufficient prospect of gathering more evidence to prosecute successfully. Although there are potentially thousands of cases, most cannot be considered because the availability of evidence is too limited.[128] To a certain degree, the question of who to prosecute will also often be driven by the prosecutors' practical considerations concerning their specific strategy in certain cases. As such, the experience of Jan D'Oliveira has shown that it is often advisable in cases involving different levels of command to prosecute the operatives first in order to be able to establish a solid case against their superiors.[129] Nevertheless, with regard to those cases that would provide a reasonable practical prospect of success, those arguing against trials in the public debate frequently express doubts as to whether it is possible to decide whom to prosecute and whom not to prosecute using consistent criteria.[130] Should the focus be on those who created the policies of apartheid or those who executed orders and should liberation movement members be put on trial in an 'even-handed' way like apartheid agents?[131] Selective prosecutions could fail to establish accountability where the command and political responsibility actually lay.[132] The gross human rights violations committed in the name of the apartheid state were not

[128] Interview with Torie Pretorius and others in Pretoria (May 2, 2006).

[129] Interview by Gerhard Werle with Jan D'Oliveira in Pretoria (March 2004).

[130] Interview with Jan Wagener in Pretoria (May 8, 2006).

[131] See on such strategic dilemmas N. Rousseau 'Prosecutions' in E. Doxtader (ed) *Provoking questions* (2005) 37 at 44–45.

[132] See also A. du Bois-Pedain *Transitional amnesty in South Africa* (2007) 345.

a range of isolated acts but flowed from a systematic pattern of abuse that resulted from political guidelines and often from the orders of superiors. Although operatives are generally more easily implicated by evidence, to prosecute them alone and not also those from the higher ranks would, thus, not do justice to the systematic nature of apartheid policies. The question, thus, that needs to be addressed is which criteria should be used to identify higher priority cases.

With the prosecution guidelines for TRC-related cases, a rather inappropriate attempt was made to create prioritisation criteria. The following subchapter will deal with the issue of how to differentiate between cases on a consistent normative basis and will highlight ways concerning how to deal with limited evidence and the need to encourage further perpetrator disclosures.

3.1 *Prioritisation*

A very noteworthy approach to prioritisation has been presented by a lawyer closely involved with TRC matters.[133] It is suggested that generally the egregiousness and the rank and authority of the perpetrator should govern the decision whether to focus on a case or not. As such, it is viewed as a mitigating factor when a junior perpetrator has acted on the basis of specific instructions issued to him or when a crowd involved in mob violence is concerned. Aggravating circumstances include situations in which the perpetrator acted in a position of great influence, authority and leadership, thus, a position of high personal responsibility that enabled the perpetrator to determine whether and how the specific operation takes place, and which, therefore, could have allowed him to resort to legal means. The egregiousness of the offence in question should be determined on the basis of the proportionality test similar to that outlined for the granting of amnesty by the Amnesty Committee

[133] H. Varney *Exploring a prosecutions strategy in the aftermath of South Africa's Truth & Reconciliation Commission* discussion paper presented at the Foundation for Human Rights and International Centre for Transitional Justice conference 'Domestic prosecutions and transitional justice conference' (Magaliesburg, May 16–19, 2005)(on file with author).

according to section 20(3)(f) of the TRC Act.[134] Accordingly, an offence should be considered egregious if the political objective pursued is out of proportion to the gravity of the offence, which is determined by the scope and value of the violated human rights. On this basis, three categories of priority are identified: low priority cases involve non-egregious offences committed by junior perpetrators; middle order priority cases involve egregious offences committed at least by low ranks; and high priority cases concern egregious offences committed by senior perpetrators. Low priority cases should not be prosecuted at all. Most attention should be paid to high priority cases and middle order priority cases should be pursued when there are practical demands to do so or when resources allow it.

A number of examples suffice to illustrate the point.[135] The attempted murder of Frank Chikane is a high priority case. It involved a number of high-ranking security force officials, infringed against a high legal value and, considering the fact that Chikane was clearly a non-violent opponent and the objective of the offence was to protect the racist and oppressive apartheid regime, the offence was disproportionate.[136] Generally, an aggravating factor with regard to security forces crimes is that they could have resorted to far less violent means to achieve their goal. Especially during the many states of emergency during the 1980s, the state had a huge range of official legal tools at hand to quash resistance, such as detention for indefinite periods without charge or

[134] In terms of the TRC Act the proportionality test determined, *inter alia*, the polical character of the crime. It is important to remember that the Amnesty Committee applied the proportionality test very generously so that crimes that were clearly disproportionate to their aims were still considered to be politically motivated (A. du Bois-Pedain *Transitional amnesty in South Africa* (2007) 121–26. The practical implementation of the proportionality test by the Amnesty Committee thus cannot be adopted by the NPA when prioritising cases.

[135] H. Varney *Exploring a prosecutions strategy in the aftermath of South Africa's Truth & Reconciliation Commission* discussion paper presented at the Foundation for Human Rights and International Centre for Transitional Justice conference 'Domestic prosecutions and transitional justice conference' (Magaliesburg, May 16–19, 2005)(on file with author).

[136] Ibid.

trial and the banning of persons believed to be a security risk. Notwithstanding these options the security police often chose instead to murder their enemies.

The refusal of amnesty to 37 ANC leaders which might relate to the bombing and landmine campaigns and other violent acts ordered during the armed struggle of the ANC is also significant. It is contended that the overwhelming majority of such offences committed under orders of the NEC must be classified as non-egregious since they were proportional to the objective pursued.[137] The objective of the ANC was to liberate the country from an internationally condemned regime of racism and oppression of the population's majority and to establish a system based on democracy and human rights. It must also be pointed out that the liberation movement tried in vain to achieve its goals by means of public and non-violent political protest and only when after decades of massive oppression and intransigence of the apartheid government this proved fruitless did they resort to violent means of protest. Violent acts were overwhelmingly directed at state facilities and police or military personnel. They generally attempted, though often unsuccessfully, to avoid harm to civilians. Such acts, accordingly, cannot be seen as egregious, they should be of low priority. However, there were occasionally individual acts that were primarily directed at civilians that went beyond official ANC policy. Any conscious attack of liberation fighters on defenceless civilians, regardless of ethnic group, cannot be seen as proportional in terms of the struggle for liberation.[138]

The outlined criteria of this prioritisation proposal[139] seem to offer a consistent and plausible way of prioritising factors, as the personal responsibility of commanders is generally greater.

3.2 *The call for even-handedness*

The considerations regarding prioritisation according to egregiousness and the statements concerning the distinction between the liberation

137 Ibid.
138 Ibid.
139 Ibid.

movement and state forces also find support in the framework of the Constitution. The South African state is, according to section 1 of the Constitution, founded on the values of human dignity, freedom, equality, non-racialism, democracy and the advancement of human rights. In light of these parameters, acts of murder, torture and abduction, which were committed by the state security forces in order to oppress free and democratic political developments and to maintain a system of racism, inequality and violation of basic human dignity, in legal terms, cannot simply be equated with acts that were committed in a violent liberation struggle, conducted as a last resort and aimed only at state forces in order to establish these very constitutional values.

The decisive circumstance regarding the legal evaluation of 'even-handedness' lies, however, with the relevance of international law. As has been outlined above, the systematic, large-scale and widespread use of torture, extra-judicial killings and kidnapping of opposition activists by the state security forces are covered by an international law obligation to prosecute. In contrast to this, liberation movement crimes are not crimes under international law or crimes against humanity, since they were not orchestrated by state organs or on behalf of a state. From an international law viewpoint, the liberation movement conducted a lawful and legitimate struggle.[140] This strongly underlines the comparatively higher egregiousness of security forces crimes. In order for South Africa to fulfil its international law obligations, the NPA's first priority must be to prosecute the outlined systematic crimes orchestrated by the apartheid state forces.

It certainly does not mean that there is no criminal liability concerning e.g. the many civilians who fell victim to the landmine campaign by the ANC. It does, however, mean that on the basis of constitutional requirements as well as of international law requirements, the NPA's primary focus must be on prosecuting criminal acts committed by the security forces in the furtherance of apartheid. Constitutional Court

[140] M.R. Rwelamira 'Punishing past human rights violations: considerations in the South African context' in M.R. Rwelamira and G. Werle (eds) *Confronting past injustices* (1996) 3 at 16.

judge Albie Sachs underlined this perception when he made it clear that securing accountability for the clandestine use of state power to murder and dispose of opponents 'goes at the heart of South Africa's constitutional order'.[141]

However, the request for 'even-handedness' was nevertheless based on section 9 of the Constitution.[142] Section 9(1) of the Constitution states that everyone is equal before the law and section 9(3) prohibits the unfair discrimination through the State. It would certainly be unacceptable under section 9 to indemnify certain criminals generally while others are held criminally liable. Yet this does not answer the question of which cases must be considered more appropriate for prosecution. Section 9(1) of the Constitution only rules out differentiations that are not justified on reasonable grounds.[143] The abovementioned legal circumstances in international and constitutional law clearly provide such reasonable grounds for a differentiation.

The request for even-handedness towards apartheid crimes and liberation movement crimes, thus, is not of perceptible legal merit and must be considered as merely political. It should not be considered in any decision-making process of the prosecution authorities concerning on which cases to focus. There is no legal authority demanding equal prosecution of liberation movement and security force members and the process of post-TRC prosecutions would not be discredited in legal terms should the NPA primarily focus on former state forces. Nevertheless, for other societies in transition, opting for a similar system to deal with past atrocities, one must conclude that the new rulers and former liberation fighters must participate in the process unequivocally so that they are not exposed to political claims of unjust proceedings and a lack of 'even-handedness' in prosecutions and to avoid political obstacles to trials.[144]

---

141 See *supra* Chapter 4 note 32.

142 Interview with Jan Wagener in Pretoria (May 8, 2006).

143 See J. de Waal et al., *The Bill of Rights handbook* 4ed (2001) 199–222.

144 It must, however, be pointed out that the ANC did support the TRC amnesty proceedings and encouraged its members to apply for amnesty. Nevertheless there obviously were gaps, as highlighted by the applications of the 37 ANC leaders.

3.3 *Limited evidence*

In terms of strategy, another issue needs to be addressed, which is general paucity of evidence in TRC-related cases and the often heavy demands such cases place on prosecutors. Various high profile trials that failed, like those of Malan and Basson but also the Chikane case, where the convictions of Vlok and van der Merwe were not reached due to strong evidence, are proof of such difficulties.

Generally, the crimes of the security forces were committed in great secrecy and evidence was meticulously concealed and never properly investigated by the police.[145] Witnesses of the criminal acts were mostly involved in the deeds themselves. Urging them to cooperate with the State, would require prosecutors to find evidence, which implicates the potential state witnesses themselves.[146] Problems of evidence increase, the higher one looks in the chain of command of the apartheid state. Written orders or records of policy directives to combat the liberation movement by criminal means are rarely obtainable.[147] Furthermore, before the first democratic government was constituted in 1994, apartheid government and security force agents destroyed huge amounts of sensitive documents.[148]

Where the prospect of a successful conviction is limited due to the insufficient capacity to compile more evidence, such difficulties could, at least to a certain degree, be countered by an extended use of plea and sentence agreements in terms of section 105A of the Criminal Procedure Act.[149] The agreements might deal with far reaching issues, such as an admission of the accused regarding the details of the crime.[150] In exchange, the accused could be rewarded with a significantly reduced

---

[145] N. Rousseau 'Prosecutions' in E. Doxtader (ed) *Provoking questions* (2005) 37 at 45.

[146] Interview with Torie Pretorius and others in Pretoria (May 2, 2006).

[147] N. Rousseau 'Prosecutions' in E. Doxtader (ed) *Provoking questions* (2005) 37 at 46.

[148] See *TRC Report*, vol. 1, chap. 8, paras. 1–106; and *TRC Report*, vol. 5, chap. 6, para. 105.

[149] See also *supra* Chapter 2(9.2).

[150] Du Toit et al., *Commentary on the Criminal Procedure Act* service 35 (2006) § 105A 15–7.

sentence.[151] Thus, perpetrators willing to make disclosures regarding offences they were involved in could do so in exchange for a suspended and/or greatly reduced sentence under a plea bargain, as was already done in the Chikane case. The declared intention of the government to offer incentives for perpetrators to come forward and disclose could thereby be met. The extended use of plea-bargaining could be accompanied by specifically drafted directives applicable only for post-TRC criminal cases in order to meet the specific demands and challenges of post-TRC prosecutions.[152] According to section 105A(11) of the Criminal Procedure Act, the NDPP with the concurrence of the Minister of Justice can issue binding directives for the use and implementation of plea and sentence agreements. Consistent criteria could, thus, outline how to apply plea-bargaining to TRC-related cases, to treat and test information that is provided and to reward perpetrators willing to make full disclosures. It could also provide for victim participation and publication of information.

These measures could also easily replace the policy approach which the government considered, as perpetrators would be encouraged to make full disclosures. The benefit would be that for plea-bargaining the participation of victims is legally required,[153] the court proceedings and its records are accessible to the public, perpetrators have to admit their guilt publicly and although they might only receive low or suspended sentences, are held criminally liable, which avoids complete impunity. Since a court tests the validity of the agreement and assesses the guilt of the accused in a plea-bargaining situation, possibly also through a process of questioning and considering evidence,[154] such procedures certainly have far greater legal legitimacy with regard to the principle of the rule of law under section 1(c) of the Constitution than decisions

---

[151] Ibid., 15–5.

[152] L. Fernandez 'Post-TRC prosecutions in South Africa' in G. Werle (ed) *Justice in transition* (2006) 65 at 69–70.

[153] E. Du Toit et al., *Commentary on the Criminal Procedure Act* service 35 (2006) §105A 15-7.

[154] Ibid.

of the NDPP to grant impunity under unknown and untested circumstances. Plea-bargaining certainly cannot replace trials completely but is advisable where resources and evidence are limited, there is an increased interest for victims to reveal the facts of the case and the interest in avoiding years long, possibly futile, criminal proceedings.

Furthermore, it is trite to point out that the challenges of prosecuting higher echelons of the command structures could, to a certain degree, be met by the use of section 204 of the Criminal Procedure Act. According to section 204(2)(a) of the Criminal Procedure Act, a witness who testifies on behalf of the State shall be discharged from prosecution for the offence in question if the court is satisfied that he has answered all questions put to him frankly and honestly. The provision is designed to protect perpetrators of a crime from criminal liability who have testified for the prosecution against their co-perpetrators.[155] Especially lower level operatives, who are generally more easily implicated since they were the ones carrying out the operations, can be offered indemnity from prosecution should they testify against those from whom they received their orders. As has already been mentioned, the mechanism continues to be of enormous practical value for the PCLU.

The above discussion shows that there are worthwhile strategy approaches for TRC-related cases. However, it is important to remember that an imminent threat of prosecution will nevertheless usually still be required since it is rather unlikely that a perpetrator who previously refused to take part in the amnesty process would, subsequently, volunteer to cooperate with the NPA without such incentive.[156]

4. *General Prospects for Further Trials*

The fact that dozens of amnesty applications concerning *prima facie* politically motivated offences were refused due to a lack of full disclosure

---

[155] Ibid., service 33 (2004) § 204 23–50B.

[156] L. Fernandez 'Post-TRC prosecutions in South Africa' in G. Werle (ed) *Justice in transition* (2006) 65 at 70.

suggests that, potentially, a great number of cases could still be dealt with by the PCLU. Furthermore, in many instances of politically motivated human rights violations, amnesty was not applied for at all. Thus, from her experience during the TRC, a former Commissioner consequently estimated that a great number cases could still warrant further investigation.[157] This is also suggested by the fact that the TRC handed to the NPA a list containing over 300 references to criminal incidents, which came to light during the TRC investigations and hearings.

However, it has already been pointed out that the actual prospects for further trials depend on the availability of evidence and the willingness of co-perpetrators to testify on behalf of the State, among other things. It has been mentioned in the preceding paragraphs that evidence is often highly limited, especially when it comes to those who occupied the higher echelons of the state. That other former officials of the apartheid government would be willing to follow the example of Vlok's and van der Merwe's voluntary admissions in the Chikane case appears rather unlikely. The two had already cooperated greatly in the process during the TRC, at least compared to other leading apartheid officials and politicians, and were, thus, possibly more willing to cooperate again with the PCLU. Especially leading figures in the ranks of the SADF, who obviously also played a central role in the Chikane case, are likely to continue to refuse to cooperate in even the slightest regard, as was already the case during the TRC proceedings. The continued lapse of time aggravates problems concerning evidence gathering, as witnesses' memory of the crimes, which often happened over 20 years ago, diminish. Some potential witnesses may have passed away, as well as certain alleged perpetrators, such as Gideon Nieuwoudt or security police general Nicolaas van Rensburg. The delay also has other negative consequences, since public and political awareness generally decline.

Another vital precondition for the conduct of successful prosecutions, is that there are sufficient investigative resources and skilled and experienced investigators available to tackle the intricate cases of apartheid

[157] Interview with Yasmin Sooka in Pretoria (May 3, 2006).

era crimes. However, these are not in place.[158] It has been outlined above that the PCLU generally does not have sufficient investigative resources and funding to conduct prosecutions on a broader basis than has already happened. The PCLU is rather modest and small compared to the task it has to face.[159] Furthermore, apart from TRC cases, it was also assigned other significant responsibilities that demand a lot of its resources.[160] Thus, there is certainly also a need for greater numbers of experienced prosecutors and investigators to conduct the proceedings. Considering these shortcomings in terms of resources, it appears rather unlikely that the PCLU will be capable to proceed with more than a few cases at a time or to guarantee that a broader spectrum of crimes can be prosecuted during a short time frame.

Given these realities, the number of cases that potentially could be prosecuted diminishes significantly in comparison to what could be expected from the number of refused amnesty applications. Consequently, at one stage the PCLU referred to only 16 cases it considered at all prosecutable, five of which were of high priority and had already been investigated to an advanced stage.[161] It is certainly possible that more cases could be pursued, were there more resources available. Thus, in general, apart from problems of evidence, the prospects of further successful trials hinge on whether the government has the political will to promote prosecutions and whether it will assign more resources to the NPA.[162] Yet as has been shown above, the government is clearly lacking political will to support prosecutions and to assign sufficient resources to the process. Moreover, considering the overall resource constraints of the judicial system in the face of the extraordinarily high present-day crime rate, it is unlikely that significantly more resources

---

[158] Interview with Anton Ackermann in Pretoria (May 11, 2006); Interview with Torie Pretorius and others in Pretoria (May 2, 2006).

[159] See N. Rousseau 'Prosecutions' in E. Doxtader (ed) *Provoking questions* (2005) 37 at 47.

[160] See *supra* Chapter 2(1.2).

[161] Ibid.

[162] D. Ntsebeza 'The legacy of the TRC' in C. Villa-Vicencio and E. Doxtader (eds) *The provocations of amnesty* (2003) 23 at 25.

will be assigned to the PCLU in the future.[163] Should possible future mechanisms of the kind that the government adopted with the prosecution policy amendment prevail over legal challenges, it would have the effect that many cases would not reach the court room.

As has been outlined above, the bleak prospects for further trials will also remain unaffected by the legal option to conduct private prosecutions, since victims and NGOs do not have the means necessary for such proceedings.[164]

Further trials might also potentially be interrupted by certain perpetrators from the ranks of the security police, exercising their right to apply for a review of their amnesty refusal, should they have been clients of Jan Wagener, with the consequences highlighted by the PEBCO-Three prosecution.[165] With regard to the need to have a consistent and short period of prosecutions, it was a bad decision to create the option to apply for a review of certain amnesty decisions years later.

Essentially, we must conclude that, although constitutional as well as international law requires the government to pursue post-TRC prosecutions vigorously, in the circumstances, the prospects for a significant number of further trials are absolutely minimal. However, it is still possible that a small number of cases will nevertheless be prosecuted.

5. *Non-Prosecutions*

The following subchapter will outline the practical prospects of further proceedings by describing an array of exemplary cases. Given the practical realities such as evidence, the choice of cases is not necessarily what might be desired by specific groups or the public generally. Thus, for instance, the prominent Steve Biko case, which many had expected to be prosecuted, will not go ahead. The popular political activist Steve Biko was the founder of the Black Consciousness movement. He was severely

---

163 N. Rousseau 'Prosecutions' in E. Doxtader (ed) *Provoking questions* (2005) 37 at 47.

164 See text accompanying *supra* Chapter 3 note 230.

165 See *supra* Chapter 2(7.2).

assaulted and tortured in police custody and died as a result thereof in 1977.[166] Five amnesty applications were refused in this matter, among those that of since deceased Gideon Nieuwoudt.[167] The NPA, however, stated that a prosecution would not be sustainable since sufficient evidence was not available to prove charges relating to the death, and other charges, such as assault, had lapsed under the statute of limitation.[168] As mentioned above, others have called for the prosecution of leading ANC members. The possible grounds for this have already been outlined.[169] However, the list of priority cases at the PCLU allegedly does not contain cases of ANC members[170] and the PCLU has, as had already been mentioned, denied that sufficient evidence would exist to prosecute any of the ANC leaders who were denied amnesty.

Although the NPA has not made public which are its priority cases, the media referencing NPA sources reported that it would focus on, *inter alia*, the cases of the St. James Church massacre, Nokuthula Simelane, both of which will be described below, and the Cradock-Four.[171] Yet charges in a number of other cases could potentially be pursued. More indications to the practical scope of a possible prosecution can be found regarding the cases outlined below.

5.1 *The cases of missing Simelane and Morudu*

Cases in which the whereabouts of the victim and the exact circumstances of his or her death remain unknown are of specific relevance.

---

[166] See *TRC Report*, vol. 2, chap. 3, paras. 184–85; *TRC Report*, vol. 4, chap. 5, para. 12; *TRC Report*, vol. 3, chap. 2, para. 120.

[167] Decision no. AC/99/0020.

[168] N. Rousseau 'Prosecutions' in E. Doxtader (ed) *Provoking questions* (2005) 37 at 47.

[169] See *supra* Chapter 3(4.).

[170] Interview with Sheila Camerer in Cape Town (March 30, 2006) (Camerer claims to have had insight in the list). See also C. Terreblanche *Apartheid massacres go to court* The Sunday Independent, April 23, 2006.

[171] C. Terreblanche *Apartheid massacres go to court* The Sunday Independent, April 23, 2006.

5.1.1 *The Nokuthula Simelane case*

An example for this is the case of Nokuthula Simelane, which many people, such as the former TRC commissioner Yasmin Sooka, believe should be investigated and prosecuted at the PCLU. The case is an example of a very egregious, yet not untypical, act of security police violence against anti-apartheid activists.

Nokuthula Simelane acted as a courier for MK and was based in Swaziland.[172] Through covert agents of the security police branch of Soweto, Simelane was lured into a trap while she was on a mission in Johannesburg in September 1983. According to the findings of the TRC in this case, Simelane was abducted and brought to a remote farm in the north-west of South Africa, where she was held captive for a period of approximately five weeks. During this period, the security police attempted to get information from her and to recruit her as an informer for the police. She was continuously and seriously assaulted and tortured until she was almost unrecognisable and could barely walk. Yet according to the TRC's findings, all attempts to get information and to recruit her remained fruitless. After Simelane's torture ordeal on the farm, she was taken away without a trace. Her exact fate has never been established with any certainty. It is, however, quite clear that she is dead.

The Amnesty Committee received eight amnesty applications in connection with the events, among them those of the three white security police officers Willem Coetzee, Anton Pretorius and Frederick Mong,[173] who were given the task of overseeing and directing the operation. Applications were also received from two black policemen, Veyi and Selamolela. All, except Veyi, participated in the abduction as well as in the subsequent torture. Compelling differences emerged in the testimonies of the black and white policemen. Whereas the white policemen maintained that Simelane was only tortured during the first

---

[172] Unless otherwise is cited, the information concerning the Simelane case derives from *TRC Report*, vol. 6, s. 3, chap. 1, paras. 199–206 and *TRC Report*, vol. 2, chap. 3, paras. 287–92.

[173] Applications no. AM/4122/96; AM/4389/96; AM/4154/96.

week of her detention and that she eventually agreed to cooperate as an informer, whereafter she had been returned to Swaziland, the black policemen denied Simelane ever agreed to cooperate. According to them she was held captive for several weeks, during which she was continuously tortured, allegedly also with electric shocks, which was denied by the white policemen. The last time the black policemen saw Simelane was when she was loaded into the boot of Coetzee's car and taken away. She was allegedly in such a bad state that it would have been absolutely impossible to return her to Swaziland. They claim to have been told by another black policeman, who has since died, that Simelane was subsequently shot by Pretorius and Coetzee and buried near Rustenburg.

The Amnesty Committee found strong indicators that the versions of the white security policemen were false and accordingly refused to grant them amnesty for the torture. Amnesty was, however, granted to all applicants regarding the abduction.[174] No conclusion could be reached on her eventual fate but it is highly likely that Simelane was murdered after being kept on the farm.

Although the case is certainly being considered by the PCLU and an investigation had already started before the TRC hearings, which was then pending the amnesty decisions, the case was simply not taken further by the NPA after the Amnesty Committee eventually refused amnesty in May 2001. This inexcusable failure has grave consequences since prospects for a successful prosecution now seem limited. Possible criminal conduct in the Simelane matter concerns kidnapping, assault, assault causing grievous bodily harm and murder. The NPA, however, refuses to investigate charges of assault because of the limitation period of section 18 of the Criminal Procedure Act, according to which the right to pursue assault charges lapses after 20 years.[175] As the torture of Simelane constituted assault in a legal sense, the possibility to charge the white policemen, who had been denied amnesty for the torture, lapsed after 20 years in September 2003. They can also not be

[174] Decision no. AC/2001/185.

[175] Interview with Howard Varney in Johannesburg (May 6, 2006).

prosecuted for kidnapping, since they all were granted amnesty for Simelane's abduction.[176] What possibly remains are charges of murder. Yet a possible murder seems very hard to prove, as there is apparently not enough evidence and possible witnesses are not forthcoming or have meanwhile passed away.[177]

The case, thus, drastically illustrates the grave consequences of the massive delay of prosecutions. Had the NPA pursued assault charges before 2003, a conviction might have been achieved. Likewise, the alleged perpetrators could have possibly been urged to testify against each other concerning the murder or to fully disclose their knowledge in a plea and sentence agreement. The NPA has also been asked to initiate investigations into the involvement of other security branch members, who possibly participated in the abduction, such as Msebenzi Radebe and Willem Schoon, neither of whom even applied for amnesty.[178]

5.1.2 *The Moss Morudu case*

Many similar cases exist in which the exact facts concerning the fate of still missing victims remain unknown.[179] One such case is that of the MK operative Moses "Moss" Morudu, in which the notorious and infamous Northern Transvaal security branch was involved. The security police believed that Morudu was part of a special MK unit, the so-called "Icing Unit", which was engaged in eliminating black collaborators with the apartheid regime such as black policemen.[180] On the instruction of Captain Hendrik Johannes Prinsloo, Morudu was abducted in October 1986 from his home in Mamelodi/ Pretoria

---

176 The attorney Howard Varney, who is presently acting for the Simelane family, has pointed out that the decision to grant amnesty for the abduction was flawed in a legal sense, since the Committee basically failed to distinguish between the two legal terms abduction and kidnapping. The attorney of the family at the time failed to apply for a review of the amnesty decision in this regard on behalf of the relatives. The possibility to apply for review has since lapsed. The option to apply for condonation has been assessed and found not to be promising.

177 Interview with Howard Varney in Johannesburg (May 6, 2006).

178 Ibid.

179 See generally *TRC Report*, vol. 6, s. 4, chap. 1.

180 *TRC Report*, vol. 6, s. 3, chap. 1, para. 269.

and taken to a farm.[181] He was interrogated and brutally tortured for approximately one week.[182] What happened to him afterwards remains unknown. His family, however, had been deceived into believing he had gone into exile.[183]

The only amnesty applications concerning this incident were tendered by three black former security police members.[184] They only applied for their role in the abduction and later captivity of Morudu on the farm and claimed to have no knowledge of what eventually happened to Morudu, since they had not been present or involved for the whole time. They implicated the other security police operatives Hechter, Ludick, dos Santos, Mokhaba, Joe Mamasela and especially Captain Prinsloo, who was allegedly in charge of the operation. All of them denied any involvement.[185] Another officer believed to have been present during the interrogation is Northern Transvaal security branch constable van Vuuren.[186] The applicants claimed that at some point Morudu was taken away from the farm while they themselves had not been present and that Prinsloo had thereafter simply ordered them to remove all signs of their presence on the farm. It still remains unclear what eventually happened to Morudu. It is, however, again highly probable that he was executed and his remains were disposed of somewhere.

The problems in prosecuting this case are similar to those in the Simelane matter, since there is not any proper evidence of a murder and the possibility of prosecuting for assault has lapsed. Yet in this case, the alleged perpetrators, such as Prinsloo, had not applied for amnesty and might possibly, providing there was evidence to support the charge, be prosecuted for the kidnapping.

Commentators close to the TRC claimed that the Northern Transvaal security police's activities were generally not properly investigated by the TRC and that prosecutions should focus more on this area, since

---

[181] Ibid., para. 272.

[182] Ibid.

[183] Ibid., s. 4, chap. 1, para. 1.

[184] Applications no. AM/3756/96, AM/3755/96, AM/6064/97.

[185] Decision no. AC/2000/010.

[186] *TRC Report*, vol. 6, s. 3, chap. 1, para. 272.

amnesty applications were often not submitted.[187] As such, especially Prinsloo is believed to be a very worthwhile target for prosecution.[188]

5.1.3 *The relevance of prosecution in missing persons cases*

The family of Nokuthula Simelane and especially her mother suffers severely, mentally and physically, from the lack of closure.[189] According to Simelane's sister, it is extremely important for the family to find out the whole truth of Simelane's probable murder and to see the perpetrators admit their guilt. Only by discovering the full truth and being able to retrieve the remains for a proper burial could the family find closure and leave their grief behind. The yet unresolved situation prevents them from doing so and is a continuous source of pain.[190] This example is representative for others. The relatives of Moss Morudu experience similar problems.[191] It is generally essential for victims' families to get to know the exact fate and whereabouts of the remains of family members for whose disappearance is still unaccounted.[192] Otherwise they are unable to find closure.[193] As the TRC Report aptly put it, families remain 'trapped in the past, unable to move on' and 'constantly caught between near certainty that the missing person has not survived and hope that he or she will return'.[194]

---

187 Interview with Madeleine Fullard in Pretoria (May 4, 2006).

188 Ibid. See further *TRC Report*, vol. 6, s. 3, chap. 1, paras. 267–77.

189 T. Nkadimeng (sister of N. Simelane) *Panel presentation at the Institute for Justice and Reconciliation conference 'The TRC: ten years on'* (April 20, 2006).

190 Ibid.

191 See for an account of equal suffering caused by the unresolved situation for the relatives of missing former activist Moss Murudu: S. Russouw *'All I want is to bury my son'* The Star, March 31, 2007. See for an exemplary account from a victim's point of view on this issue and the implications for reconciliation with regard to victims: Y. Sooka 'Apartheid's victims in the midst of amnesty's promise' in C. Villa-Vicencio and E. Doxtader (eds) *The provocations of amnesty* (2003) 309 at 312.

192 *TRC Report*, vol. 6, s. 4, chap. 1, para. 115.

193 Y. Sooka *Panel presentation at the Institute for Justice and Reconciliation conference 'The TRC: ten years on'* (April 20, 2006).

194 *TRC Report*, vol. 6, s. 4, chap. 1, para. 7.

Although in such cases it is generally more important for victims to get to know all the facts than to see the perpetrator being sentenced to a long jail term,[195] criminal proceedings are nevertheless an important tool to extract this very information. In both above examples, the possible perpetrators are not willing to cooperate with the NPA or the victims' relatives to clarify the facts. An imminent threat of prosecution is absolutely critical in presenting an incentive to move the perpetrators to disclose information.

Both cases have shown the grave consequences that the non-investigation of security police violence during the apartheid years and the statute of limitation has with regard to torture. On the basis of the above elaborations,[196] it can be argued that the limitation period should be extended. Furthermore, in terms of the above outlined prioritisation approach, both cases should be considered as of high priority for the PCLU, since the crimes in question are very egregious and can qualify as crimes against humanity. Both cases also give proof that it is worthwhile to explore an extended use of plea-bargaining. Perpetrators could be offered a suspended or reduced sentence in exchange for a full disclosure on the victims' fates.

5.2 *The Cradock-Four case*

The Cradock-Four case is a well-known case, typical of police violence against opposition activists.[197] Four leading UDF members of the Eastern Cape town of Cradock, Matthew Goniwe, Sparrow Mkhonto, Fort Calata and Sicelo Mhlauli, were abducted and executed by the security police in 1985.[198] All four had already previously been frequently arrested,

---

[195] Interview with Marjorie Jobson in Pretoria (May 9, 2006); Interview with Y. Sooka in Pretoria (May 3, 2006).

[196] See *supra* Chapter 4(3.).

[197] See on the case *TRC Report*, vol. 2, chap. 3, paras. 245–52; *TRC Report*, vol. 3, chap. 2, paras. 294–98. The Motherwell-Four case is connected to this case, since there the killings took place to prevent revelations concerning the Cradock-Four murders (*TRC Report*, vol. 3, chap. 1, appendix, page 28).

[198] *TRC Report*, vol. 3, chap. 2, para. 295.

tortured and harassed by the police.[199] On 27 June 1985, after returning from a UDF meeting in Port Elizabeth, they were abducted by the security police and shortly thereafter shot or stabbed to death.[200] To avert suspicion from the security police their bodies and the car were burned.[201] The corpses were later found in the vicinity of Port Elizabeth.[202] In 1987 an inquest into the matter did not find any indications of security force involvement in the murders. However, in 1993 a secret document containing a message of the regional SADF command to the State Security Council secretariat was found, which called for the 'permanent removal from society' of the four activists.[203] Thereafter the inquest was reopened. The inquest judge found that there was *prima facie* evidence that the security forces carried out the murders and recommended the institution of criminal proceedings.[204]

Prompted by later investigations of the Transvaal Attorney-General in the case,[205] the Amnesty Committee received amnesty applications in relation to the murders from six security police officers: Hermanus du Plessis, Gerhardus Johannes Lotz, Harold Snyman, Johannes Martin van Zyl, all of whom had also been involved in the PEBCO-Three case, which happened only six weeks beforehand, Eric Taylor and General Nicolaas van Rensburg.[206] All applications with regard to the abduction and killing were refused in 1999 since the Committee was not convinced the applicants had made a full disclosure.[207] Snyman and van Rensburg have since passed away. Thus, the PCLU could potentially prosecute the four remaining security police perpetrators. However, since the amnesty refusals, the NPA has not made an attempt to lay charges.

---

199 *TRC Report*, vol. 2, chap. 3, para. 247.

200 Ibid., para. 250.

201 Ibid.

202 *TRC Report*, vol. 3, chap. 2, para. 296.

203 *TRC Report*, vol. 2, chap. 3, para. 248.

204 Ibid.

205 *TRC Report*, vol. 6, s. 3, chap. 1, para. 17.

206 Applications no. AM/4384/96, AM/3921/96, AM/3918/96, AM/5637/97, AM/3917/96, AM/3919/96.

207 Decision no. AC/99/0350.

The Cradock-Four case must be considered as egregious and of high priority, since it involves systematic, ordered and very grave police violence against opposition members. However, should a prosecution be initiated, at least with regard to van Zyl, and possibly also with regard to some of the other alleged perpetrators, if they are clients of the lawyer Jan Wagener, the agreement to apply for a review of the amnesty refusal could again come into play and possibly delay or even prevent the start of a trial, as was the case in the PEBCO-Three matter.[208]

5.3 *The St. James Church massacre*

Among the cases believed to be under close scrutiny by the PCLU, there is at least one case that concerns the former liberation movement, the St. James Church massacre. The massacre was committed by members of the APLA, the military wing of the PAC. On 25 July 1993, a service congregation of St. James Church in Kenilworth, a district in Cape Town with predominantly white inhabitants, was stormed by APLA members.[209] The attackers opened machine gun fire and threw hand grenades at the about 1000 churchgoers. Eleven people were killed and fifty-eight were wounded.[210]

Four people applied for amnesty in relation to the attack, among them Letlapa Mphahlele,[211] former APLA commander and later president of the political party PAC. Mphahlele was director of operations of the APLA at the time of the massacre.[212] He was allegedly involved in the planning and authorisation of the attack.[213] Mphahlele later effectively withdrew his application before a decision of the Committee was handed down.[214] According to him, this was done in protest against a

[208] See *supra* Chapter 2(7.2).
[209] *TRC Report*, vol. 2, chap. 7, para. 472.
[210] Ibid.
[211] Application no. AM/3018/96.
[212] F. Kutz *Amnestie für politische Straftäter in Südafrika* (2001) 271.
[213] Ibid., 277.
[214] *TRC Report*, vol. 6, s. 3, chap. 4, para. 114.

perceived lack of objectivity of the TRC.[215] All other applicants were granted amnesty.[216]

The APLA attack was exceptionally brutal. It appeared highly senseless and totally unjustifiable in terms of the struggle against apartheid. The only reason for the APLA to attack the church was allegedly that white churches were used to legitimise apartheid and were, thus, perceived to be a means of oppressing the black population.[217] However, this specific church community consisted of very liberal whites, who actively engaged in cooperating with black church communities in poor areas of Cape Town.[218] Furthermore, about one third of the congregation consisted of people of colour.[219] The massacre also happened at a time when the Interim Constitution was about to enter into force and the transition to democracy was well under way. It was presumed by many that the attack was an attempt to thwart the negotiations, which were not supported by the PAC.

The APLA was also responsible for a number of other attacks during the negotiation period, which were only aimed at killing civilians. Among those are the Heidelberg Tavern massacre of December 1993 and the King William's Town Golf Club attack of November 1992, both of which left four people dead.[220]

In September 2006 Mphahlele was elected president of the political party PAC.[221] His prosecution was apparently high on the PCLU's list of priority cases. It remains to be seen whether these brutal attacks on unarmed civilians will indeed be prosecuted. However, since the targets of the attack were totally defenceless civilians, the case must be considered as being egregious and of high priority.

---

215 Ibid.

216 Decision no. AC/1998/018.

217 *TRC Report*, vol. 2, chap. 7, para. 475.

218 F. Kutz *Amnestie für politische Straftäter in Südafrika* (2001) 275.

219 *TRC Report*, vol. 6, s. 3, chap. 4, para. 125.

220 See *TRC Report*, vol. 2, chap. 7, paras. 466–96; *TRC Report*, vol. 6, s. 3, chap. 4, paras. 89–167.

221 See *PAC elects new president* SAPA, Sep. 26, 2006.

5.4 *Cases involving former security police leaders*

In the Chikane case further proceedings are apparently envisaged concerning a very high-ranking former security force official. As such there are obviously plans to charge the former head of the apartheid security police, General Sebastiaan "Basie" Smit, since part of the plea agreement in the case was that the accused undertook to act as state witnesses in the event of a prosecution of General Smit.[222] As mentioned above, Smit eventually issued the order to murder Chikane.[223] The plea bargain also clearly indicated that other figures from the higher echelons of authority, probably including the highest levels of the apartheid government and the command of the SADF, were involved. It remains to be seen if the PCLU will follow up on such leads and charge these persons who may have been behind Chikane's assassination.

One of those concerned in the Chikane case, General Johan van der Merwe, could be a focus point for the PCLU, also with regard to at least one other case.[224] He was refused amnesty for a failure to make full disclosure concerning his involvement in organising a cross-border raid into Lesotho.[225] In December 1985 a group of security police operatives secretly entered Lesotho with the aim of executing various MK members who had planned to enter South Africa. During the attack nine people were murdered, among them uninvolved civilians.[226] However, it must be remembered that van der Merwe was one of the very few high-ranking security force officials who cooperated with the TRC extensively. His general openness to cooperate with the state in clarifying apartheid atrocities has also been shown in the Chikane case. The focus should rather be on those leaders, who, thus far, have yet to cooperate.

Another possible prosecution could again target General Smit and

---

[222] See *supra* Chapter 2(9.3).

[223] Ibid.

[224] As a leading security police official during the 1980s, van der Merwe was probably involved in or must have had knowledge of a number of criminal security police operations (see various mentioning of van der Merwe in *TRC Report*, vol. 6).

[225] Decision no. AC/2001/231.

[226] Decision no. AC/2001/231.

a further former high-ranking officer of the security police, General "Krappies" Engelbrecht, for their involvement in instigating "third force" violence during the early 1990s. Engelbrecht had been the last head of the notorious C section of the security police, which the Vlakplaas unit was a part of, and was, as such, also the direct superior of Eugene de Kock.[227] In this, he was certainly involved in a number of the criminal activities of Vlakplaas. However, the TRC, specifically, found evidence of Smit and Engelbrecht having been involved in the provision of arms to Inkatha fighters to support their attacks on ANC sympathisers during the bloody conflicts raging during the early 1990s.[228] The Goldstone Commission had in 1994 found indications of the two generals having initiated, authorised and supervised a project, which involved the production of home-made guns as well as the importing of large amounts of weapons from Namibia.[229] Allegedly the arms were directly provided to senior members of the IFP, such as Themba Khosa, to be used in their brutal slaying of ANC supporters.[230] A central figure in these activities was Eugene de Kock, who testified against the two at the TRC.[231] The involvement of Engelbrecht and Smit could merit, to say the least, a charge of incitement and/or aiding and abetting the murder of thousands of ANC supporters.

An investigation against Engelbrecht was already completed by the D'Oliveira team in 1999 and there were plans to charge Engelbrecht by April 2000.[232] However, strangely nothing has happened thus far, which might be due to the overall pattern of delay and the flaws in providing for proper continuity between the prosecution teams. Whether a trial of Engelbrecht is still planned is unknown.

---

[227] *TRC Report*, vol. 2, chap. 3, appendix, para. 19.

[228] *TRC Report*, vol. 6, s. 3, chap. 1, para. 132. See especially *TRC Report*, vol. 2, chap. 7, paras. 100–123.

[229] *TRC Report*, vol. 3, chap. 6, para. 546.

[230] Ibid.

[231] Ibid.

[232] V. Nerlich *Apartheidkriminalität vor Gericht* (2002) 155 and 220. It cannot be said, however, which conduct was planned to be concerned by the charges.

5.5 *The State Security Council and the apartheid government*

In public debates on the topic many human rights activists and victim representatives have called for more prosecutions of figures from the higher ranks of the apartheid regime and political leaders of the former governments, notwithstanding the practical challenges in targeting the command and political level of the former apartheid regime. Many have claimed that it would be necessary to investigate the involvement of former President F.W. de Klerk in apartheid atrocities.[233] Whereas the former Director-General of de Klerk's presidential office, Dave Steward, maintained that de Klerk could not be prosecuted since he had not been aware of any crimes committed by the security forces during his tenure, human rights activists claimed that his accountability could be established on the basis of his involvement in the State Security Council (hereinafter SSC).[234]

The SSC was a board of leading security force members and politicians, including de Klerk from the late 1980s, which was established to advise the government and security forces on security issues.[235] The TRC expressed great surprise that members of the SSC, who always maintained that they had no knowledge of criminal conduct, had never investigated or followed up the clear indications of crimes committed within the security structure they commanded.[236] Former leading NP member Leon Wessels, himself a member of the SSC, doubted the argument that SSC members could not have known of the crimes, which at least indirectly resulted from its policy directives.[237] With regard to former President F.W. de Klerk, the TRC had lamented that during his testimony before the TRC he did not give a truthful and full account of his knowledge of gross human rights violations committed by senior

[233] Interview with Yasmin Sooka in Pretoria (May 3, 2006); Interview with Howard Varney in Johannesburg (May 6, 2006); Interview with Marjorie Jobson in Pretoria (May 9, 2006).

[234] H. Varney *De Klerk and the Truth Commission* The Guardian, Aug. 17, 2007.

[235] See *TRC Report*, vol. 2, chap. 3, appendix, paras. 1–6.

[236] *TRC Report*, vol. 6, s. 3, chap. 1, para. 357.

[237] *TRC Report*, vol. 5, chap. 6, para. 77.

government members and the SAP.[238] As such, the Commission proposed to make a finding that he had known of the bombing of Khotso house in Johannesburg, the headquarters of the South African Council of Churches which was very active in anti-apartheid opposition, through the security police in 1988.[239]

The TRC also found that 22 members of the SSC were accountable for the violence of Inkatha groups against anti-apartheid organisations, especially the ANC, as the government had provided equipment, training and financial resources to IFP hit-squads.[240] It further found that the SSC, among others, pressured the security forces to act robustly against the liberation movement, used language that could easily be understood as orders to eliminate anti-apartheid activists and failed to prevent the commission of crimes by security force operatives.[241] Such conduct could possibly constitute criminal liability, such as incitement to commit the political crimes in question or make the involved politicians accessories to the fact. However, the exact scope of involvement of apartheid politicians in criminal acts cannot be determined here.

5.6 *The Steyn-Report concerning criminal SADF activities*

The potential to investigate cases of criminal SADF activities was again highlighted by the declassification of a report on alleged dangerous activities of SADF components in early 2006.[242] SADF general Pierre Steyn had in the early 1990s been assigned by former President de Klerk with the task of following up and investigating allegations that SADF

---

238 The respective paragraph of *TRC Report*, vol. 5, chap. 6, para. 104 containing these findings on de Klerk had to be blacked out before publication following a court order de Klerk had applied for.

239 *TRC Report*, vol. 6, s. 1, chap. 4, para. 29. See further *TRC Report*, vol. 2, chap. 3, paras. 521–29.

240 *TRC Report*, vol. 2, chap. 5, para. 249.

241 *TRC Report*, vol. 5, chap. 6, paras. 99 and 102.

242 Staff paper prepared for the Steyn commission on alleged dangerous activities of SADF components, December 1992 (on file with author).

elements attempted to thwart the negotiations in the early 1990s and destabilise the country. During the mid-1990s, the report was handed to the TRC from which it was, after being considered highly sensitive, moved to the Department of Justice. It had only been declassified after the South African History Archives had lodged a legal challenge for its release against the Department of Justice.

The report outlines detailed yet uncorroborated indications of far-reaching and intense involvement of the SADF in third force violence, such as provision of weapons to IFP members, instigation of the so-called train murders and hostel violence in the Witwatersrand area, setting up of weapon caches, incitement to kill ANC members and various murders. The report also alleges that there had been plans for a right wing *coup d'État* as well as that support had been given to opposition movements in neighbouring countries. It details a wide range of names of officials and their specific alleged conduct.[243]

Criminal investigations concerning the SADF activities interrogated by Steyn had allegedly already been conducted in the early 1990s, apparently without results.[244] However, the concrete indications of intense and far reaching involvement of some very high-ranking SADF officials in high profile political crimes, which emerged through the Steyn report, appear to offer grounds on which the PCLU can initiate further investigations.[245]

[243] Strangely and apparently due to a lapse the names had not, at least in the English version, been masked by the NPA which eventually released the document.

[244] C. Carter *Apartheid army's deadly secrets* The Sunday Independent, April 30, 2006.

[245] However, the report itself points out that criminal proceedings might be difficult due to destroyed evidence and the role players protecting each other.

Chapter Five

Conclusion

This book was written to document and evaluate the progress, and lack thereof, which has been made in establishing criminal accountability for politically motivated gross human rights violations of the apartheid era, for which amnesty was not granted by the TRC. This process of establishing accountability is not isolated. Post-TRC prosecutions are part of South Africa's model of dealing with crimes committed during the apartheid conflict and, thus, must be put in context with the TRC's conceptual and legal regime on amnesty. Such prosecutions potentially impact on South Africans' attitude towards the TRC process and reconciliation generally, since many expect trials as part of this process. On the other hand, the former apartheid establishment and parts of the white population may see trials as yet another confirmation of their perception of victor's justice. The following will summarise the main conclusions and results reached in this book and will comment on the conduct of post-TRC prosecutions and their impact on the process of dealing with the past.

1. *Summary of Results*

The deadline to apply for amnesty was 30 September 1997. On the release of the TRC Report in 1998, the TRC and President Mandela made strong recommendations for criminal proceedings to be instituted where there was evidence of gross human rights violations (Chapter 1).

However, the government and the NPA implemented the recommendations very reluctantly (Chapter 2). In 1999 the Human Rights Investigative Unit was established to oversee investigations into and the prosecution of TRC-related cases. Thereafter matters were moved to the DSO ("Scorpions"). Not one prosecution was instituted by these units. Only when the last volumes of the TRC Report were issued in 2003 was a more appropriate unit, the PCLU, established.

The PCLU nevertheless only concluded three criminal proceedings during its five years of existence. In all, during almost one decade after the conclusion of the TRC, prosecutions have been initiated in only eight cases. Seven proceedings were finalised in court, four of which resulted in the conviction of all accused parties. Four of the finalised cases were conducted by regional prosecution offices.

There has, therefore, been a minimal number of criminal proceedings conducted after the conclusion of the TRC. Provisions for the appropriate conditions for the units to perform the necessary tasks involved in prosecutions were totally insufficient. For the sake of the country to achieve quick closure on the past, as President Mandela had rightly suggested already in 1998, it would have required a clear commitment in 1998, consistent strategic decisions, the definition of priority criteria, the assignment of better and more resources, more continuity and cooperation between the D'Oliveira Unit and possibly only one successor unit instead of various different ones.

The lack of a clear commitment and concentrated efforts after 1998 essentially reveal a lack of political will from the government to properly support post-TRC prosecutions (Chapter 3). This lack of political will has found expression when the government intervened in a specific case and interrupted all proceedings for 13 months by imposing a moratorium without compelling reasons, thereby further delaying trials from taking place. However, most indicative of the lack in political will were the consultations of government and leading ANC representatives with groups of former apartheid security force leaders, which aimed to reach agreement on new indemnity mechanisms to circumvent trials. Eventually, the Prosecution Policy was amended to the effect that specific guidelines, which reproduced the TRC's indemnity mechanism and aimed to avoid large-scale prosecutions, shall govern the discretionary decision on whether to prosecute a TRC-related case. It was found to have potentially negative consequences for the establishment of criminal accountability after the TRC. With the suspension of the amendment by the High Court of Pretoria, the government suffered a serious blow in its ambitions to introduce new indemnity mechanisms.

The South African handling of post-TRC prosecutions violates the Constitution wherever proceedings are not instituted despite the existence of evidence which would warrant further investigation or prosecution (Chapter 4). By granting *de facto* indemnity to many authors of gross human rights violations, South Africa is also in breach of its obligations under international humanitarian and human rights law, should the crimes in question constitute grave breaches of the Geneva Conventions or crimes against humanity.

There are practical and strategic difficulties in the approach to post-TRC prosecutions, which should be an incentive to explore legally appropriate solutions, allowing prioritisation of cases, embracing the practical needs as well as the interests of victims and that do justice to the Constitution. On this basis, there are sound legal grounds to place higher priority on systematic crimes of state forces.

The prospects for a significant number of cases to be dealt with are bleak. Better progress would require the state to increase resources significantly, which, in the face of a lack of political will, limited resources and a very high present-day crime rate, is unlikely to happen. Among such cases that could already have been tackled, are the St. James church massacre, the Simelane case, the Cradock-Four case and many other cases from the PCLU's priority list of 16 cases, which allegedly are cases that have already been prepared to an advanced stage, as well as the many cases, which had already been prepared for prosecution by the D'Oliveira Unit, such as the case of General Engelbrecht.

Even under the difficult conditions in present-day South Africa, a limited amount of the most egregious cases of gross human rights violations could have been and can still be targeted. Nevertheless, many cases which actually warrant further investigation and provide the prospect of a successful prosecution on the basis of available evidence will remain unpursued. The book has practically been closed on post-TRC accountability.

2. *The Conduct of Prosecutions in the Context of the TRC Process*

While the appropriate course of transitional justice will always depend on the specific circumstances in the country concerned, there are general considerations either speaking for or against prosecutions in transitional societies.[1] However, any academic assessment concerning the advantages or disadvantages of prosecutions in South Africa's transition to democracy is now anachronistic. The course of transitional justice and dealing with the crimes under apartheid, which South Africa chose, means that prosecutions must take place where amnesty was not granted.

The systematic requirement of prosecutions to take place is obvious. However, the question needs to be addressed to what extent the minimal conduct of post-TRC prosecutions impacts on the overall assessment of the TRC and its amnesty proceedings. Some suggest that abandoning the idea of prosecutions would 'make a mockery of the process',[2] and even that the entire TRC might unravel into a farce.[3] Certainly, the granting of amnesty on conditions simply does not make any sense if there are no consequences in terms of criminal proceedings attached to the non-compliance with one or more of the requirements. However, it can hardly follow from this that the entire legitimacy of the TRC would be obliterated. This would mean that the justice of amnesty depends fundamentally on post-TRC prosecutions being implemented. This certainly is not the case. It has been pointed out at the outset that the granting of amnesty was necessitated by the political realities during the negotiation period. Nevertheless, with the conditional model a successful attempt was made to avoid blanket amnesty, which in itself is an achievement. The great strength of the amnesty proceedings above was that they encouraged perpetrators to disclose information about their deeds, which might otherwise not have been forthcoming. Thousands

---

[1] See A. Boraine *A country unmasked* (2000) 280–81; E. Hahn-Godeffroy *Die Südafrikanische Truth and Reconciliation Commission* (1998) 39–43.

[2] Interview with Yasmin Sooka in Pretoria (May 3, 2006).

[3] L. Fernandez 'Post-TRC prosecutions in South Africa' in G. Werle (ed) *Justice in transition* (2006) 65 at 79.

participated in the process. It was often suggested that the model was ideal to meet the demands of the South African transition and even superior to prosecutions.[4] There was, therefore, strong justification for the amnesty proceedings on their own, regardless of the overall context of accountability.

Nevertheless, amnesty and prosecutions were both integral parts of the South African system. The offer of amnesty was fundamentally premised on the fact that, without it, criminal proceedings would be instituted if there was sufficient evidence to support a prosecution. Many relied on this premise. 'Amnesty is not cheap', as former TRC chair Desmond Tutu repeatedly pointed out.[5] Yet this statement only rings true for those who participated in the process. For those who did not participate but who are not prosecuted, indemnity was obtained cheaply. Perpetrators who participated in the process may now ask themselves why they did so at all. Those who scoffed at the TRC are, in contrast, validated in their decision not to cooperate. This makes it clear that failing to institute prosecutions contradicts the system of accountability, which South Africa chose to adopt as a transitional justice scheme. Thus, if it is not the entire legitimacy of amnesty which is at stake, it is certainly the perceived credibility and justice of the process. What is therefore also at stake, is the overall assessment of the success of South Africa's attempt to deal with its past and the perception of many concerned South Africans that a consistent and just way of dealing with the past has been implemented.[6]

Consistency and credibility in the process is especially relevant with regard to victims' position in the legal setup of amnesty. Their sacrifice of retributive justice and redress was meant to be compensated with a concrete claim to the full truth regarding the crimes they had to endure. This benefit of the amnesty procedures for victims was, according to the Constitutional Court, of central relevance for the scheme's legal

[4] See A. du Bois-Pedain *Transitional amnesty in South Africa* (2007) 344–45.

[5] See G. Werle 'Neue Wege' in P. Bock and R. Wolfrum (eds) *Umkämpfte Vergangenheit* (1999) 269 at 279.

[6] See G. Werle 'Alternativen zur Aufarbeitung von Systemunrecht' in H. Hof and M. Schulte (eds) *Wirkungsforschung zum Recht* vol. III (2001) 291 at 297.

justification.[7] It follows from this logic that should this benefit fail to materialise, either because the full truth was not told or amnesty was not applied for, these victims have a right to call for the normal course of criminal justice to proceed.[8]

In terms of consistency of the process, we must also conclude that the positive international perception of transitional justice in South Africa must be altered. The great international reputation the TRC gained with regard to amnesty was premised on the fact that blanket indemnity was avoided.[9] Especially with regard to the amnesty scheme's legal evaluation in terms of South Africa's international law obligations to prosecute, this structure was considered as the basis for the TRC's legal legitimacy in comparison to other societies in transition.[10] This, however, only rings true if the conditional model is conducted consistently. This is not the case. South Africa does not properly comply with its international law obligations to conduct post-TRC prosecutions properly. Thus, whereas the TRC's scheme on amnesty was seen by many as a role model, which could provide many lessons for transitional societies,[11] South Africa's actual conduct cannot properly function as a role model since it sends out the message that those who refused the offer of amnesty will still not be held accountable for their actions.

Nevertheless, it was often argued in the case against post-TRC prosecutions, that in terms of dealing with the past and promoting reconciliation and nation-building, the achievements of the TRC were

---

7 *The Azanian Peoples Organisation and others v The President of South Africa and others* (CC) Case no. CCT 17/96 25 July 1996 at para. 17.

8 Ibid., at para. 20.

9 Interview with Desmond Tutu in Cape Town (March 22, 2006); L. Fernandez 'Post-TRC prosecutions in South Africa' in G. Werle (ed) *Justice in transition* (2006) 65 at 79.

10 R.A. Wilson *The politics of truth and reconciliation in South Africa* (2001) 23.

11 S. Garkawe 'The South African Truth and Reconciliation Commission: a suitable model to enhance the role and rights of victims of gross human rights violations?' (2003) 27 *Melbourne University Law Review* 334 at 335; P. Hayner 'Same species, different animal: how South Africa compares to truth commissions worldwide' in W. Verwoerd and C. Villa-Vicencio (eds) *Looking back reaching forward* (2000) 32 at 33.

sufficient.[12] Trials are seen by many as detrimental to these achievements of the TRC. Certainly, prosecutions concentrating on former security police members, who were mostly recruited from the white Afrikaans speaking population, would be perceived by many South Africans of that ethnicity as yet another attack of the new ruling class on their group.[13] However, it would seem that such perceptions, especially among the Afrikaans speaking population, generally stem from affirmative action measures and the feeling that their language and heritage are predominantly pushed away from schools, universities, city names or memorial sites. Prosecutions would rather be a merely insignificant addition to these circumstances.

Furthermore, it fails to take into account what victims are required to do to reconcile the gross human rights violations they, or their family members, had to endure. Their ability to do so is certainly dependent on accountability being established for the crimes,[14] since what was for perpetrators a very generous offer to come clean on their criminal deeds,[15] was hard to accept for victims and often highly contested.[16] Unless proceedings are instituted, a balance cannot be struck between the concessions made by victims and the offers made to perpetrators.[17] To abandon post-TRC trials would, thus, be considered as 'a slap in the face' to victims.[18] Under such circumstances, it is hardly possible to expect victims to reconcile themselves with the past if perpetrators

[12] G. Bizos *Why prosecutions are necessary* in C. Villa-Vicencio and E. Doxtader (eds) *The provocations of amnesty* (2003) 5 at 7 refers to this notion of many others.

[13] The activities of the predominantly Afrikaans advocacy group "Afriforum", especially around the Chikane litigation, demonstrate the mingling of anti-prosecution with pro-Afrikaans advocacy efforts.

[14] R.C. Slye 'Amnesty, truth and reconciliation' in R.I. Rotberg and D. Thompson (eds) *Truth v. justice* (2000) 170 at 179. See also K. Marxen and G. Werle *Die strafrechtliche Aufarbeitung von DDR-Unrecht* (1999) 246.

[15] Interview with Desmond Tutu in Cape Town (March 22, 2006).

[16] A. Gutmann and D. Thompson 'The moral foundations of truth commissions' in R.I. Rotberg and D. Thompson (eds) *Truth v. justice* (2000) 22 at 24.

[17] M.E. Bennun 'Some procedural issues relating to post-TRC prosecutions of human rights offenders' (2003) 16 *South African Journal of Criminal Justice* 17 at 36.

[18] Interview with Desmond Tutu in Cape Town (March 22, 2006).

simply get away with their deeds scot-free without the state making sufficient efforts for prosecutions.[19] The deep divide between the government and apartheid victims, mainly caused by the highly reluctant payout of reparations, will deepen further.

The proposition of prosecutions harming the achievements of the TRC also forgets that the amnesty proceedings had significant gaps, since many perpetrators of politically motivated gross human rights violations did not submit amnesty applications. Prosecutions can function to fill some of these gaps. They can, to some extent, clarify the facts regarding past atrocities[20] and should occur where the TRC has not been successful.

3. *Closing Remarks*

The assessment of the conduct of post-TRC prosecutions in South Africa in this study is negative. However, the moral and/or legal desirability of criminal accountability is certainly restricted by the adverse practical realities and conceptual difficulties that have been acknowledged. Certainly, only a relatively small number of cases could still be tackled under the present circumstances. The question which ultimately needs to be addressed is, whether these practical burdens and theoretical dilemmas can, in terms of this evaluation, trump criminal accountability and justify not instituting more proceedings. Can the fact that the vast majority of crimes cannot be prosecuted lend support to the contention that it would then be better not to prosecute at all? Must one conclude that the prosecution of only a small number of cases is actually not worth the effort, today, fifteen years into the new democracy?

The answer clearly must be, no. Limited resources and strategic demands can, by no means, be a reason not to institute proceedings at all. Many victims still have no answers to what happened to their

---

[19] R.C. Slye 'Amnesty, truth and reconciliation' in R.I. Rotberg and D. Thompson (eds) *Truth v. justice* (2000) 170 at 179.

[20] See also K. Marxen and G. Werle *Die strafrechtliche Aufarbeitung von DDR-Unrecht* (1999) 245.

family members, although in many cases the perpetrators are known to the NPA. What is fundamentally at stake is not only the aforementioned consistency and reputation of the TRC process and, partially, the success of the process of dealing with the past, but also the substance and credibility of South Africa's commitment to the enforcement of a culture of human rights. The new South Africa was, in its renunciation of the politics of apartheid, eager to support international human rights law. Respect for human rights has found expression in the Constitution as a fundamental basis for the new democratic order.[21] The current practice of *de facto* indemnity, however, furthers a disreputable tradition of impunity for state orchestrated gross human rights violations, which was adopted during apartheid.[22] It renders meaningless and undermines the human rights protection in international, as well as constitutional law.

Finally it must be pointed out that to rely on forgetfulness in dealing with the past, which by many is seen as the ideal option in the interest of the country, has hardly ever proved to be successful as many countries provide an example that their violent past refuses to rest until it has sufficiently been dealt with and acknowledged. Reconciliation and closure on the past on an individual and national level are prevented by official forgetting.[23] Thus, avoiding the assignment of criminal accountability serves short term practical interests but in the long run will not be in the interest of the country to leave its past behind effectively. Although South Africa made an important step against total impunity with the TRC, too many crimes yet remain unrevealed and unaccounted for.

Almost 10 years after conclusion of the TRC, post-TRC prosecutions have not been conducted successfully and the South African process of dealing with past gross human rights violations, therefore, cannot be seen as concluded.

---

[21] See also T.M. Grupp *Südafrikas neue Verfassung* (1999) 27–28.

[22] See F. Kutz *Amnestie für politische Straftäter in Südafrika* (2001) 29–63; P. Parker 'The politics of indemnities, truth telling and reconciliation in South Africa' (1996) 17 1–2 *Human Rights Law Journal* 1 at 1.

[23] K. Marxen and G. Werle *Die strafrechtliche Aufarbeitung von DDR-Unrecht* (1999) 255.

Bibliography

A selection of largely unpublished judicial and other documents cited in this book is available for download at the edoc-server of Humboldt University (edoc.hu-berlin.de). The material can be found under the search form keyword "post-TRC prosecutions" and will be updated appropriately.

Ambos, Kai. *Straflosigkeit von Menschrechtsverletzungen—Zur "impunidad" in südamerikanischen Ländern aus völkerstrafrechtlicher Sicht* (1997) Freiburg im Breisgau.

Beck, Roger B. *The history of South Africa* (2000) Westport, Connecticut—London.

Beinart, William and Dubow, Saul (editors). *Segregation and apartheid in twentieth-century South Africa* (1995) London.

Bekker, Peet M./ Geldenhuys, Tertius/ Joubert, J.J./ Swanepoel, J.P./ Terblanche, S.S./ van der Merwe, Steph E. *Criminal procedure handbook* seventh edition (2005) Cape Town.

Bennun, Mervyn E. 'Amnesty and international law' in Charles Villa-Vicencio and Erik Doxtader (editors). *The provocations of amnesty—Memory, justice and impunity* (2003) Cape Town, pages 92–114.

——. 'Some procedural issues relating to post-TRC prosecutions of human rights offenders' *South African Journal of Criminal Justice* volume 16 (2003) pages 17–37.

Bizos, George. 'Why prosecutions are necessary' in Charles Villa-Vicencio and Erik Doxtader (editors). *The provocations of amnesty—Memory, justice and impunity* (2003) Cape Town, pages 5–9.

Bonner, Philip/ Delius, Peter/ Posel, Deborah (editors). *Apartheid's genesis—1935-1962* (1993) Johannesburg.

Boraine, Alex. *A country unmasked—Inside South Africa's Truth and Reconciliation Commission* (2000) Oxford.

——. 'Truth and reconciliation in South Africa—The third way' in Robert I. Rotberg and Dennis Thompson (editors). *Truth v. justice—The morality of truth commissions* (2000) Princeton and Oxford, pages 141–157.

Braude, Claudia and Spitz, Derek. 'Memory and the spectre of international justice: a comment on AZAPO' *South African Journal on Human Rights* (1997) pages 269–282.

Cassese, Antonio. *International criminal law* (2003) New York.

Coleman, Max (editor). *A Crime against humanity—Analysing the repression of the apartheid state* (1998) Johannesburg and Cape Town.

Corder, Hugh. 'Towards a South African constitution' *The Modern Law Review* volume 57, no. 4 (1994) pages 491–533.

Crocker, David A. 'Truth commissions, transitional justice, and civil society' in Robert I. Rotberg and Dennis Thompson (editors). *Truth v. justice—The morality of truth commissions* (2000) Princeton and Oxford, pages 99–121.

Davenport, Rodney and Saunders, Christopher. *South Africa—A modern history* fifth edition (2000) Basingstoke.

De Lange, Johnny. 'The historical context, legal origins and philosophical foundation of the South African Truth and Reconciliation Commission' in Wilhelm Verwoerd and Charles Villa-Vicencio (editors). *Looking back reaching forward—Reflections on the Truth and Reconciliation Commission of South Africa* (2000) Cape Town, pages 14–31.

De Waal, Johan/Currie, Iain/Erasmus, Gerhard. *The Bill of Rights handbook* fourth edition (2001) Lansdowne.

De Waal, Johan and Currie, Iain. *The new constitutional and administrative law* volume 1 (2001) Lansdowne.

Du Bois-Pedain, Antje. *Transitional amnesty in South Africa* (2007) Cambridge.

Dugard, John. 'Dealing with crimes of a past regime. Is amnesty still an option?' *Leiden Journal of International Law* volume 12 (1999) pages 1001–1015.

——. *International law—A South African perspective* (1994) Kenwyn.

——. 'Is the truth and reconciliation process compatible with international law? An unanswered question' *South African Journal on Human Rights* (1997) pages 258–268.

Du Toit, Etienne/de Jager, Frederick J./Paizes, Andrew/St Quintin-Skeen, Andrew/van der Merwe, Steph. *Commentary on the Criminal Procedure Act* service 33 (2004), service 35 (2006), service 36 (2006) Cape Town.

Fenwick, Mark. 'Dilemmas of transitional justice—Criminal prosecutions or truth commissions?' *The Seinan Law Review* volume 35, no. 3–4 (2003) pages 1–24.

Fernandez, Lovell. 'Post-TRC prosecutions in South Africa' in Gerhard Werle (editor). *Justice in transition—Prosecution and amnesty in Germany and South Africa* (2006) Berlin, pages 65–81.

Friedland, Martin L. *Double jeopardy* (1969) Oxford.

Fullard, Madeleine and Rousseau, Nicky. 'An imperfect past: the Truth and Reconciliation Commission in transition' in John Daniel, Adam Habib and Roger Southall (editors). *State of the nation—South Africa 2003–2004* (2003) Cape Town, pages 78–104.

——. 'Truth, evidence and history—A critical review of aspects of the amnesty process' in Charles Villa-Vicencio and Erik Doxtader (editors). *The provocations of amnesty* (2003) Cape Town, pages 195–216.

Garkawe, Sam. 'The South African Truth and Reconciliation Commission: a suitable model to enhance the role and rights of victims of gross human rights violations?' *Melbourne University Law Review* volume 27 (2003) pages 334–380.

Graybill, Lyn S. *Truth and reconciliation in South Africa: miracle or model?* (2002) Boulder.

Grupp, Thomas Michael. *Südafrikas neue Verfassung* (1999) Baden-Baden.

Gutman, Amy and Thompson, Dennis. 'The moral foundations of truth commissions' in Robert I. Rotberg and Dennis Thompson (editors). *Truth v. justice—The morality of truth commissions* (2000) Princeton and Oxford, pages 22–44.

Hahn-Godeffroy, Emily. *Die südafrikanische Truth and Reconciliation Commission* (1998) Baden-Baden.

Hayner, Priscilla B. 'Fifteen truth commissions—1974–1993: a comparative study' in Neil J. Kritz (editor). *Transitional justice—How emerging democracies reckon with former regimes* volume I (1995) Washington, pages 225–261.

——. 'Same species, different animal: how South Africa compares to truth commissions worldwide' in Wilhelm Verwoerd and Charles Villa-Vicencio (editors). *Looking back reaching forward—Reflections on the Truth and Reconciliation Commission of South Africa* (2000) Cape Town, pages 32–41.

Kiss, Elizabeth. 'Moral ambition within and beyond political constraints—Reflections on restorative justice' in Robert I. Rotberg and Dennis Thompson (editors). *Truth v. justice—The morality of truth commissions* (2000) Princeton and Oxford, pages 68–98.

Klaaren, Jonathan and Varney, Howard. 'A second bite at the amnesty cherry?—Constitutional and policy issues around legislation for a second amnesty' in Charles Villa-Vicencio and Erik Doxtader (editors). *The provocations of amnesty—Memory, justice and impunity* (2003) Cape Town, pages 265–293 (The same text was also published in *South African Law Journal* volume 117 (2000) pages 572–593).

Koppe, Karoline. *Wiedergutmachung für die Opfer von Menschenrechtsverletzungen in Südafrika* (2005) Berlin.

Kreicker, Helmut. 'Die völkerstrafrechtliche Unverjährbarkeit und die Regelung im Völkerstrafgesetzbuch' *Neue Justiz* (2002) pages 281–286.

Kress, Claus. 'War crimes committed in non-international armed conflicts and the emerging system of international criminal justice' *Israel Yearbook on Human Rights* volume 30 (2000) pages 103–177.

Kritz, Neil J. (editor). *Transitional justice* volume I (1995) Washington.

Kutz, Florian. *Amnestie für politische Straftäter in Südafrika—Von der Sharpeville-Amnestie bis zu den Verfahren der Wahrheits- und Versöhnungskommission* (2001) Berlin.

Law Reform Commission of Canada (editor). *Double jeopardy, pleas and verdicts* working paper 63 (1991) Ottawa.

Marxen, Klaus and Werle, Gerhard. *Die strafrechtliche Aufarbeitung von DDR-Unrecht—Eine Bilanz* (1999) Berlin and New York.

McAdams, A. James (editor). *Transitional justice and the rule of law in new democracies* (1997) Notre Dame.

McGregor, Lorna. 'Individual accountability in South Africa: cultural optimum or political facade?' *The American Journal of International Law* volume 95 (2001) pages 32–45.

Meron, Theodor. 'International criminalisation of internal atrocities' *American Journal of International Law* volume 89 (1995) pages 554–577.

Motala, Ziyad. 'The Promotion of National Unity and Reconciliation Act, the Constitution and international law' volume 28 (1995) *Comparative and International Law Journal of Southern Africa* pages 338–362.

Naudaschder-Schlag, Kyra and Schillinger, Huber Rene. 'Von der Rassentrennung zur Regenbogennation' in Rainer Zugehör (editor). *Kap der Besseren Hoffnung?* (1994) Unkel/Rhein and Bad Honnef, pages 9–62.

Nerlich, Volker. *Apartheidkriminalität vor Gericht—Der Beitrag der südafrikanischen Strafjustiz zur Aufarbeitung von Apartheidunrecht* (2002) Berlin.

——. 'Lessons for the International Criminal Court: the impact of criminal prosecutions on the South African amnesty process' in Gerhard Werle (editor). *Justice in transition—Prosecution and amnesty in Germany and South Africa* (2006) Berlin, pages 55–63.

Ngesi, S'fiso. 'The presidential pardons and the media—Healing a wound with salt' in Charles Villa-Vicencio and Erik Doxtader (editors). *The provocations of amnesty—Memory, justice and impunity* (2003) Cape Town, pages 294–308.

Ntsebeza, Dumisa. 'The legacy of the TRC' in Charles Villa-Vicencio and Erik Doxtader (editors). *The provocations of amnesty—Memory, justice and impunity* (2003) Cape Town, pages 23–26.

——. 'The uses of truth commissions—Lessons for the world' in Robert I. Rotberg and Dennis Thompson (editors). *Truth v. justice—The morality of truth commissions* (2000) Princeton and Oxford, pages 158–169.

Omar, Abdullah Mohammed. 'Foreword by A.M. Omar' in Medard R. Rwelamira and Gerhard Werle (editors). *Confronting past injustices—Approaches to amnesty, punishment, reparation and restitution in South Africa and Germany* (1996) Durban, pages vii–xii.

Orentlicher, Diane F. 'Settling accounts: the duty to prosecute human rights violations of a prior regime' *The Yale Law Journal* volume 100 (1991) pages 2537–2615.

Parker, Peter 'The politics of indemnities, truth telling and reconciliation in South Africa—Ending apartheid without forgetting' *Human Rights Law Journal* volume 17, no. 1–2, (1996) pages 1–13.

Pedain, Antje. 'Was amnesty a lottery? An empirical study of the decisions of the Truth and Reconciliation Commission's Committee on Amnesty' *South African Law Journal* volume 121 (2004) pages 785–828.

Ratner, Steven R. and Abrams, Jason S. *Accountability for human rights atrocities in international law—Beyond the Nuremberg legacy* second edition (2001) New York.

Richings, F.G. 'The prosecutor's discretion: a plea for circumspection' *South African Journal of Criminal Law and Criminology* volume 1, no. 2 (1977) pages 143–146.

Rousseau, Nicky. 'Prosecutions' in Erik Doxtader (editor). *Provoking questions—An assessment of the Truth and Reconciliation Commission's recommendation and their implementation* (2005) Institute for Justice and Reconciliation.

Rwelamira, Medard R. 'Punishing past human rights violations: considerations in the South African context' in Medard R. Rwelamira and Gerhard Werle (editors). *Confronting past injustices* (1996) pages 3–19.

Sarkin, Jeremy. *Carrots and sticks: the TRC and the South African amnesty process* (2004) Antwerp and Oxford.

——. 'The amnesty hearings in South Africa revisited' in Gerhard Werle (editor). *Justice in transition—Prosecution and amnesty in Germany and South Africa* (2006) Berlin, pages 43–53.

——. 'The trials and tribunals of South Africa's Truth and Reconciliation Commission' *South African Journal on Human Rights* volume 12, part 4 (1996) pages 617–640.

Schabas, William A. *An introduction to the International Criminal Court* third edition (2007) Cambridge.

Scharf, Michael. 'The letter of the law: the scope of the international legal obligation to prosecute human rights crimes' *Law & Contemporary Problems* volume 59 (1996) pages 41–61.

Schönteich, Martin. *Lawyers for the people—The South African prosecution service* (2001) Pretoria.

Slye, Ronald C. 'Amnesty, truth and reconciliation—Reflections on the South African amnesty process' in Robert I. Rotberg and Dennis Thompson (editors). *Truth v. justice—The morality of truth commissions* (2000) Princeton and Oxford, pages 171–188.

——. 'Apartheid as a crime against humanity: a submission to the South African Truth and Reconciliation Commission' *Michigan Journal of International Law* volume 20 (1998–1999) pages 267–300.

——. 'Comment on the papers by Lovell Fernandez, Jeremy Sarkin and Volker Nerlich' in Gerhard Werle (editor). *Justice in transition—Prosecution and amnesty in Germany and South Africa* (2006) Berlin, pages 83–91.

Sooka, Yasmin. 'Apartheid's victims in the midst of amnesty's promise' in Charles Villa-Vicencio and Erik Doxtader (editors). *The provocations of amnesty—Memory, justice and impunity* (2003) Cape Town, pages 309–314.

Stadler, H.D. *The other side of the story—A true perspective* (1997) Pretoria.

Stuckenberg, Carl-Friedrich. *Double jeopardy—Das Verbot doppelter Bestrafung und Strafverfolgung im US-amerikanischen Recht* (2001) Heidelberg.

Swart, Mia. 'Sorry seems to be the hardest word: apology as a form of symbolic reparation' *South African Journal on Human Rights* volume 1 (2008) pages 50–70.

——. 'The Wouter Basson prosecution: the closest South Africa came to Nuremberg?' *Heidelberg Journal of International Law* volume 68, no. 1 (2008) pages 209–226.

Tomuschat, Christian. 'The duty to prosecute international crimes committed by individuals' in Hans-Joachim Cremer, Thomas Giegerich, Dagmar Richter and Andreas Zimmermann (editors). *Tradition und Weltoffenheit des Rechts—Festschrift für Helmut Steinberger* (2002) Berlin.

Truth and Reconciliation Commission (editor). *Truth and Reconciliation Commission of South Africa report* volumes 1–5 (1998) Cape Town, volumes 6 and 7 (2003) Cape Town.

Van Niekerk, Phillip and Ludman, Barbara (editors). *A-Z of South African politics 1999—The essential handbook* (1999) Johannesburg.

Van Zyl Smit, Dirk and Steyn, Esther. 'Prosecuting authority in the new South Africa' *Centre for the Independence of Judges and Lawyers Yearbook* volume 8 (January 2000) pages 137–155.

Varney, Howard and Sarkin, Jeremy. 'Failing to pierce the hit-squad veil: an analysis of the Malan-trial' *South African Journal of Criminal Justice* volume 10 (1997) pages 141–161.

Verwoerd, Wilhelm and Villa-Vicencio, Charles (editors). *Looking back reaching forward—Reflections on the Truth and Reconciliation Commission of South Africa* (2000) Cape Town.

Werle, Gerhard. 'Alternativen zur Strafjustiz bei der Aufarbeitung von Systemunrecht—Die Amnestieverfahren der südafrikanischen Wahrheits- und Versöhnungskommission' in Hagen Hof and Martin Schulte (editors). *Wirkungsforschung zum Recht* volume III (2001) Baden-Baden.

——. (editor). *Justice in transition—Prosecution and amnesty in Germany and South Africa* (2006) Berlin.

——. 'Neue Wege—Die südafrikanische Wahrheitskommission und die Aufarbeitung von schweren Menschenrechtsverletzungen' in Petra Bock and Rüdiger Wolfrum *Umkämpfte Vergangenheit* (1999) Munich.

——. *Principles of international criminal law* (2005) The Hague.

——. 'Without truth no reconciliation—The South African "Rechtsstaat" and the apartheid past' *Verfassung und Recht in Übersee—Law and Politics in Africa, Asia and Latin America* volume 29 (1996) pages 58–72.

Wilson, Richard A. *The politics of truth and reconciliation in South Africa—Legitimizing the post-apartheid state* (2001) Cambridge.

Press Reports

Adams, Sheena. *Drama in Chikane's poison case* The Star, November 11, 2004.

ANC member charged with murder of farm couple Cape Times, July 7, 2004.

Apartheid crimes a political issue—Maharaj SAPA, August 1, 2007.

Battersby, John. *Call to stop apartheid prosecutions* The Sunday Independent, July 24, 1999.

Carter, Chiara. *Apartheid army's deadly secrets* The Sunday Independent, April 30, 2006.

——. *No truth for the thousands of apartheid dead* Cape Argus, April 8, 2006.

Chikane poison case not closed, say Scorpions SAPA, November 11, 2004.

Chikane's would-be assassins on NPA's list SAPA, January 24, 2005.

Court date for Vlok expected Tuesday: NPA SAPA, June 25, 2007.

Da Costa, Wendy Jasson and Mtshali, Thokozani. *Prosecuting apartheid's soldiers 'divisive'* Pretoria News, February 8, 2007.

Defence confirms Basson's suspension payments SAPA, September 13, 2006.

De Klerk, Frederik Willem. *Amnesty rules for all* Financial Mail, July 27, 2007 (available at http://secure.financialmail.co.za/07/0727/features/hfeat.htm).

Dickson, Peter. *ANC to seek broad national amnesty* Cape Times, December 11, 2002.

End of the road for Scorpions SAPA, October 10, 2008.

Feud builds up over Kirkwood murders The Herald, available at http://www.theherald.co.za/herald/2004/07/08/news/n06_08072004.htm.

I know who tried to kill me—Chikane SAPA, October 2, 2006.

Joubert, Jan-Jan and Jordaan, Willem. *Cops up for apartheid crimes* Beeld, February 7, 2007.

Joubert, Jan-Jan and Muller, Annelie. *Versoening in gedrang* Beeld, February 12, 2004.

Mackay, Moses Mdewu Mthetheleli. *Outrage as amnesty reject gets off in court* Cape Argus, May 7, 2002.

Menges, Werner. *'Dr Death' is off the hook in South Africa* The Namibian, October 24, 2005.

Momberg, Eleanor and Terreblanche, Christelle. *Alleged NPA deal may let Vlok off the hook* The Sunday Independent, February 25, 2007.

Mtshali, T. *Pebco Three: old cops face charges* The Sunday Times, July 17, 2007.

Naidoo, Edwin. *No general amnesty for apartheid crimes* The Sunday Independent, July 3, 2005.

Nieuwoudt case will drive home a message Cape Times, February 13, 2004.

Nieuwoudt charged with murder SAPA, February 11, 2004.

NPA apartheid-era prosecutions to start SAPA, January 24, 2006.

NPA won't prosecute ANC 37 SAPA, June 2, 2004.

Oelofse, Louis. *NPA may have found bodies of Pebco Three* SAPA, July 16, 2007.

PAC elects new president SAPA, September 26, 2006.

Pigou, Piers. *Unfinished business* Mail & Guardian, September 21, 2002.

Presidential pardons in the spotlight SAPA, November 15, 2007.

Russouw, Sheree. *'All I want is to bury my son'* The Star, March 31 2007.

SA 'should try apartheid-era torturers' SAPA, November 25, 2006.

Steinberg, Jonny. *Amnesty quandary looms for judges* Business Day, June 8, 1999.

——. *Juggling justice, practically* Business Day, June 21, 2001.

Terreblanche, Christelle. *Apartheid massacres go to court* The Sunday Independent, April 23, 2006.

——. *Back door amnesty plan revealed* The Sunday Independent, November 27, 2005.

——. *New deal for apartheid abuse perpetrators* The Sunday Independent, April 20, 2003.

Terreblanche, Christelle and Quintal, Angela *NPA feels the heat on amnesty* The Sunday Independent, November 28, 2004.

Terreblanche, Christelle. *Tutu warns against blanket amnesty* The Sunday Independent, April 18, 2004.

Theatre of differences outside Vlok trial SAPA, August 16, 2007.

Tutu slates SA's lack of apartheid prosecutions SAPA, December 15, 2005.

Varney, Howard. *De Klerk and the Truth Commission* The Guardian (UK), August 17, 2007.

Victim's to fight amnesty Mail & Guardian, June 7, 2002.

Villa-Vicencio, Charles. *Let apartheid-era perpetrators be heard* The Sunday Independent, January 29, 2006.

——. *The TRC still has lessons for our future* The Sunday Times, April 23, 2006.

Vlok apologises for atrocities SAPA, August 26, 2006.

Vlok trial: different conclusions drawn SAPA, August 20, 2007.

Webb, Boyd. *Tit-for-tat threat by apartheid generals* Sunday Tribune, July 20, 2008.

Wouter Basson to defend himself against complaints SAPA, February 26, 2007.

Interviews

Interview with *Anton Ackermann*, head of the Priority Crimes Litigation Unit, on 11 May 2006 in Pretoria.

Telephone interview with *Johan Bezuidenhout*, Director of Public Prosecutions in the Eastern Cape, June 2006.

Interview with *Sheila Camerer*, justice spokesperson of the Democratic Alliance party, in Cape Town on 30 March 2006.

Interview with *Dr. Jan D'Oliveira*, former attorney-general of the Transvaal and former deputy NDPP, *Dr. Torie Pretorius* and *Susan Bukau*, prosecutors at the PCLU, on 2 May 2006 in Pretoria.

Interview by Prof. Dr. Gerhard Werle with *Dr. Jan D'Oliveira* in March 2004 in Pretoria.

Interview with *Madeleine Fullard*, former investigator at the TRC, presently head of the exhumation team of the NPA, on 4 May 2006 in Pretoria.

Interviews with *Jan Geldenhuys*, former chief of the SADF, on 10 May 2006 and 15 May 2006 in Pretoria.

Interview with *Marjorie Jobson*, director of the Khulumani Support Group, in Pretoria on 9 May 2006.

Interview with *Jürgen Kögl*, facilitator in consultations between ANC and government representatives and former SADF generals, on 12 May 2006 in Johannesburg.

Telephone interview with *Jürgen Kögl* on 14 June 2006.

Interview by Prof. Dr. Gerhard Werle with *Chris McAdam, Dr. Silas Ramaite* and *Anton Ackermann* on 27 February 2004 in Pretoria.

Interview with *Johan van der Merwe*, former head of the security branch of the SAP and former national commissioner of the police, on 5 May 2006 in Pretoria.

Interview with *Piers Pigou*, former researcher at the TRC and currently director of the South African History Archives (SAHA), on 6 May 2006 in Johannesburg.

Telephone interview with Advocate *Quitsi*, attorney of Tyani and Gumengu, in June 2006.

Interview with *Vincent Saldanha*, former head of the Human Rights Investigative Unit, on 26 April 2006 in Cape Town.

Interview with *Yasmin Sooka*, executive director of the Foundation for Human Rights and former TRC commissioner, on 3 May 2006 in Pretoria.

Interview with *Desmond Tutu*, former chairperson of the TRC, on 22 March 2006 in Cape Town.

Interview with *Howard Varney*, attorney in Johannesburg, on 6 May 2006 in Johannesburg.

Interview with *Themba Velem*, prosecutor in Worcester and Paarl, on 21 June 2006 in Paarl.

Interview with *Charles Villa-Vicencio*, former executive director of the Institute for Justice and Reconciliation and former head of the TRC Research Department, on 29 March 2006 in Cape Town.

Interviews with *Jan Wagener*, attorney in Pretoria, on 8 May 2006 and 16 May 2006 in Pretoria.

E-Mail Correspondence

E-mails from *Shaun Abrahams*, prosecutor at the PCLU, of 30 May 2007 and 6 June 2007.

E-mails from *Anton Ackermann* of 10, 18 and 21 October 2005 and 19 June 2006.

E-mail from *Jürgen Kögl* of 26 June 2006.

E-mails from *Johan van der Merwe* of 31 May 2006 and 4 June 2006.

E-mail from *Sheila Camerer* of 13 June 2006.

E-mail from *Charles Villa-Vicencio*, executive director of the Institute for Justice and Reconciliation, of 31 May 2006.

E-mails from *Jan Wagener* of 12 and 16 February 2007 and 13 September 2007.

Statements, Papers and other Documents

Amnesty International and Human Rights Watch, briefing paper *Truth and justice: unfinished business in South Africa* (February 2003) (available at http://www.hrw.org/backgrounder/africa/truthandjustice.htm).

Edwin, Valnora; Goldstone; Richard; Gyimah-Boadi, E.; Méndez, Juan E.; Pajibo, Ezekial; Saki, Otto; Suma, Mohammed. *Letter to President Thabo Mbeki, President of South Africa* (April 7, 2006) (available at http://www.ictj.org/images/content/6/2/624.pdf).

Ellis, Mark S. (executive director of the International Bar Association). *Letter to Brigitte Mabandla* (Minister of Justice and Constitutional Development) (March 14, 2006) (on file with author).

Freedom Front Plus, press statement. *FF Plus says NPA must prosecute Mbeki and other ANC* (January 25, 2006).

Institute for Justice and Reconciliation. *Statement: the IJR conference on the TRC: ten years on—actions required to ensure the TRC's success* (available at http://www.ijr.org.za/pastevents/finalstatement/view).

International Bar Association, press statement. *IBA critical of amendments to South Africa's prosecution policy* (March 29, 2006) (available at http://www.ibanet.org/images/downloads/hri/PR_South%20Africa_March_06.pdf).

Jobson, Marjorie. *Panel presentation at the Institute for Justice and Reconciliation conference "The TRC: ten years on"* (April 20, 2006) (relating paper available at http://www.ijr.org.za/pastevents/trcconference/papers/marjoreijobson/view).

Justice and Constitutional Development Portfolio Committee. *Briefing and deliberation on the amendment of the prosecuting policy to provide for directives for the prosecution of matters before 11 May 1994* (January 17, 2006) (protocol of minutes available at http://www.pmg.org.za).

Khulumani Support Group, press statement. *Khulumani Support Group rejects the finding of the Pretoria High Court today* (August 17, 2007).

National Prosecuting Authority, press statement. *NPA decides not to re-charge Wouter Basson* (October 19, 2005).

National Prosecuting Authority. *Presentation at the tabling of the prosecution policy amendment in the justice portfolio committee* (January 17, 2006) (available at http://www.pmg.org.za).

National Prosecuting Authority. *Annual report 2002/2003* and *Annual report 2005/2006.*

National Prosecuting Authority, press statement. *Amended prosecution policy and directives relating to prosecution of criminal matters arising from the conflicts of the past* (January 24, 2006).

Nkadimeng, Thembisile (sister of Nokuthula Simelane). *Panel presentation at the Institute for Justice and Reconciliation conference 'The TRC: ten years on'* (April 20, 2006).

Opening address by President Nelson Mandela in the special debate on the report of the Truth and Reconciliation Commission (National Houses of Parliament) (February 25, 1999) (available at http://www.pmg.org.za).

Pretorius, Dr. Torie. *Panel presentation at the Institute for Justice and Reconciliation conference "The TRC: ten years on"* (April 20, 2006) (transcript on file with author).

Sooka, Yasmin. *Letter to the Minister of Justice and Constitutional Development* (September 8, 2005) (on file with author).

——. *Panel presentation at the Institute for Justice and Reconciliation conference "The TRC: ten years on"* (April 20, 2006) (transcript available at http://www.ijr.org.za/pastevents/trcconference/papers/yasminsooka/view).

Staff paper prepared for the Steyn commission on alleged dangerous activities of SADF components (December 1992) (on file with author).

Statement by President Thabo Mbeki to the National Houses of Parliament and the Nation, at the Tabling of the Report of the Truth and Reconciliation Commission (April 15, 2003) (available at http://www.pmg.org.za).

Stewart, Dave. *Panel presentation at the Institute for Justice and Reconciliation conference "The TRC: ten years on"* (April 20, 2006) (relating paper available at http://www.ijr.org.za/pastevents/trcconference/papers/amnesty/view).

Varney, Howard. *Exploring a prosecutions strategy in the aftermath of South Africa's Truth & Reconciliation Commission* discussion paper presented at the Foundation for Human Rights and International Centre for Transitional Justice conference 'Domestic prosecutions and transitional justice conference' (Magaliesburg, May 16–19, 2005) (on file with author).

——. *Memorandum on discussion concerning the prosecution policy amendment—attended by Yasmin Sooka, Marjorie Jobson, Howard Varney, Ahmed Motala (executive director of the CSVR), Jody Kollapen (chair of the South African Human Rights Commission)* (December 9, 2005) (on file with author).

Vlok, Adriaan; van der Merwe, Johan; Smith, Chris; Otto, Gert and van Staden, Manie; press statement (Aug 17, 2007) (on file with author).

Index

www.ingramcontent.com/pod-product-compliance
Lightning Source LLC
Chambersburg PA
CBHW071433230926
51846CB00001B/214
9789004177031